CRASH PROOF 2.0

How to Profit from the Economic Collapse

PETER D. SCHIFF
with John Downes

A Lynn Sonberg Book

WILEY

John Wiley & Sons, Inc.

Published by John Wiley & Sons, Inc., Hoboken, New Jersey.
Published simultaneously in Canada.

The first edition of this book, *Crash Proof: How to Profit from the Coming Economic Collapse*, was published in 2007.

For general information on our other products and services or for technical support, please contact our Customer Care Department within the United States at (800) 762-2974, outside the United States at (317) 572-3993 or fax (317) 572-4002.

Wiley also publishes its books in a variety of electronic formats. Some content that appears in print may not be available in electronic books. For more information about Wiley products, visit our web site at www.wiley.com.

ISBN 978-0-470-47453-2 (cloth); ISBN 978-1-118-15200-3 (pbk);
ISBN 978-0-470-55056-4 (ebk); ISBN 978-0-470-55057-1 (ebk);
ISBN 978-0-470-55058-8 (ebk)

Printed in the United States of America

SKY10062699_121423

*To my father, Irwin Schiff, whose influence and guidance
concerning basic economic principles enabled me to see clearly
what others could not; to my son Spencer,
in whom I hope to instill a similar vision; and to
his and future generations of Americans, who
through hard work and sacrifice might one
day restore this nation to her former glory*

Disclosure

Data from various sources was used in the preparation of this book. The information is believed to be reliable, accurate and appropriate but it is not guaranteed in any way. The forecasts and strategies contained herein are statements of opinion, and therefore may prove to be inaccurate. They are in fact the author's own opinions, and payment was not received in any form that influenced his opinions. Peter Schiff and the employees of Euro Pacific Capital implement many of the strategies described. This book contains the names of some companies used as examples of the strategies described, as well as a mutual fund that can be sold only by prospectus; but none can be deemed recommendations to the book's readers. These strategies will be inappropriate for some investors, and we urge you to speak with a financial professional and carefully review any pertinent disclosures before implementing any investment strategy.

In addition to being the President, Peter Schiff is also a registered representative and owner of Euro Pacific Capital, Inc (Euro Pacific). Euro Pacific is a FINRA registered Broker-Dealer and a member of the SIPC. This book has been prepared solely for informational purposes, and it is not an offer to buy or sell, or a solicitation to buy or sell, any security or instrument, or to participate in any particular trading strategy. Investment strategies described in this book may ultimately lose value even if the opinions and forecasts presented prove to be accurate. All investments involve varying amounts of risk, and their values will fluctuate. Investments may increase or decrease in value, and investors may lose money.

Contents

Author's Note, *Crash Proof 2.0*   vii

Preface   xv

Introduction: America.com: The Delusion of Real
Wealth   xxi

1 The Slippery Slope: Consumers, Not Producers   1

2 What Uncle Sam, the Mass Media, and Wall Street
Don't Want You to Know   33

3 For a Few Dollars More: Our Declining Currency   63

4 Inflation Nation: The Federal Reserve Fallacy   91

5 My Kingdom for a Buyer: Stock Market Chaos   129

6 They Burst Bubbles, Don't They?: The Coming
Real Estate Debacle   159

7 Come On In, the Water's Fine: Our Consumer
Debt Problem   199

8 How to Survive and Thrive, Step 1: Rethinking
Your Stock Portfolio   237

9 How to Survive and Thrive, Step 2: Gold Rush—
Be the First Person on Your Block to Stake a Claim   283

10 How to Survive and Thrive, Step 3: Stay Liquid   317

Epilogue 339
Books for Further Reading 345
Glossary 349
Index 353

Author's Note, *Crash Proof 2.0*

Ever since the first version of *Crash Proof* was published in February of 2007 I have been credited as one of the few widely visible analysts to have clearly foreseen the great unraveling of the U.S. economy. And while I'm not known primarily for modesty, I have to admit that the most dire predictions I made in that first edition have yet to happen. However my convictions have never been stronger that real economic catastrophe is an event of the future, not of the past.

I was certainly not the only person to have warned about a general economic slowdown after years of record "growth" in the middle years of the George Bush presidency. But I was the accuracy of my predictions concerning the real estate and credit busts put me on a very different level. I knew that homes had become massively overvalued, and as a result I saw a string of events that would bring the curtain down on an era of easy wealth and stunning blindness.

To a chorus of laughter and derision I predicted how a 30 to 50 percent decline in national real estate prices would spark a wave of foreclosures, a collapse of the mortgage market, the demise and nationalization of Fannie and Freddie, widespread failures of banks and financial institutions, an implosion of the credit markets, and ultimately the deepest recession since the Great Depression. Those forecasts now read like history.

But of greater concern were my predictions as to how the federal government would destroy any remaining economic vitality through misguided stimuli. I believed that a campaign of printing, spending, and borrowing would destroy the dollar, causing both consumer prices and interest rates to spike. The crash I spoke of in *Crash Proof* was not a housing collapse but a collapse in American living standards. In the most part, that has yet to happen.

When I published *Crash Proof 2.0* in mid-2009, more than two years after the collapse of Bear Stearns, the business and investment shelves of bookstores had become filled with titles analyzing the calamities of the previous two years and offering various theories about the future. With all due respect to my fellow authors, most of them were writing after the fact and starting from the premise that the crisis could not have been predicted.

As 2009 wore on, and red ink piled up on the federal balance sheet, the economic crowd turned surprisingly optimistic. The watchwords of the day were "green shoots," and by year end much ink had been being spilled about how the Fed would engineer an "exit strategy" to withdraw liquidity it had previously pumped into the system. Stunningly, the media gave great credence to this message, even though the messengers themselves had been blind to the crash in the first place. At the time I was warning that any signs of recovery were an illusion and that the Fed had no exit strategy. Instead I forecast further easing (later called "quantitative easing") and no end to the debt, deficits, dollar debasement, and stagnation. I was ignored almost as completely as I was in 2007.

Most believed then, and continue to believe now, that the economic collapse had ended. I believe that we have merely seen the events that have set the collapse in motion. It will take some time for all of the dominoes to fall. But fall they will, perhaps even more spectacularly than I initially envisioned back in 2005.

In 2009 testimony before Congress, Federal Reserve chairman Ben Bernanke claimed that aggressive Fed action and government intervention had averted economic catastrophe. Two years later we can say with high confidence that rather than being averted, the catastrophe has been postponed, and its severity has been worsened. But this isn't the first time that "the Bernank" (as he is now known) has been spectacularly wrong.

Back in July 2005, as I began writing the first draft of *Crash Proof* (which includes an entire chapter on the pending real estate debacle), Bernanke told CNBC's Maria Bartiromo that a decline in national house prices was highly unlikely, and that any future real estate-related slowdown would not cause the economy to veer from its full-employment path. Incredibly, Bernanke is still calling the economic shots.

In mid-2008, investors around the world reacted perversely to a collapsing American financial system. Like horses running back into a burning barn, they dumped commodities and foreign stocks and poured funds into U.S. dollars and U.S. Treasury securities. Several factors explained the move:

- A credit crunch that amounted to a global margin call caused forced massive selling of gold and other viable assets that had high liquidity;
- America's trading partners were instinctively inclined to prop up their best customer and continued buying American debt regardless of its diminishing creditworthiness; and
- the dollar was falsely perceived as a safe haven by short-term investors waiting for the storm to pass.

In March 2009, as these market trends were still in force, I was writing an update of *Crash Proof*, which became for *Crash Proof 2.0*. In that edition I advised readers to seize the opportunity to buy foreign stocks, gold, and other commodities at fire-sale prices. By buying at that time, I argued that investors could capture currency gains, capital gains, and rising dividends as the dollar weakened and foreign economies revived. In the second quarter of 2009 the markets behaved as I predicted. By the summer, with *Crash Proof 2.0* on the way to the printer, I added a brief update to the author's note in which I assured readers that although the fire sale had largely passed, the arguments behind my investment strategy remained stronger than ever. I continue to believe that today.

For *Crash Proof 2.0* I decided to keep the original *Crash Proof* text unchanged by adding updated commentary at the end of each chapter. My reasoning had partly to do with the time-honored rule of not fixing something that wasn't broken. My other reason was to lay out the basic economic thinking that underlies my accurate predictions. Anyone can be a Monday-morning quarterback. It's another thing to call the plays on Sunday afternoon. Leaving the original text intact enabled readers to see that our problems then, and now, are the consequences of pernicious fundamental trends that I had recognized and warned about for years.

It's also important to note how my thinking separates me from the "perma-bears," those chronic pessimists whose uniformly negative predictions, like a stopped clock, are accurate twice a day. It may surprise some that I have been very bullish on investments in overseas markets. And while it's true that many of these investments saw oversize declines in 2008, their recovery in 2009 and 2010 was oftentimes astounding. I have equal confidence that my current predictions will be borne out over the long haul.

As I write this in the latter half of 2011 the U.S. economy is essentially comatose. As I forecast two years ago, unemployment has stayed high, the work force has atrophied, the housing market has continued to drift downward, and debt levels continue to mount. But, amazingly we continue to be spared the gravest consequences that I described in the original *Crash Proof*. Many people may find it hard to believe that things could be worse. Trust me, they could be.

While I knew that unending stimuli and deficit spending would sap our economy (as it has in Japan for more than 20 years), and encourage a stampede into gold, I did not properly reckon with the power of the status quo and I overestimated the ability of the establishment to finally recognize the bubble after it burst. I did not imagine that investors the world over would run toward the exploding financial time bomb that has Wall Street and Washington as its twin epicenters. It never occurred to me that yields on U.S. Treasury debt could sink to all-time lows as the U.S. government added more than $1.5 trillion of new debt every year and spectacularly failed to deal with our long-term fiscal imbalances. It never occurred to me that consumer prices would stay relatively flat while the Fed pursued the easiest monetary policy in the world, printed trillions of dollars, and monetized the federal debt. But that's exactly what has happened in 2009, 2010, and 2011.

As a result, Americans can still borrow money at the lowest rates in our history. Foreign exporters are still willing to sell goods to Americans on credit, and the dollar has held a good deal of its value. I believe that this good fortune comes from a combination of luck, habit, political will, market timidity, and abject economic ignorance. We have dodged the bullets for now, but sooner or later we are going to step on a land mine.

With the benefit of hindsight, it now appears to me that emotion can trump reason for a longer time period than I had anticipated. The saying goes that the markets can stay irrational longer than you can stay solvent. But I still believe that over time people will wake up and rub the sand from their eyes. The strangeness of our economic times is manifested in the increased volatility of the financial markets. During times of panic, investors seek safety in assets that inspire confidence. But inspiration can change. A look at the last three market corrections of 15 percent or more reveals some important clues.

Between January 2, 2009, and March 6, 2009, the S&P 500 sold off more than 21 percent. During that time, the U.S. dollar rallied by 9 percent and gold just under 8 percent. In contrast, foreign currencies sold off heavily, including a 7 percent drop for the vaunted Swiss franc. The next major correction in stocks showed a slightly different result. Between April 23, 2010, and July 2, 2010, the S&P 500 dropped 16 percent. During that time, the dollar rallied just 3 percent. Notably, this time around, the Swiss franc did not sell off, but rather rallied by about 1 percent. More importantly, gold rallied nearly 5 percent, taking from the U.S. dollar the title of "fear asset of choice."

These trends gained momentum in 2011. The worst carnage of the year (thus far) came between April 29 and August 8, when the S&P 500 lost almost 18 percent. During that time, the dollar managed just a skimpy 2 percent gain. Meanwhile, the Swiss franc jumped almost 13 percent and gold surged 12 percent. It does appear that the crowd has changed at least some of its assumptions. It no longer runs blindly into U.S. dollars. It considers other options.

As these assumptions slowly change we can continue to enjoy relatively good fortune. Meanwhile, the economic pillars that should be healing are rotting instead. We should have repaired our communal balance sheet. But as a people and a government, we are taking on unsustainable levels of debt. At the same time, the non-productive sectors of the economy—government, health care, and education—have grown, while the productive sectors—manufacturing, resource development, and agriculture—have contracted. An activist federal government, intent on engineering a recovery, has taken the wheel, and has relegated private enterprise to the back seat. The central planning tendencies of the Obama administration are leading our economy down a blind alley.

Based on the faulty assumption that spending is the key to economic growth, current economic policy involves getting Americans to borrow and spend. But we dug ourselves into an economic hole by borrowing and spending too much. We will never get out by digging deeper. Instead we have to produce our way out. That requires more saving and more investment, which necessitates less spending.

We must also recognize that government interference in our economy created the problems that free market forces would have prevented. The housing bubble and ensuing financial crisis were not a failure of capitalism, but of government's failure allow capitalism to work. Rather than learning from past mistakes, current policy involves stricter regulations on business and preferential treatment for politically favored sectors. But the hopes for real recovery lie only in the strength and dynamism of free markets and unregulated entrepreneurship.

Back in 2008, governments bailed out failing banks, transforming bad private debt into bad public debt. Now entire governments need bailouts. This is new territory for the world economy. For now, creditor nations such as China and Germany are willing to throw good money after bad. We can only hope their largesse has no limits. But I am convinced they will one day throw in the towel. When they do, the purchasing power of the U.S. dollar will reflect the underlying fundamentals of the American economy. Those fundamentals are bad and are getting worse.

In addition, sovereign debt problems abroad are temporarily overshadowing the larger sovereign debt problem looming here at home. As with the mortgage crisis, the "experts" are convinced that sovereign debt problems are "contained" to subprime nations like Greece, Ireland, and Portugal. In contrast, I correctly pointed out then that subprime was merely the tip of a mortgage-crisis iceberg. Similarly, the sovereign debt crisis is not just confined to Europe's fringes. All overly indebted nations will have their day of reckoning and the largest debtor of them all will not be spared.

In the meantime worries about the Euro provide more temporary support for the dollar. But this borrowed time comes with a heavy price tag. It amounts to more rope with which to hang ourselves. Once the side show in Europe ends, the curtain will rise on the main event here in the United States.

A debased currency and sky high inflation will bring American living standards down to levels not seen in recent memory. Your investment capital provides you with a means of escape. Use it wisely. The window of opportunity won't stay open for ever.

Peter Schiff
September 2011

Preface

When I began this book early in 2006, I didn't plan to have a Preface. My goal was to explain in a readably informal, easy-to-understand way why America's persistent and growing imbalance of imports over exports—its trade deficit—would cause the dollar to collapse, forcing the American public to accept a drastically lower standard of living and years of painful sacrifice and reconstruction. Seven chapters would show the various ways the world's greatest creditor nation had become, in the incredibly short space of some 20 years, the world's largest debtor nation while the public's attention was focused on other things. My challenge, as I saw it, was to create public awareness, where it didn't exist, of an impending economic crisis for which I have been helping my clients prepare for years. My final three chapters would share investment strategies already being used successfully by my several thousand brokerage clients, so that readers could avoid the dollar debacle and position themselves to profit during the rebuilding.

That's the book you are about to read. Why this Preface?

Because as I write this in the final days of 2006, with the book scheduled for publication a month or so from now, everybody has started talking about the trade deficit. Virtually ignored for years, it has suddenly become a subject of public debate. And while there is a growing consensus that the problem is deadly serious, there's a concurrently emerging consensus, mainly representing Wall Street with its vested interest in the status quo, making the opposite argument that trade deficits are a sign of economic health—that American consumption is the engine of economic growth. It's this group that I want to take on at the very outset. Their arguments are self-serving nonsense. If I can convince you of that here and now, you can get the full benefit of the wisdom and guidance I humbly set forth in the coming pages.

I'll get to some more comprehensive examples in a minute, but for sheer pithiness it would be hard to improve on a pronouncement made last week by Lawrence Kudlow, the genial host of CNBC's daily program *Kudlow and Company*. Opening the program, Kudlow welcomed his viewers, and then brazenly intoned: "I *love* trade deficits. Why? Because they create capital account surpluses."

In the way of background, the balance of payments, the bookkeeping system for recording transactions between countries, is made up, among other items, of a trade account, which is the part of the current account that nets out imports and exports, and a capital account, which nets investment flows between countries. Because dollars we send abroad in payment for goods and services are returned as investments in U.S. government securities and other assets, one account can be viewed as the flip side of the other. A country, like the United States, that is a net importer will therefore typically have an offsetting capital balance, the trade account being a deficit and the capital account a surplus.

But "surplus" as it is used here is a bookkeeping term meaning simply that more cash flowed in than flowed out. The reason cash flowed in is that an asset, say a Treasury bond, was purchased by a foreign central banker. But selling a bond doesn't make us richer; it creates a liability. Sure, we initially have cash in hand as a result of the sale, but it's money we are obligated to pay back with interest.

So the word "surplus" has a positive ring to it, but a capital surplus has the opposite meaning of, say, a budget surplus. Surpluses can be bad or good. A surplus of water in a reservoir during a drought is good, but when it's in your basement during a rainstorm, it's bad.

Now Larry Kudlow is a smart guy, and I'm not suggesting he doesn't know what the word means. But in his opinion, a capital surplus is evidence of our country's creditworthiness. The implication is that we can depend on that to keep the music playing. That's where I think he's wrong. Our trading partners are quite free to invest elsewhere, and that's just what they'll do when they realize the United States, with $8.5 trillion in funded debt ($50 trillion including unfunded obligations) and persistent budget deficits that add to that figure annually, is no longer creditworthy. It's not as though they are getting higher yields by investing here; our markets are underperforming all the other major markets in the world, and that's been true for six or seven years now.

The continued demand for U.S. government investments among central bankers has its explanation, I think, in robotic bureaucratic momentum. Private foreign investors steer clear. But for Wall Street and its media cheerleaders, who would get killed if trade deficits translated into market pessimism, "capital surplus" is a term coined in heaven.

Another, more comprehensive, argument that trade deficits are desirable was made in a December 21, 2006, *Wall Street Journal* op-ed piece titled "Embrace the Deficit" by Bear Stearns's chief economist, David Malpass.

Mr. Malpass writes at some length, but his argument is pretty well summarized in his opening paragraph: "For decades, the trade deficit has been a political and journalistic lightning rod, inspiring countless predictions of America's imminent economic collapse. The reality is different. Our imports grow with our economy and population while our exports grow with foreign economies, especially those of industrial countries. Though widely criticized as an imbalance, the trade deficit and related capital inflow reflect U.S. growth, not weakness—they link the

younger, faster-growing U.S. with aging, slower growth economies abroad."

With due respect to Mr. Malpass, I couldn't disagree with him
more. Although his point about demographics may have some
limited validity, he ignores the fact that underlying the trade deficit is a shrinking manufacturing base, and relies heavily on the
familiar but erroneous argument that declining savings rates are
belied by high household net worth figures, which we know reflect inflated housing and paper asset values. He confuses consumption with growth and credits high competitive yields with
attracting foreign investment, when we know major foreign
markets outperform ours substantially when exchange rates are
factored in. His view of inflation ignores past monetary policy. I
could go on, but rather suggest that my entire book is a refutation
of his point of view. His article is an exquisite example of Wall
Street's self-serving effort to gild the economic lily.

In general, the ridiculous notion that American consumption
is driving the global economy is regularly reinforced by the mass
media. On a recent airing of the Fox News business program
Bulls and Bears the panelists were asked to nominate a "person of
the year." The unanimous choice: the American shopper.

In the same vein, I am always struck by how the televised
media characterize the American economy by showing images
of sales clerks frantically stocking shelves and shoppers swiping
their credit cards. In contrast, the economies of Japan or China
are portrayed with images of billowing smokestacks, busy production lines, robots assembling, and people actually making
things. The most amazing part of the farce is that no one even
recognizes just how ridiculous these segments are. If Longfellow
was right that "whom the gods destroy they first make mad,"
we must surely be on the eve of our economic destruction, as we
are clearly a nation gone completely insane.

Fortunately, there are a few among us who still have their
wits about them. Recently there has been increasing recognition

from qualified and impartial opinion leaders that trade imbalances are in fact detrimental and that the resulting dollar decline could have serious consequences. Unfortunately, their cries fall on deaf ears and their warnings go unheeded.

In a December 11, 2006, Bloomberg article, former Fed Chairman Alan Greenspan, speaking now as a private citizen, was quoted as telling a business conference in Tel Aviv by satellite that the U.S. dollar will probably keep dropping until the nation's current-account deficit shrinks. "It is imprudent to hold everything in one currency," he was reported as saying. A Reuters report on the same conference quoted Greenspan as saying, "There has been some evidence that OPEC nations are beginning to switch their reserves out of dollars and into euro and yen [so a dollar moving lower] will be the experience of the next few years."

Former Treasury Secretary Robert E. Rubin and former Federal Reserve Chairman Paul Volcker have reportedly expressed similar concerns about the dollar. Volcker was quoted in a November 1, 2006, *New York Times* article, "Gambling Against the Dollar," as saying circumstances were as "dangerous and intractable" as any he can remember.

Warren Buffett had weighed in back on January 20, 2006, saying, according to an Associated Press report, "The U.S. trade deficit is a bigger threat to the domestic economy than either the federal budget deficit or consumer debt and could lead to political turmoil. . . . Right now, the rest of the world owns $3 trillion more of us than we own of them."

To my knowledge, nobody has ever asked Warren Buffett, "If you're so smart, why ain't you rich?" If he and the aforementioned think there's a problem, it's pretty good confirmation that there is one. In the following pages, you'll learn why the U.S. economy is in real trouble and how you can avoid loss and enjoy continued prosperity.

INTRODUCTION

America.com: The Delusion of Real Wealth

When business in the United States underwent a mild contraction . . . the Federal Reserve created more paper reserves in the hope of forestalling any possible bank reserve shortage. The "Fed" succeeded; . . . but it nearly destroyed the economies of the world, in the process. The excess credit which the Fed pumped into the economy spilled over into the stock market—triggering a fantastic speculative boom. Belatedly, Federal Reserve officials attempted to sop up the excess reserves and finally succeeded in breaking the boom. But it was too late: . . . the speculative imbalances had become so overwhelming that the attempt precipitated a sharp retrenching and a consequent demoralizing of business confidence. As a result, the American economy collapsed.

The above quotation is not a forecast of what might happen, but a summary of something that actually did happen. It was written more than 40 years ago in reference to 1920s America. The writer was a young economist by the name of Alan Greenspan.

(The article was "Gold and Economic Freedom," *The Objectivist*, 1966, reprinted in Ayn Rand's *Capitalism: The Unknown Ideal*, New York: Penguin, 1987.)

The former Fed chairman's words apply to current conditions as aptly as they did to the Roaring Twenties, but with a major difference. The difference is that as Fed chairman between 1987 and 2006, Greenspan acted even more irresponsibly than the officials he was criticizing. Rather than "sopping up the excess reserves," Greenspan added even more, morphing a stock market bubble into a housing and consumer spending bubble of unprecedented proportions.

According to Greenspan, the Great Depression of the 1930s resulted from the unwinding of the speculative imbalances caused by the excess liquidity created by the Fed during the 1920s. Given that Greenspan created even more excess liquidity during his tenure and that the speculative imbalances that resulted were that much greater, what dire economic consequences might the Maestro, as journalist Bob Woodward dubbed the one-time professional saxophone player, believe await the United States today?

From Greenspan's perspective, that question will likely remain rhetorical, as his monetary high-wire act continues under his successor, Chairman Ben Bernanke, with the same apparent confidence that it can go on indefinitely.

But I see things differently. In the following chapters I will not only answer the question myself, but I will provide the reader with a comprehensive financial plan to help weather the coming economic storm. Make no mistake; extremely difficult times lie ahead. Our nation's character will be tested like never before. Whether it will rise to the occasion or be found wanting remains to be seen. While we can all hope for the best, the pragmatist in me suggests that we had better prepare for the worst.

For years I have been conducting workshops entitled "America's Bubble Economy: Implications for Your Investments

When It Finally Bursts," helping thousands of my clients prudently invest their savings, while making sure they steer clear of Wall Street's many investment land mines. I have never allowed popular delusion to cloud my judgment, nor fads to influence my recommendations.

During the 1990s, as most of my colleagues eagerly bought into the "new era" tech stock hype, I held steadfastly to sound investment principles, urging all who would listen to sell. The outlook for the U.S. economy today is strikingly similar to the outlook for Internet stocks in the 1990s.

Just as stock market analysts believed then that traditional measures of valuation such as earnings, cash flow, dividend yield, price to sales, price to book, internal rate of return, and return on equity no longer applied, economists today dismiss as passé the concerns we traditionalists have about such economic fundamentals as savings rates, manufacturing activity, federal deficits, unfunded liabilities, counterparty risks, consumer debt, and trade and current account deficits. To modern economists, we are now living in a new era where Americans can consume and borrow indefinitely while the rest of the world saves and produces in their stead.

This book aims to shatter that myth once and for all, and show that this so-called "new era," like all those that preceded it, will fade as quickly as it appeared—that "America.com" is no more viable than any of the now-bankrupt dot-coms that once populated the investment landscape.

When reality finally sets in, those who have read this book and followed my advice will be well positioned to profit during the difficult times that lie ahead.

While most germane to investors, this book is also written for a broader audience. My goal here is not simply to provide an investment survival guide, but to expose and illuminate the grave economic weaknesses that make survival the issue.

A proper understanding of the true state of the American economy is vital to investors and noninvestors alike.

For our nation to travel the road back to true prosperity, we must first rediscover the road and understand how we got so far off course in the first place.

Nations are not served by citizens who refuse to face the truth. Blind optimism, shrouded typically in patriotism, abounds and is going to lead us to disaster.

My warnings are based on realism, and the passion I bring to them is the greater because I love my country and have no higher goal than to see it thrive. But to be viable and to enjoy its traditional glory, it has to return to traditional values.

Arguments such as mine are sobering and not calculated to be popular. As such, they tend to fall on the deaf ears of a brainwashed public that understandably would prefer to feel good about itself.

Because my positions are so unconventional and therefore sensational, I am trotted out by the media with increasing frequency to balance prevailing opinion. CNBC has labeled me Dr. Doom and gives me the friendly needle for being a modern-day Chicken Little.

I take it all in fun, but recognize our economic realities are hardly a laughing matter. I strongly believe my arguments are demonstrably valid and will soon become the prevailing opinion. I only hope that by then it is not too late. Unfortunately, this may finally be a case where the little chicken has it right. The sky actually may be falling after all.

1

The Slippery Slope: Consumers, Not Producers

If the United States economy was a prizefighter and I was the referee, I would have mercifully stopped the carnage while the old pug still had his champion's pride and all his marbles. But the mismatch has been allowed to continue, round after bloody round. Past glory can get in the way of accepting present realities.

The economy of the United States, long the world's dominant creditor, now the world's largest debtor, is fighting a losing battle against trade and financial imbalances that are growing daily and are caused by dislocations too fundamental to reverse.

I'm not talking abstract economics here. Unless you take measures to protect yourself—and this book will tell you what those measures are—your dollar-denominated assets are going to collapse in value and your standard of living will be painfully lowered. I can't pinpoint the date this will happen—the government has been successful in hiding the problem and buying time—but there is going to be a day of reckoning and it's already overdue.

In the short space of a couple of decades, and causing surprisingly little anxiety among economists, the nation has undergone a radical transformation in terms of its economic infrastructure and its economic behavior. A society that saved, produced, created wealth, and was a major exporter has become a society that stopped saving, shifted from manufacturing to nonexportable services, has run up record national and personal indebtedness, and uses borrowed money to finance excessive consumption of unproductive imported goods.

On a national level, our circumstances are similar to those of a philandering playboy who inherits a huge fortune and then proceeds to squander it. During the dissipation period, he lives the good life, and by all appearances he seems prosperous. But his prosperity is a function of the hard work of his ancestors rather than his own. Once the fortune is gone, so too will be the gracious lifestyle that it helped support. The problem is that most Americans, including most economists and investment advisers, have confused conspicuous consumption with legitimate wealth creation. Our impressive gross domestic product (GDP) growth, dominated as it is by consumption, is not a measure of how much wealth we have created but of how much we have destroyed (see Figure 1.1).

The result: a trade deficit of some $800 billion annually, a budget deficit running $300 billion to $400 billion, and a national debt of $8.5 trillion. (Of course, when unfunded liabilities, such as Social Security obligations, are included, the real national debt exceeds $50 trillion, or over six times the official estimates). Had the past two decades been characterized by genuine prosperity, we would have run trade surpluses and still be the world's largest creditor, rather than its greatest debtor. I believe that we are

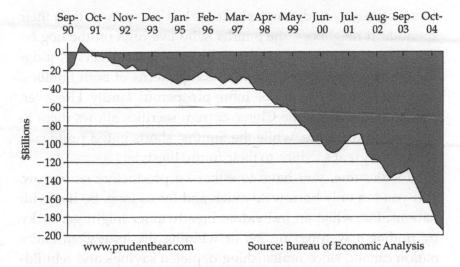

| | Sep-90 | Oct-91 | Nov-92 | Dec-93 | Jan-95 | Feb-96 | Mar-97 | Apr-98 | May-99 | Jun-00 | Jul-01 | Aug-02 | Sep-03 | Oct-04 |

www.prudentbear.com   Source: Bureau of Economic Analysis

FIGURE 1.1 *U.S. current account balance, 1990–2005.* The U.S. current account deficit has exploded in recent years, with annual red ink now flowing at a rate close to $1 trillion. Such an abysmal economic performance is a national disaster of unparalleled proportions.
Source: Reprinted by permission from David L. Tice and Associates (www.prudentbear.com).

fast approaching a perfect storm scenario, with a monetary collapse the most likely way it will play out.

It's analogous, I think, to a family—let's call them the Smiths—whose breadwinners have lost their jobs. To keep up appearances and maintain the same lifestyle, the family resorts to borrowing and goes deeper and deeper into debt. It is a situation that cannot go on indefinitely. Unless the breadwinners get jobs that enable them to repay their debt and legitimately finance their previous lifestyle, the family faces painful and humiliating adjustment.

Contrast this to a family—let's call them the Chins—who sacrifice, underconsume, and live below their means in order to accumulate a significant financial nest egg. During the accumulation period, they appear far less prosperous than their spendthrift neighbors, the Smiths, who live high on the hog on credit card and mortgage debt. To the casual observer, judging only by the relative consumption patterns of both families, the Smiths appear to be the more prosperous family. However, beneath the surface, the Chins' current sacrifice allows them to build a bright future, while the Smiths' shortsighted profligacy comes at a great sacrifice to their future lifestyle.

To consume, you have to either be productive or borrow, and you can only borrow so much and for so long. So it is with nations. But while an individual breadwinner might get lucky by finding a well-paying job or winning the lottery, an entire nation cannot, since replenishing depleted savings and rebuilding a deteriorated manufacturing base will take time and require great sacrifice.

Because Americans are not saving and producing but are borrowing and consuming, we have become precariously dependent on foreign suppliers and lenders. As a result, we are facing an imminent monetary crisis that will dramatically lower the standard of living of Americans who fail to take action to protect themselves (see Figure 1.2).

WHY THE GLOOM? THE GOVERNMENT SAYS THE ECONOMY'S FINE

If you're wondering why you keep reading and hearing that the economy is doing just fine, don't think you're hallucinating or that I am. Modern politics is premised on the high expectations of American consumers, and the government has mastered the art of making bad economic news look like good economic news, thereby keeping the public happy and the politicians in office. (The midterm elections of 2006 that changed the leadership

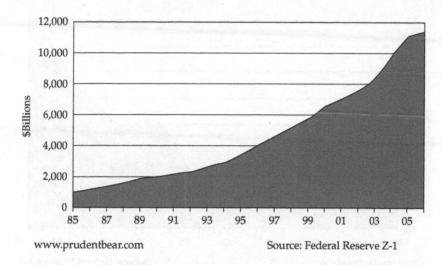

www.prudentbear.com   Source: Federal Reserve Z-1

FIGURE 1.2   *Rest of the world holdings of U.S. financial assets, 1985–2006.*
America's unprecedented consumption and borrowing binge has
put record amounts of liabilities in foreign hands. If not repudiated,
servicing this debt will suppress national income and domestic
consumption for generations to come.
Source: Reprinted by permission from David L. Tice and Associates
(www.prudentbear.com).

of the House and Senate might indicate the public is waking
up.) Government officials—aided by an accommodative Federal
Reserve empowered to create credit—manipulate economic data
routinely to simultaneously maintain the domestic consumer
confidence and foreign lender confidence required to keep the
party going. But with every bit of time they buy, the basic problems worsen.

For their part, the foreign central banks continue to use
accumulated dollars to buy our Treasury and mortgage-backed
securities, helping finance our growing deficits and keeping
our housing market propped up (see Figure 1.3). They get the
same sunny economic news we do, and they also have the naive
belief, although there are signs that this belief is beginning to

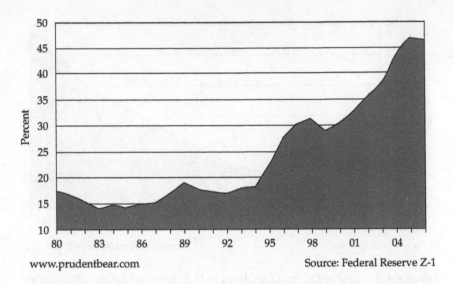

www.prudentbear.com   Source: Federal Reserve Z-1

FIGURE 1.3 *Foreign holdings of U.S. Treasuries as percent of total, 1980–2006.* Due to insufficient domestic savings and profligate government spending, an increasing percentage of U.S. Treasury debt is now held abroad. We certainly do not "owe it to ourselves" anymore.

Source: Reprinted by permission from David L. Tice and Associates (www.prudentbear.com).

waver, that the U.S. economy is too big to fail. If they woke up to what's actually happening and stopped buying our Treasury securities, our choice would be to further tax an already over-burdened citizenry or default like Russia did in the later 1990s. We are in a real mess.

That brings me back to my prizefighter analogy. Remember when Iron Mike Tyson wore the heavyweight crown, was knocking out everybody in sight, and was so fearsome it seemed inconceivable he could lose? Well, as always happens eventually, he finally met his match. Buster Douglas beat him, and after that he just kept getting beaten. It was the same Mike Tyson, but Buster had broken a psychological barrier.

Any reality check that pierces the myth that the American economy is too big to fail could begin the process of unraveling.

Our days as the dominant economic power are numbered. The dollar is going to collapse, and Americans are going to experience stagflation on an unprecedented scale in the form of recession and hyperinflation. Those of you who act smartly and quickly by taking measures I outline later in this book not only will avoid loss of wealth but also will have positioned yourselves to prosper while your neighbors suffer a painful period of reconstruction and reform.

It is important to remember that in market economies living standards rise as a result of capital accumulation, which allows labor to be more productive, which in turn results in greater output per worker, allowing for increased consumption and leisure. However, capital investment can be increased only if adequate savings are available to finance it. Savings, of course, can come into existence only as a result of underconsumption and self-sacrifice (see Figure 1.4).

The fatal flaw in the modern economy is that any attempt to save and under consume, which would surely bring about a badly needed recession, is resisted by government policy, the sole purpose of which is to postpone the inevitable day of reckoning. In their selfish attempt to secure reelection, American politicians have persuaded their constituents that they should indulge their every whim and that self-sacrifice or underconsumption are somehow un-American, a character flaw uniquely Asian.

As a result, those same American politicians, with the help of the Federal Reserve, will succeed in doing what no foreign power ever could have: They will bring the U.S. economy to its knees, as sacrifice and underconsumption will ultimately define the U.S. economy for generations to come.

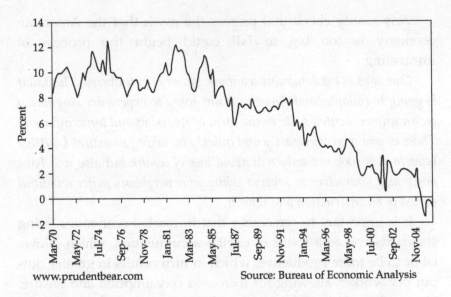

www.prudentbear.com   Source: Bureau of Economic Analysis

FIGURE 1.4 *U.S. savings rate, 1970–2006.* The collapse of personal savings has led to the unprecedented accumulation of external liabilities and the demise of the U.S. industrial base. Rebuilding national savings and the capital investment it finances will be a hallmark of the coming economic austerity.

Source: Reprinted by permission from David L. Tice and Associates (www.prudentbear.com).

HOW WE GOT INTO THIS MESS

In a very real way, our success as a military and industrial power and the period of great affluence that followed World War II seeded the developments that have caused the fix we're in and allowed it to fester.

Reserve currency status, a badge of America's preeminence, has been both a blessing and a curse. Bestowed on the United States by the Bretton Woods agreement of 1944 (see Chapter 3) and still enjoyed by the United States today thanks to complacent central bankers abroad, the U.S. dollar's status as the world's reserve currency has shielded the United States from the consequences of persistent and growing trade imbalances.

The Bretton Woods accords made the U.S. dollar the currency used by other governments and institutions to settle their foreign exchange accounts and to transact trade in certain vital commodities, such as gold and oil. It thus behooved countries involved in international trade to accumulate dollars and build ample reserves. That the dollar was originally accepted by the world as its reserve currency was due to America's unequaled industrial might, its status as both the world's leading exporter of manufactured goods and its greatest creditor, and the fact that its currency was fully backed by, and redeemable in, a fixed quantity of gold. None of these attributes currently exist, and the dollar would not qualify for comparable status were a similar accord attempted today.

However, because its reserve currency function was inseparable from its own import/export activities, the United States was permitted to run trade deficits exempt from the free market forces that would otherwise have forced their adjustment. Thus we were spared the economic impact that a devaluation of the dollar would have caused.

Our trading partners could, under the Bretton Woods rules, force us to deal with the issue, but bureaucratic central bankers have so far been complacent and allowed our deficit to reach increasingly dangerous levels.

But that complacency could change. There is also speculation that reserve currency status might be transferred to the euro or to a combination of foreign currencies. In any event, the U.S. dollar's status as a reserve currency immune from market pressures cannot last indefinitely. When it ends, all those surplus dollars will come home to roost, creating hyperinflation domestically.

The shift from manufacturing to services caused growing trade deficits. The erosion of our manufacturing base with its value as a producer of exportable goods and a source of high wages was the result of a number of factors. Aggressive labor unions demanding worker benefits, increased government regulation, higher taxation, aging plants and equipment, a "bigger is better" attitude that allowed too much waste and encouraged too little conservation and discipline, a smugness with respect to quality and design—these and other factors put U.S. manufacturing at a disadvantage to competitors abroad that were playing catch-up.

Abroad, in contrast, there was a spirit of rebuilding, an awareness that natural resources were scarce and must be conserved, lower taxes and wages, and generally fewer government obstacles to economic development. America's most formidable overseas competitor was Japan, whose answer to America's "bigger is better" was "higher quality is better." Gas-guzzling, chrome-laden "Detroit iron" was suddenly challenged by durable, economical, electronically sophisticated competition from Toyota and others. Resources, human and natural, were to be used with more care, more skill, and more discipline not to make money but to make products of greater excellence that in turn would make money. Nor was the Japanese government averse to self-serving trade policies, which the United States was willing to tolerate in exchange for an ally in its all-consuming war in Vietnam.

David Halberstam, in his book, *The Next Century* (Morrow, 1991), observed:

> *America in the postwar years became a political society that assumed the essential health and bountiful quality of the American economy. Japan, by contrast, was an economic society, where wealth had to be renewed each day by the nation's most talented people. . . . We were obsessed with the cold war then the hot war, but the Japanese were obsessed with commerce.*

As our manufacturing base shrank, a service economy expanded in its place. Service economies do not reduce trade

deficits. Consisting of businesses such as retailing and wholesal-
ing, transportation, entertainment, personal services, and other
intangible and intellectual property, the service sector not only
produces fewer exportable goods but also makes us dependent
on goods imported from economies that do save and produce.
How would we otherwise stock our shelves?

The popular notion that in the postindustrial service economy money-valued services are an acceptable substitute for
goods because both generate money ignores the distinction
between money and wealth. Money is a medium of exchange.
Wealth is what is received in that exchange.

I agree with those who argue that information technology
can be an exportable product equal to goods, but I don't agree
that we can ever replace manufacturing with information.
There is simply an insufficient quantity of such products, and
the diversity of cultures abroad limits the marketability of the
entertainment and educational output coming from the United
States. The facts speak for themselves. We are simply not exporting enough information technology to pay for the real goods that
we import. The resulting trade deficits prove that our so-called
information/service economy is in reality a sham.

Another problem with an economy based primarily on services is that jobs in that sector pay less than manufacturing jobs.
Making matters worse, there are high-end and low-end, skilled
and unskilled jobs in the service sector, and in the United States
the growth is in the low-end jobs. When we talk services, we're
talking mainly about flipping hamburgers.

Debunking a Popular Fallacy

A popular fallacy is that America's transition from a manufacturing-
based to a service-based economy is an example of progress comparable to its transition during the nineteenth century from an
agrarian-based to a manufacturing-based economy. During the

nineteenth century, efficiencies made possible by capital investment financed with savings enabled more food to be produced by fewer farm workers. This increased farm productivity freed up labor to make a transition into higher-paying manufacturing jobs similarly created by capital investment financed by savings. The growth in farm productivity that made the industrial revolution possible also resulted in huge exports of American agricultural products and agricultural trade surpluses.

Contrast that with the modern transition from a manufacturing-based to a service-based economy. In this case, labor was freed up because American manufacturers, increasingly burdened by high taxes, excessive regulation, and trade union demands tantamount to extortion, were driven out of business by more efficient foreign manufacturers, resulting in huge trade deficits as we imported all the stuff we could no longer produce competitively at home. The fact that those displaced factory workers were forced to accept lower-paying jobs in the service sector is indicative not of progress but of colossal failure.

Another fallacious comparison was made during an interview I had with Mark Haines, host of CNBC's *Squawk Box*. Mark misinterpreted my position that the United States cannot hope to pay for imports solely through reliance on the service sector as my advocating that the country return to the equivalent of a buggy whip economy. His "buggy whip" reference is to the classic example of creative destruction, a concept of economist Joseph Schumpeter, whereby an innovation such as the automobile represents an improvement so major that it causes the destruction of a mature industry, such as whips for horse-drawn buggies.

The application of the creative destruction concept to the atrophy of manufacturing in the United States is flawed, however. When buggy whip companies went out of business, Americans did not start importing foreign-made buggy whips.

American businesses stopped making buggy whips because the invention of the automobile made them obsolete. Today, the very same highly desirable, state-of-the-art consumer goods that were formerly produced in the United States are now being produced abroad.

That's very different from the creative destruction of manufacturers of obsolete buggy whips by manufacturers of innovative automotive supplies. Today's example is pure destruction. There is absolutely nothing creative about it.

Baby Boomers are Consumers, Not Savers

Born to a generation of people who lived though a depression and then returned from a world war to a victorious country offering the GI Bill and a future filled with possibility, the baby boomers, as the bulging population born following World War II became known, grew up knowing affluence and building it into their life expectations. Those expectations naturally became the promises of the politicians they elected. Amid a business boom driven by leverage and making credit an integral and acceptable part of modern life, financial services organizations, now deregulated and free to expand and diversify, relaxed their lending standards and aggressively foisted auto loans, credit cards, mortgages, and home equity loans on a market as vulnerable as it was demographically irresistible. With personal expectations now tantamount to a sense of entitlement, the stage was clearly set for the spending binge we have today.

Savings? Who needs savings when you own stocks that can only go up in price and a home that gains equity every year? Let the dismal scientists worry that stock values or home equity might simply be the result of inflationary bubbles created by an irresponsible Federal Reserve, or that when the bubbles burst, all that will remain are the debts they collateralized.

WHAT'S TO WORRY ABOUT? WITHOUT THE UNITED STATES THE ASIAN PRODUCERS WOULD BE ALL DRESSED UP WITH NOWHERE TO GO. NO?

You hear this argument all the time, and if you believe it I've got some oceanfront property in Indiana to talk to you about.

The world no more depends on U.S. consumption than medieval serfs depended on the consumption of their lords, who typically took 25 percent of what they produced. What a disaster it would have been for the serfs had their lords not exacted this tribute. Think of all the unemployment the serfs would have suffered had they not had to toil so hard for the benefit of their lords. What would they have done with all that extra free time?

The way modern economists look at things, had the lords increased their take from 25 percent to 35 percent, it would have been an economic boon for the serfs because they would have had 10 percent more work. Too bad the serfs didn't have economic advisers or central bankers to urge such progressive policies.

Here's my favorite analogy to illustrate why it's idiotic to think the world benefits from Americans' excess consumption and would suffer without it (see Figure 1.5).

Let's suppose six castaways are stranded on a desert island, five Asians and one American. Their problem is hunger. So they sit down and divide labor as follows: One Asian will do the hunting, another will fish, the third will scrounge for vegetation, the fourth will cook dinner, and the fifth will gather firewood and tend the fire. The sixth, the American, is given the job of eating.

So five Asians work all day to feed one American, who spends his day sunning himself on the beach. The American is employed in the equivalent of the service sector, operating a tanning salon that has one customer: himself. At the end of the day, the five Asians present a painstakingly prepared feast to

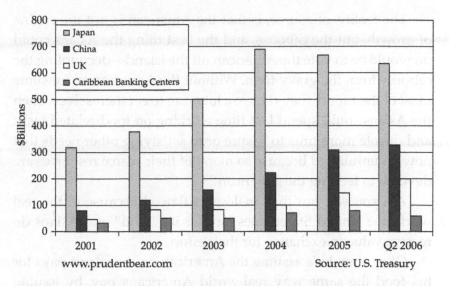

www.prudentbear.com   Source: U.S. Treasury

FIGURE 1.5 *Holdings of U.S. Treasuries by selected countries, 2001–2006.*
The significant percentage of Treasuries purchased by Asian nations,
in particular Japan and China, represents the greatest international
subsidy since the Marshall Plan, the main difference being that the
United States intended its aid to be charity, whereas Japan and China
actually expect to be paid back.
Source: Reprinted by permission from David L. Tice and Associates
(www.prudentbear.com).

the American, who sits at the head of a special table built by the
Asians specifically for this purpose.

Now the American is practical enough to know that if the
Asians are going to continue providing banquets they must also
be fed, so he allows them just enough scraps from his table to
sustain them for the following day's labor.

Modern-day economists would have you look at the situation just described and believe that the American is the lone
engine of growth driving the island's economy; that without the
American and his ravenous appetite, the Asians on the island
would all be unemployed.

The reality, of course, is that the American is not the engine of growth, but the caboose, and the best thing the Asians could do would be to vote the American off the island—decoupling the caboose from the gravy train. Without the American to consume most of their food, they'd have a lot more to eat themselves. Then the Asians could spend less time working on food-related tasks and devote more time to leisure or to satisfying other needs that now go unfulfilled because so many of their scarce resources are devoted to feeding the American.

Ah, you say, but that analogy is flawed because in the real world the United States does pay for its "food" and Asians do receive value in exchange for their effort.

Okay, then let's assume the American on the island pays for his food the same way real-world Americans pay, by issuing IOUs. At the end of each meal, the Asians present the American with a bill, which he pays by issuing IOUs claiming to represent future payments of food.

The castaways all know that the IOUs can never be collected, since the American not only produces no food to back them up, but also lacks the means and the intention of ever providing any. But the Asians accept them anyway, each day adding to the accumulation of worthless IOUs. Are the Asians any better off as a result of this accumulation? Are they any less hungry? Of course not.

Suppose an Asian central banker suddenly washes up onto the island and volunteers his services. Now each day the central banker taxes the other Asians on the island by confiscating a portion of the scraps of food the American throws them each day from his table. The central banker then agrees to return these morsels to the other Asians each day, in exchange for each Asian's daily accumulation of the American's IOUs, less a small percentage for himself because he, the central banker, also has to eat.

Does the existence of a central banker change anything? Do the Asians have any more to eat because their own central banker gives them back a portion of the food he took from them in the first place? Do the American IOUs have any more value because they can now be exchanged in this manner? Of course not.

THE ASIANS WILL BE BETTER OFF WITHOUT US

The real-world lesson is that if it doesn't make sense for the six make-believe Asians to support one make-believe American, it does not make sense for billions of real-world Asians to support millions of real-world Americans. The fact that they do so in exchange for worthless IOUs in no way alters this reality.

There is no question that in the short run, by allowing U.S. dollars to collapse (in effect, voting millions of Americans off the island), there will be some disruptions of Asian economies. Of course, there will be some initial losers, particularly among those Asians who currently profit from the present arrangement. However, these profits come only at the expense of greater losses borne by the entire Asian population.

In the end, the cessation of America's excess consumption, which is not a benefit Asians enjoy but rather a burden they now disproportionately bear, will be the best thing that can happen to them. Like the serfs being liberated from their lords, their scarce resources will be freed to satisfy their own needs and desires, and their standards of living will rise accordingly. As their savings finance increased capital investment, rather than being squandered on American consumption, their future standards of living will rise that much faster as well.

CHINA'S "WARTIME" ECONOMY

As noted earlier with reference to Asia in general, the mainstream of economic thinking holds that China will continue to finance the U.S. current account deficit indefinitely because American consumption is vital to the survival of China's export-driven economy. Quite to the contrary, China's own capacity to consume is much greater than ours and the productive capacity needed to serve it is already in place—in China!

In many ways the modern Asian economies are reminiscent of the wartime economy of the United States during World War II, when the nation's industrial might was concentrated on supplying the war effort. We had 10 million men under arms spread across three continents, our ships patrolled the Atlantic and Pacific Oceans, and our bombers blackened the skies. Factories that had previously produced passenger cars, sewing machines, and farm equipment had been retooled to make fighter planes, jeeps, tanks, rifles, bullets, artillery shells, destroyers, aircraft carriers, submarines, uniforms, helmets, boots, mess kits, and military radios.

At the time we were a very busy nation. Our factories were in operation 24/7, and more people than ever before were working, including legions of women previously absent from the workforce.

Given this full-throttle activity, economists of that time period might have argued that we never should have stormed the beaches at Normandy or Iwo Jima. After all, if the war ended, a disaster would befall our wartime economy. Millions of soldiers and factory workers would lose their jobs and corporate profits would collapse, as there would be no more demand for all the weapons and military equipment they were producing. Because victory abroad would surely bring recession at home, the war needed to be waged indefinitely.

As ridiculous as this argument sounds, it is exactly what most believe the Chinese should do today, as in reality their export-driven economy is basically no different from our wartime economy in 1944.

During the war, American consumers did not receive any direct economic benefit from their hard work and economic activity. In fact, they sacrificed greatly. Because factories were producing military goods, consumer goods were in short supply. In addition, scores of common staples, such as butter, nylon stockings, and gasoline, had to be rationed so that they or the resources needed to produce them would be readily available for the military. Similarly, Chinese citizens now produce export goods from which they themselves derive no direct economic benefit. In effect, consumer goods are rationed in China so as to make them plentiful in the United States.

However, when World War II ended, American factories didn't shut down; they merely returned to consumer goods production. Soldiers didn't lose their jobs; they merely put their labor to more productive uses. Instead of being wasted on a war (which unfortunately had to be fought), resources were applied to civilian purposes, leading to a postwar economic boom.

The same would apply in China today. As Americans once sacrificed to defeat the Nazis and Imperial Japan, the Chinese now sacrifice merely to support the purchasing power of Americans. If China allowed the dollar to decline against the yuan, American purchasing power would by definition be transferred to the Chinese. In China, factors of production would therefore be reallocated as they were during the postwar period in the United States. Factories would retool and labor would seek more productive employment. Instead of wasting scarce resources producing goods to export, China would instead produce goods for domestic consumption.

The time has come for China, and the rest of Asia for that matter, to redirect their vast resources to raising their own standards of living rather than propping up the living standards of Americans. As soon as the Chinese stop producing goods for Americans they can finally begin producing more for themselves.

It's time for China to declare peace. Unfortunately, as Americans are the principal profiteers in China's war, we stand to lose the most when it ends. So while peace means China's days of sacrifice, rationing, and underconsumption will soon end, it means ours are about to begin.

Unfortunately for Americans, being decoupled from the Asian gravy train means it's time to get back to work. In the simple terms of our island castaways analogy, this means a whole lot more hunting and fishing (in the commercial sense) and a whole lot less eating.

REBUILDING A PRODUCTIVE ECONOMY

For Americans to revert from consumers to savers following the economic collapse will probably be less difficult than one might imagine. It is in their fairly recent tradition to be savers, and it will also be a matter of survival.

But rebuilding a manufacturing base from the investment of those savings will be a daunting challenge and will take years to accomplish. Although the devalued dollar will create a favorable environment for exports once factories are up and running, rebuilding modern manufacturing facilities that can compete successfully with those in other countries is largely a matter of building from the ground up. Much of the existing equipment is now obsolete. The government will have to adopt policies that relax onerous and costly regulations, provide tax relief, and generally encourage economic development, which includes having a role in the education of appropriately skilled workers.

Manufacturing anything is a complex process requiring natural and human resources and the presence of a community of supporting industries and services. Just take something as simple as an ordinary lead pencil. To make it you need incense cedar, specially grown, harvested, and selected in a form and grade suitable for the product; lead, which is graphite obtained from mines around the world; metal (for the erasure ferrule); rubber for the eraser; and various stains, glues, and paints. The manufacturing process involves mixing graphite and clay; baking it; cutting, slating, grooving, gluing, and milling wood; fabricating metal and rubber; painting; and engraving.

I'll spare you my comparison to the automobile as an example of complexity at the other extreme, since I've hopefully made my point: Once a particular manufacturing industry (which, to be competitive, is really a community of related industries contributing in various ways) has been dismantled, recreating it is a formidable undertaking, requiring capital investment and years of time.

COMPARING APPLES AND ORANGES: A CLARIFYING PARABLE

The issue of our enormous trade deficit is central to our economic crisis, and Wall Street has gone to mind-blowing lengths to minimize the importance of it. I will conclude by sharing a simple analogy I use in my seminars to illustrate a complex subject and put it into its proper perspective.

A Tale of Two Farmers

Farmer Chang grows only oranges. Farmer Jones grows only apples. Each grows only the fruit he produces most efficiently, trading his surplus for the fruit grown by the other. Both farmers benefit from comparative advantage and free trade. The sole reason that Farmer Chang "exports" oranges is so that he can afford to "import" apples, and vice versa.

Suppose that one year a flood wipes out Farmer Jones' apple crop. Not having any fruit to trade, but hungry nevertheless, he proposes to trade apple IOUs for Farmer Chang's oranges. Since Farmer Chang cannot eat all the oranges he grows anyway, and since Farmer Jones' IOUs will pay 10 percent interest (in extra apples, of course), he accepts.

Farmer Chang accepts Farmer Jones' offer only because of the apples that Farmer Jones' IOUs promise to pay. By themselves, the IOUs have no intrinsic value. Farmer Chang cannot eat them. It is the promise to pay additional apples that gives the IOUs their value.

When Farmer Jones issues his apple IOUs in exchange for real oranges, he does not actually pay for the oranges. Payment will not really be made until the following year when Farmer Jones redeems his notes by giving Farmer Chang all the apples his IOUs obligate him to pay. Only then can the notes be retired and the transaction be completed.

Now suppose that the following year Farmer Jones' crop is again destroyed, this time by a hurricane. He and Farmer Chang once again make the same deal, with Farmer Jones getting more of Farmer Chang's oranges, and Farmer Chang accepting more of Farmer Jones' IOUs.

Further suppose that similar natural disasters continue to besiege Farmer Jones for several more years, until it finally dawns on him that he is eating pretty well, without actually farming. He therefore decides to turn his apple orchard into a golf course and simply play golf all day while enjoying farmer Chang's oranges. In other words, Farmer Jones now operates as a service economy.

Farmer Chang, by contrast, is so busy growing all those oranges that he never gets a chance to play Farmer Jones' course. In fact, he has been accepting Farmer Jones' IOUs for so long that he no longer remembers his original reason for doing so. He now counts his wealth based solely on his accumulation of Farmer Jones' IOUs. Farmer Jones actually enjoys such a good reputation within the farming community that Farmer Chang is able to trade some of Farmer Jones' IOUs for goods and services provided by other farmers and merchants. However, as a result of Farmer Jones' good reputation, no one notices that his apple orchard has been turned into a golf course. His IOUs are now worthless since Farmer Jones no longer possesses the ability to redeem them with actual apples.

Some might argue that the entire community now depends on Farmer Jones and his worthless IOUs and that Farmer Chang and the others will simply accept them indefinitely to avoid acknowledging the reality of their folly. Of course, were these revelations to occur, any unfortunate holders of Farmer Jones' IOUs would officially be forced to realize their losses. However, their true financial situations would improve, as any further accumulation of worthless IOUs would end. As for Farmer Chang, he would once again, literally, enjoy all the fruits of his labor.

The real loser, of course, would be Farmer Jones, for without a viable apple orchard or the ability to buy oranges on credit, he would starve. It would take years to transform his golf course back into an orchard, regain his lost knowledge of farming, and replace his obsolete and dilapidated farming equipment (provided he hadn't already traded it in for golf carts and titanium clubs).

In the end, Farmer Jones' only alternative might be to sell his golf course to Farmer Chang and take a job picking fruit in his orange grove.

2009 UPDATE

The slope was slippery, all right! The ink in *Crash Proof* was hardly dry before the phony, borrow-and-consume U.S. economy began to unravel. As I had predicted, it started when the real estate bubble, already leaking air, finally burst in 2007, triggering a credit crunch that quickly became global and plunged the American economy into deep recession and virtual bankruptcy. In a paradox as valid as it is bizarre, that's actually the good news!

The failing banks, corporate and personal bankruptcies, massive layoffs, falling stock, and real estate prices, home foreclosures, and other consequences of the current economic collapse, however painful the personal and social effects, are free-market forces trying to correct economic imbalances and restore economic viability. An overleveraged economy—leverage referring to debt—is trying now to reverse its errant ways by deleveraging. What is perceived as the problem is really the solution. The problem is what I described earlier in this chapter. The government should get out of the way and let the markets rebalance our economy. It won't, though, and that is the bad news.

Keeping Our Collapses Straight

The collapse I was predicting when I chose my original title, *Crash Proof: How to Profit from the Coming Economic Collapse*, hasn't happened yet. It is largely still ahead of us. The ill-fated dollar, after a bear market rally in 2008, still has a long way to fall. Inflated bond prices, the inverse result of artificially low interest rates, are a bubble still searching for a pin, with effects potentially more devastating than the real estate meltdown.

Maybe a couple of fairy tales will help clarify my point. The mess we are in happened because our government defied free-market forces and tried to engineer a "Goldilocks" economy, one neither too cold nor too hot, but just right. That seemed for a while to be working, but it was actually working against us. What we had instead was a "Humpty Dumpty" economy that sat high on a wall and had a great fall. Now our friends in Washington are trying to do what all the king's horses and all the king's men couldn't do, which is to put Humpty Dumpty back together again. That exercise in futility has a price tag of trillions of dollars, which we will have to either borrow or print at the cost of crippling debt or massive inflation. When I wrote *Crash Proof*, excluding Social Security, Medicare, and other unfunded obligations, our government owed the better part of $8.5 trillion. The figure is now over $10 trillion and about to start mounting much higher. The budget deficit, which was running $300 billion to $400 billion annually, is projected to exceed $1.8 trillion this year and despite government projections, to keep growing thereafter.

The main problem is that the very individuals who assured us that all was well are the ones now entrusted to solve the problem. But how can they solve a problem they still do not understand? The Goldilocks crowd wants to rehabilitate their prodigal daughter. If they can just get her borrowing and spending again, she can once again skip blissfully picking daisies. It has not dawned on them that they embraced the wrong fairy tale and are now unknowingly scrambling to put Humpty Dumpty back together again.

The Real Estate Meltdown and Its Consequences

As I predicted, subprime mortgages granted on indiscriminate terms to unqualified borrowers, which totaled a staggering $600 billion or 20 percent of all new mortgages in 2006 alone, became a nationwide foreclosure problem in 2007. But defaults quickly spread to prime mortgages, as neighborhoods got seedier and housing prices declined, wiping out the home equity Americans relied on as a substitute for savings and a source of available credit.

Mortgage lenders and institutional investors, such as banks, Wall Street investment banks, and other investors in mortgage-backed bonds or structured mortgage-backed securities called collateralized debt obligations (CDOs), took huge write-offs that jeopardized their required leverage ratios or resulted in insolvency.

With loan portfolios full of toxic paper, banks stopped lending, not just to homeowners but to everybody, including businesses large and small and even other banks. Some got emergency cash infusions from external sources (Citigroup got $7 billion from Abu Dhabi, for example) and others from that bottomless well (of printer's ink), the United States Treasury. Such bailouts were deemed necessary because the recipients were presumed to be "too big to fail." (Paul Volcker, former Federal Reserve chairman and now economic adviser to President Barack Obama, took a small liberty with that phrase in February 2009 when he sardonically and perhaps prophetically observed they were "too big to exist," a rather profound comment when you think about it.)

The result was a global credit freeze. Businesses curtailed operations and consumers reduced spending, causing declining sales, bankruptcies, and massive layoffs. The CEOs of the big three automakers boarded separate corporate jets and flew to Washington with hats in hand, telling Congress that without a government bailout they (with the exception of Ford) would go out of business and take a network of parts suppliers and dealerships with them (Unfortunately they got their bailout money, then got even more when they filed for bankruptcy anyway several months later).

By 2009, the U.S. economy was in free fall, economies abroad were in varying degrees of distress, and states, businesses, and strapped consumers were getting more desperate by the day. In efforts to stimulate bank lending and consumer spending, the federal funds rate was cut to a range of zero to ¼ percent, rebate checks were mailed to taxpayers under a Bush program, and half of a $700 billion bank bailout bill known as the Troubled Asset Relief Program (TARP) was used to bolster the capital at several banks. None of that stimulus made a dime's worth of difference. Rather than lend the money, the banks added to their reserves or acquired other banks. Government intervention was proving impotent in the face of market forces, which were having a constructive effect, as I look at things. To my way of thinking, a bank that got into trouble making bad loans deserves applause rather than opprobrium for being unwilling to use a cash bailout to make more bad loans. Similarly, consumers who are cutting back on spending are doing what I believe they should be doing, creating savings that will become the basis for future bank lending and provide the capital investment that entrepreneurs need to create jobs and finance the production of exportable goods.

The Wrong Way to Go

The Obama administration's Economic Recovery and Reinvestment Program initially provides some $800-plus billion in combined spending and tax relief, but has the expressed aim of spending whatever money is required to create jobs, get credit flowing again, and put the economy back on track. A small but important percentage of the funds will go to states and municipalities for public works projects that will replace deteriorated infrastructure and perhaps ultimately improve productivity. The projects are supposed to be "shovel ready" and thus will create new jobs within a short time frame.

While some of the infrastructure spending is likely long overdue and badly needed, making the repairs will not help the economy. The bottom line is that we simply cannot afford to pay the bill right now. Imagine an out-of-work, overly indebted individual deciding to have her kitchen remodeled to solve her financial problems. Even if her kitchen were badly dated, with avocado appliances, orange counter tops, and dark wood-paneled cabinets, going deeper into debt to fix it up would only worsen her predicament.

The reality is there are more pressing uses for our scarce resources right now than making our roads nicer. Once we rebuild our savings and start producing stuff again, then we can afford to remodel. Until then we need the government to get out of the way and allow market forces to reallocate resources, including labor.

If that means people are going to lose jobs in the service and financial sectors, it is a sacrifice we must make. Human resources should be allocated where they are productive and contribute to a strong economy that benefits everybody. Nobody wants to see people out of work, but which is more humane: 5 million unemployed today, or 10 million unemployed a few years from now? In my view, that is the choice we face.

Lost in translation, of course, is that we do not want jobs merely to keep ourselves busy, but for the purchasing power that working at a job creates. But nonproductive government jobs, or private sector jobs subsidized by government money, confer limited purchasing power to workers; in the end we may all be employed but have little to show for our efforts.

I fear that government spending on the scale being contemplated will change the character of our economy by moving us in the direction of central planning. That is the opposite of free-market capitalism. Our economy needs to be restructured from the foundation up to regain the viability it had when profit-minded people were making the important decisions and the United States was becoming the world's leading industrial power.

Yet what the government is about to do is spend massive amounts of taxpayer money to reflate a consumer-driven bubble economy. Its objective is to get consumers using credit again, to go back to the malls, to buy more cars, to carry more credit cards, and to take out more student loans. But buying stuff we couldn't afford with money we didn't have was what got us into this fix. We've consumed too much and have more than we need, and until we stop consuming and start saving and producing, our economy will never enjoy a real recovery.

Get credit flowing again? There's nothing to flow. The banks blew their money on bad loans. That money is gone. The only way we can restore our banking system is with savings. To get from here to there, we have to allow a lot of banks to fail. We can't just print money and tell banks to lend it out. There is no productivity associated with that.

It also appears that first on the agenda of Treasury Secretary Timothy Geithner is to revitalize the market for asset-backed securities. He wants to help Wall Street securitize more consumer debt (mortgages, credit cards, and auto and student loans) and sell it to leveraged hedge funds and overseas investors. In other words, he wants to re-create the very conditions that brought our economy to the brink. Rather then encouraging American borrowers to once again tap the savings of foreigners, we should allow our domestic pool of savings to be replenished. The main reason securitization flourished in the first place was that after we depleted our own savings, securitization was the best way to gain access to everyone else's. But since the money financed consumption, we simply lack the productive capacity to pay it back.

President Obama says if we don't act quickly on a rescue plan, we're in for a catastrophe. I say if we *do* intervene we're in for a bigger catastrophe, which, in a worst-case scenario, means a repeat of the Great Depression, this time with hyperinflation instead of deflation. In short, the government is about to pour gasoline on the wildfire it set.

The Hoover/Roosevelt and Bush/Obama Analogy

It's nearly everybody's understanding that the Great Depression was caused by Herbert Hoover's inaction and cured by Franklin D. Roosevelt's New Deal intervention. That enduring misconception is used all the time to support the argument that an impending depression can be averted by New Deal–type programs. The fact is that both men were interventionists, FDR more so than Hoover, but in different ways. Hoover, caricatured as the capitalist from central casting, actually distrusted free markets and favored government planning, although within strict constitutional limits. Roosevelt railed about what he saw as the abuses of capitalism and favored big government operating in experimental ways to achieve progress, even if it meant abandoning constitutional orthodoxy at times.

The asset bubble we know as the Roaring Twenties that ended with the Crash of 1929 was the result of an easy money policy not unlike the one that has led to our present crisis.

In dealing with the Crash, Hoover, far from inactive, intervened in major ways but made mistakes—ordering wages up when they wanted to go down; raising taxes when the public couldn't afford them—that turned what should have been a stock market correction, albeit a major one, into the start of an economic depression.

Roosevelt, elected in 1932, inherited the depression and proceeded to create a panoply of regulatory, relief, and aid agencies, some of which worked and some of which didn't, but in general contributed to an environment characterized by unpredictability and antibusiness bias that discouraged private investment and kept the depression going until the end of the decade.

The "depression within a depression" in 1937 was followed by heavy government spending preparatory to World War II, causing an upswing in the economy that continued when the wartime economy began in 1941.

Bottom line: When it comes to the New Deal as an antidote to depression, I ain't buying.

The Impact Abroad of the United States' Economic Problems

I am absolutely unshaken in my conviction that foreign producing economies, such as China, Japan, and other Asian and European exporters, will eventually decouple—that is, stop subsidizing U.S. consumption and begin producing for themselves. I have always said, however, that it wouldn't happen overnight. The recent rally in the dollar, something I'll get into in a later chapter update, resulted from foreign governments and investors seeking the perceived safety of U.S. Treasury securities. Here we are, virtually bankrupt and preparing to print or borrow trillions more dollars to jump-start a car clearly headed for a cliff. Yet countries with fundamentally strong economies and with trade and budget surpluses put their money here because they want to keep it safe and because they still think our consumption is vital to their economies. So their initial reaction is to prop up our economy and our currency. By doing so, they are preventing complete decoupling, because they are preventing our purchasing power from being transferred abroad. This will be the case as long as foreign central banks keep intervening to buy up dollars and keep currency pegs in effect.

They are only hurting themselves. In effect, Americans are not spending because they are out of dollars, and foreigners are not spending because they are hoarding dollars.

Financially, of course, the foreign economies are hurting. When the largest consumer and borrower goes broke, obviously suppliers and lenders are going to feel it. But ultimately they will be better off without a customer that requires vendor financing, the extended payment time a commercial seller gives a buyer that can't pay its bills. The credit crunch is global because they lent us money we can't repay and now we're asking to borrow more. Our borrowing needs are crowding out investment all over the world. And every time we pass another stimulus bill, we up the ante. So it's not the collapse of the American economy that is crippling the rest of the world, but the huge cost of trying to prop it up.

But how much longer will the rest of the world suffer to subsidize the United States? It's absolutely unarguable that they, not we, are the engine of economic growth. We are the caboose that's keeping the train from getting up to speed. As Abe Lincoln said: "It is true you may fool all of the people some of the time; you can even fool some of the people all of the time; but you can't fool all of the people all the time."

2

What Uncle Sam, the Mass Media, and Wall Street Don't Want You to Know

A little dissimulation on the part of our leaders now and then is probably something we should learn to accept, lest the natives get unnecessarily restless, but it's something else—and to my mind, downright inexcusable—to have vital economic information routinely and blatantly misrepresented.

The economic statistics put out by the U.S. government are propaganda, pure and simple. Issued by government agencies, interpreted by spokespersons for the government and the financial community, and reported by the mass media, the information we get has been manipulated to mold a public understanding favorable to the agenda of the powers that be.

Because our trading partners and the foreign central banks and other foreign investors who buy our debt get the same information we do, they continue to throw good money after

33

bad. But that can't last. When they wake up to the fact that the United States can't pay, they'll stop financing our debt and become their own consumers. Lacking the savings and production capacity to support ourselves, our economy will collapse.

Yet, the American public remains oblivious because we're not getting facts. The government, the mass media, and Wall Street have a vested interest in consumer confidence, keeping the American public assured that everything's basically okay. There may even be an element of altruism; strong economies are built on positive psychology. But too much of the data issued by government agencies is self-serving and ultimately counterproductive. Myths get reinforced and they get in the way of rational decisions. Wall Street buys in because it sells stocks and bonds when investors are optimistic, although it has been known to bet the other way with its own money. The media report the news as they understand it, but they get their understanding from the government and Wall Street.

The midterm congressional elections in 2006, I might note, seemed to offer a ray of hope that the American public is not so easily fooled. Despite administration claims that the economy was stronger than ever, most Americans voted their pocketbooks, and leadership changed in both the House and the Senate. Wall Street economists are puzzled by the discrepancy between the strength of the economic numbers and the weakness of the polling numbers representing the president's popularity. The election results are evidence that it's the economic numbers they should be questioning, not the polling numbers.

I'm not suggesting that anybody out there is nefariously scheming to collapse the American economy. Everybody, including our trading partners, wants our economy to be strong. Our politicians have to live in the economy, too, so their interest is in deferring problems so the bad news happens when somebody else is in office. But economic imbalances based on weak fundamentals get worse with time, and the potential consequences are dire.

Consider some recent examples of what Uncle Sam and Wall Street have been telling us and how these self-serving distortions compare with reality.

THE BALLOONING TRADE DEFICIT

The comforting distortion: Large trade deficits are a sign our economy is creditworthy, strong, and growing faster than the economies of our trading partners.

The disturbing reality: Our trade deficit is a huge and growing problem and threatens to ruin us.

Trade deficits occur when countries import more than they export. Ours, which is on the order of $65 billion per month, is near record levels and trending higher. Nothing moves in a straight line, however, and when we have a month in which the trade deficit ratchets back a billion or two, Wall Street uncorks champagne. Given the state of our economy, that's like celebrating the fact that your kid brought home a report card with an F instead of an F minus (see Figure 2.1).

When the upward trend resumes, administration spinmeisters tell us large deficits are a sign that our domestic economy is strong. ("Oh, and by the way, Dad, the F stands for fabulous.")

As a case in point, on January 13, 2005, the New York Times ran an article headlined "Trade Deficit at New High, Reinforcing Risk to Dollar." The piece quoted an exuberant then Treasury Secretary John Snow as saying the deficit was a sign the American economy "is growing faster than those of our trading partners in the euro zone and in Japan. . . . The economy is growing,

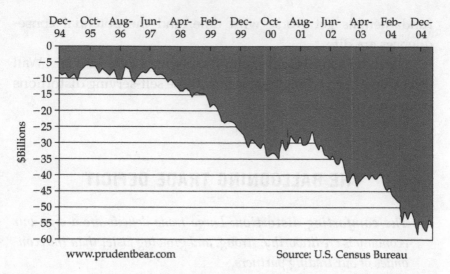

www.prudentbear.com   Source: U.S. Census Bureau

FIGURE 2.1 *U.S. trade balance, 1994–2005.* The sharp deterioration in the U.S. trade balance reflects a deindustrializing nation increasingly living beyond its means. When discipline returns, Americans will see their cost of living surge and their standard of living plunge.

Source: Reprinted by permission from David L. Tice and Associates (www. prudentbear.com).

expanding, creating jobs and disposable income and that shows up in the demand for imports."

Coincidentally, the same article also quoted me. I said: "In reaction to today's release of record trade deficit figures, Treasury Secretary John Snow continued with his Rumpelstiltskin routine of characterizing disastrous economic news as if it were just the opposite."

Mr. Snow might have been right if we were a production economy generating the wealth to finance the imports, but we're not. In the 1950s and 1960s we had budget deficits, small by today's standards but considered big at the time, but our economy was strong because we had savings and were making things. (We still do produce, of course, but not enough. The shift from manufacturing to services has gone too far.) Now long on consumption and short on production, we are financing that consumption not with money we have saved, but with money we have borrowed, mostly from the same countries we're importing from.

To make matters worse, we're borrowing short-term to finance a long-term imbalance, a hangover from the Rubinomics of the Clinton years. That keeps the interest lower, but it will make it easier for creditors to bail out when they wise up. Instead of being locked into 30-year bonds, which they'd have to sell in the secondary market, they'll just let their Treasury bills mature and move on.

No less solid a citizen than Warren Buffett was quoted in an Associated Press report dated January 20, 2006, warning, "The U.S. trade deficit is a bigger threat to the domestic economy than either the federal budget deficit or consumer debt and could lead to political turmoil. . . . Right now, the rest of the world owns $3 trillion more of us than we own of them."

INFLATION: THE CORE AND THE BUBBLE

The comforting distortion: Core inflation is moderate and well under control.

The disturbing reality: Core inflation excludes food and energy from producer and consumer price indexes that understate real inflation to begin with. Actual inflation is considerably higher and also exists big-time in the form of a housing bubble being represented as a strong housing market.

The producer price index (PPI) and the consumer price index (CPI) were designed to measure inflation as it is reflected in prices. Inflation is something we like when we're in debt, which stays in constant dollars, and need more dollars (albeit of less intrinsic value) to repay it with. Inflation is bad, however, because it reduces the dollar's purchasing power and puts upward pressure on bond rates, which have to factor in inflation protection so that real yields will be attractive to investors.

Inflation is so important that I've devoted Chapter 4 in its entirety to the subject. What we need to understand here is that our government has an interest in keeping inflation both secretly high and officially low. Here's the background:

On the one hand, Americans saw the value of their dollars decline in the rampant inflation of the 1970s and learned to dread inflation. A government that lets inflation get out of control will have to answer to a scared and angry public, so it stops at nothing to make sure CPI numbers reflect moderate inflation at worst.

On the other hand, the government has an outsized national debt and budget deficit because of the Iraq war and the failure of Americans to save and invest in productive activities that would provide a multiplied return on investment and the funds to repay debt.

Cheaper dollars mitigate the debt burden.

To continue its foreign borrowing, the government must keep the international community assured that it has its economic house in order and is creditworthy. A healthy economy is an economy that is growing, and growth is measured by consumer spending. American consumers, already in debt up to their eyeballs and earning less since we became a service-oriented economy, can keep spending only by borrowing, most recently against the equity in their homes.

The Housing Bubble

Housing prices have soared in recent years to bubble levels, spurred by mortgage rates that the Federal Reserve, again by adding liquidity (printing money), has kept artificially low. I discuss the coming real estate debacle in Chapter 6.

The Federal Reserve under Messrs. Alan Greenspan and Ben Bernanke has been creating inflation, pure and simple, in the guise of a healthy housing market. How often have you read headlines to the effect that the U.S. economy, driven by a strong housing market, has been growing at a healthy rate?

The Fed chose this course following the bursting of the dot-com bubble of the late 1990s. We should have had a corrective recession then, but really didn't. Sure, we had a couple of quarters of slightly declining growth, but only in the most technical sense could it be said we had a recession. No serious withdrawal symptoms or sobering up took place. But the oxymoronic "jobless recovery" that followed, even with lower taxes, was distinctly lackluster. Something had to be done to reignite economic growth.

So Federal Reserve Chairman Greenspan made his decision to open the monetary floodgates to keep long-term mortgage rates artificially low, and thus create an inflationary housing bubble to replace the stock market bubble.

It is noteworthy that substantial numbers of the homes bought or built were pure speculation. It cannot be seriously argued that the government's motive was to make it easier for young families to find housing. To the contrary, increased home values were used to collateralize additional household debt used for nonproductive purchases like automobiles, TV sets, and vacations.

Now the housing market is softening. A bursting of the bubble would leave homeowners looking at higher adjustable-rate mortgage payments and negative equity in their homes. What president would want that kind of train wreck on his watch?

Helicopter Ben

And how opportune that we have manning the printing press a supposedly independent Fed chairman who thinks like Alan

Greenspan. I'm referring now to Helicopter Ben Bernanke. Needless to say, I'm being sarcastic. The helicopter reference, you may remember, stems from a speech the newly appointed Bernanke gave at the National Economists Club in Washington, D.C., in which he used the metaphor of cash dropping from a helicopter to illustrate the ease with which the economy could be invigorated through government fiscal (lower taxes) and monetary (money-printing) actions. That became known as the helicopter theory and it's all about inflation.

So in case you were wondering, inflation is a problem and a particularly tricky one because the economy is too vulnerable to absorb a significant interest rate increase.

As mentioned, inflation is measured, or misrepresented to be more accurate, at the wholesale level by the producer price index (PPI) and at the consumer level by the consumer price index (CPI). Both comprise a mix of goods and commodities (no services) spread across different industries, but half of the items are creatively adjusted in different ways, making the reliability of price measurements highly suspect.

Two examples of distortions affecting the CPI were the recent declines in used car prices and rents. In the first case, zero percent financing deals on new automobiles produced a glut of used car trade-ins, causing used car prices, a component of the index, to fall dramatically, thus reducing inflation. In the other case, based on an adjustment made to the CPI dating back to the late 1970s, when politicians replaced home prices with owners' equivalent rent in an effort to mitigate the former's adverse effects on measured inflation rates, skyrocketing home prices actually caused rents to fall, thus exerting downward pressure on the CPI. As a result, despite surging house prices, quiescent owners' equivalent rent (a subjective estimate of what it would cost to rent a similar house) helped keep those rising prices from feeding into the CPI. This occurred because rock-bottom mortgage rates and lax lending standards turned renters into buyers, creating record high vacancy rates and few prospective tenants to fill them. This suppressed rents, keeping a lid on the housing component of the CPI, particularly the "core," comprised of almost 40 percent rents. Therefore, the highly inflationary monetary policy of extremely low interest rates paradoxically suppressed core consumer prices, providing justification for a continuation of the policy. In short, the more inflation the Fed created, the more downward pressure applied to the core CPI, its preferred inflation measure. As the Church Lady used to say, how convenient! Those two items alone caused a 1.7 percent drop in the core CPI between November 2001 and December 2003, according to Bill Bonner and Addison Wiggin in *Empire of Debt* (John Wiley & Sons, 2006).

Rotten to the Core

Did I say "core"? The distinction between official and core PPI and CPI numbers is another way real rates of inflation are concealed. Core inflation is measured by eliminating from the indexes items whose susceptibility to abrupt price movements might cause distortions. This always means food and energy, but may include other so-called outliers from time to time. Significantly, the recent rise in petroleum prices, even though it affects every other price to which the cost of gas is a contributing factor, is not reflected in core numbers, which get more play than "headline" numbers (the CPI figures that do include food and energy).

The only thing more disingenuous than the core CPI is reporting annual inflation rates using a 12-month trailing core. This now-common practice deceives twice. The core part hides volatile prices, while the trailing 12-month part, which would eliminate the problem of volatility anyway, weights the result with lower values, assuming inflation is rising. I like to think of core CPI as the government equivalent of the "pro forma" earnings the dot-coms used to tout during the tech bubble. Pro forma earnings are earnings that exclude all the charges that might otherwise reduce earnings. Similarly, core CPI is inflation not counting the stuff that went up.

The Importance of Oil

The misrepresentation of core inflation as the official inflation number is especially problematic in the case of oil, which is a major part of the excluded energy category. Oil prices have been volatile, to be sure, but to ignore their significance as a factor in inflation could be justified only if it could be argued that recent oil price increases are temporary and likely to be reversed in the coming years. In fact, high oil prices are not only here to stay, but are headed significantly higher than their present level of around $60 a barrel and their 2005 high of over $70.

A familiar yet extremely naive argument is that oil represents a declining percentage of gross domestic product in the increasingly service-based U.S. economy and is therefore of diminishing importance.

True, energy expenditures have declined from about 14 percent of GDP in 1980 to only 7 percent today. However, to argue that this makes the U.S. economy less dependent on oil is simplistic and fallacious. Wall Street analysts are only too eager to accept this flawed logic, as it allows them to sweep yet another major economic problem under an already lumpy rug.

Just because the United States now imports many of the goods that it formerly produced domestically does not mean that it is now less dependent on the oil used to manufacture them. In fact, due to the increased energy now required to transport these goods to America, the U.S. economy is more vulnerable than ever to rising oil prices. Although foreign oil consumption does not directly factor into U.S. gross domestic product, oil is a cost affecting the price of virtually everything we buy, whether it is produced here or imported from abroad.

For example, in 1980 a pair of shoes purchased in New Haven, Connecticut, might have been manufactured in a factory in nearby Hartford. The oil necessary to produce these shoes would have been consumed domestically, and therefore directly included in U.S. gross domestic product. However, since today that pair of shoes is likely to have been produced in China, the oil consumed in the production process is now excluded from U.S. gross domestic product. Instead, that cost is indirectly passed on to American consumers in the price of the shoes. Oil is just as significant a factor; it's just that its costs are hidden in the prices of nonoil imports.

However, since shoes manufactured in China must also be shipped across the Pacific Ocean, the oil consumed in transportation is now far more significant today than it was in 1980. The extra cost of those ships returning to China empty is also indirectly passed on to American consumers in the prices of imported shoes. Once these shoes arrive at a port in California, they must then be trucked 3,000 miles to the East Coast. The cost of oil consumed in domestic transportation, which is included as part of U.S. gross domestic product, is nevertheless significantly higher than it was in 1980, when those shoes needed to be transported fewer than 100 miles.

That the growing dominance of non-energy-intensive sectors, especially financial services, protects the overall economy from higher energy costs is also a frequently voiced but fallacious argument, as it ignores the impact rising energy costs will have on interest rates, a central cost factor in financial services and other nonmanufacturing businesses.

As higher energy costs push up consumer prices, particularly energy-intensive imports, it will be harder for the Fed to maintain the illusion that inflationary pressures are contained. As inflation expectations become more in line with inflation reality, long-term interest rates will rise substantially as well. With the Fed well behind a rapidly accelerating inflation curve, it might be forced to get extremely aggressive with short-term interest rates, potentially inverting the yield curve with both long-term and short-term rates substantially above current levels.

The impact of double-digit interest rates on financial services and other interest-rate-sensitive sectors will be severe. When factoring in their impact on highly inflated asset prices, which collateralize borrowing and finance a significant portion of consumer spending, the effects could be catastrophic.

Self-serving rhetoric notwithstanding, the truth is that U.S. dependence on oil has never been greater. Given that any significant rise in interest rates that will ultimately accompany higher oil prices will likely occur at a time when a highly leveraged American economy can least afford it, it is very dangerous to downplay the risks associated with rising oil prices.

THE DEFLATION RUSE

The comforting distortion: Increases in the CPI are an indication that the risk of deflation is being successfully combated.

The disturbing reality: Deflation risk is pure bunk designed to distract us from the real problem, which is inflation and which the Fed can't effectively counter by raising interest rates because consumers are too close to the edge.

In 2003, the Fed invoked the threat of deflation to take the stinger out of reported inflation figures. Now there's a straw man if there ever was one. Whenever inflation rates (already understated) rose, the Fed pointed to the specter of deflation and the successful fight being waged against that contrived bugaboo.

Just as inflation results from an expansion of the supply of money and credit, deflation, technically defined, is a contraction of that supply. Deflation is bad, however, only when demand disappears completely due to a collapse of income, as happened during the Great Depression. Otherwise, there is always demand at some level of prices, and deflation simply means that supply exceeds it, causing consumer prices to fall. Economists nonetheless worry about falling prices for two reasons, both of them nonsense.

The first is that people will stop spending as they anticipate cheaper prices, but there is no evidence this happens. Computers, cell phones, digital cameras, and camcorders get cheaper all the time but continue to sell like hotcakes. And how could falling gas prices be bad?

The other fear is that corporate profits would suffer, causing companies to reduce investment, production, and employment. But corporate profitability is not determined by absolute dollars. Profitability is about margins. Margins remain constant as costs and prices fall together. In fact, as falling prices result in increased sales, constant margins often lead to greater profitability. A lot more flat-screen TV sets are sold at $2,000 apiece than were sold at $10,000.

The great danger in misleading the public and the stock and bond markets about real inflation levels is that by the time inflation is recognized for the problem it is, we'll have hyperinflation and it will be too late to counteract it.

THE PRODUCTIVITY MYTH

The comforting distortion: Productivity gains mean higher sustainable growth rates, lower inflation, and lower unemployment.

The disturbing reality: What productivity gains?

So maybe we do have a problem with sustained economic growth, with inflation, and with diminished production, but won't these problems be alleviated by the technology-driven economic phenomenon known as productivity?

To dispose quickly of a question of semantics, let's be clear that productivity and production don't mean the same thing. Production has to do with quantities, productivity with efficiencies. During World War II, for example, General Motors stopped making cars and, with money no obstacle, delivered more than $12.3 billion worth of war material to lead the Allied war effort. That's production. In a recent quarterly report, the now-struggling automaker reported progress in the form of a decrease in its labor costs per vehicle. That would be a reflection of higher productivity.

A great deal has been made of U.S. productivity gains and how they are supposed to translate into sustained higher economic growth rates, lower inflation, lower unemployment, and less pronounced business cycles. Productivity enjoyed its highest level of hype just before the dot-com bust, as part and parcel of the heralded but now discredited "new economy."

Productivity means output per unit of input, input referring to labor or to time. Whatever the fallacies of the new economy argument, productivity should theoretically improve as technology enables deeper levels of analysis that managers can use to achieve higher levels of efficiency. The questions are (1) how significant a factor higher productivity has actually been and (2) why, if it is true that we are more productive than our trading partners, our trade deficit gets bigger, not smaller.

Heady Hedonics

Productivity has been widely studied, the relevant science being known as hedonics, and it's no coincidence that as computers became faster and more powerful, claims of economy-wide productivity gains became more extravagant.

In a March 2000 speech at Boston College on "The Revolution in Information Technology," as reported in an April 2001 article by the editors of Monthly Review titled "The New Economy: Myth and Reality," Alan Greenspan said:

Until the mid-1990s, the billions of dollars that businesses had poured into information technology seemed to leave little imprint on the American economy. [But since 1995] computer modeling, for example, has dramatically reduced the time and cost required to design items ranging from motor vehicles to commercial airliners to skyscrapers.

After a decade of analysis, however, it has been generally concluded that while computers and technology have accomplished wondrous things, higher industrial productivity is not notably among them.

One important reason why higher productivity became such an overrated economywide phenomenon has to do with computers themselves as one of America's leading manufactured products.

Because computer technology has advanced so rapidly, hedonics analysts decided to recognize these advances using a formula to adjust the productivity numbers of computer manufacturers. If a new computer has 10 times the power of the model it replaced, the manufacturer's productivity is increased by a factor of 10. In other words, the employee who put the computer together has improved his output 10 times over, an obvious and ridiculous (but real) distortion of the productivity statistic.

The distortion is even more egregious when the hedonic logic is carried to the consumer level. Because my new computer is 10 times more powerful than last year's model, does that mean I can type my reports 10 times faster? Of course not; I type at the same rate on both machines.

When measuring productivity, it's the production of consumer goods, not of capital goods, that counts, the sole purpose of the latter being merely to facilitate the production of the former. That is the main distinction between the two classes of goods. Consumer goods are wanted for themselves, while capital goods (also referred to as being instrumental goods) are wanted solely for the consumer goods that they are capable of producing. While personal computers are clearly consumer goods, those purchased by business are capital goods. The key factor is not how fast or sophisticated the computers themselves are, but how many more consumer goods businesses actually produce as a result of using them.

The previously referenced article in the April 2001 issue of Monthly Review quoted Alan Greenspan again as saying:

> *The elevated rates of return offered by the newer technologies in the United States are largely the result of a reduction in labor costs per unit of output. The rates of return on investments in the same new technologies are correspondingly less in Europe and Japan because businesses there face higher costs of displacing workers than we do.*

In other words, to quote from one of my own commentaries in September 2004, "Today, a company increases productivity by simply replacing domestic labor with less expensive foreign labor. The savings for America are greatly reduced as the added 'productivity' comes at the expense of a growing current account deficit. . . . So, while analysts and journalists continue praising misleading 'productivity' numbers, the American economy will continue to produce less, and the number of unemployed Americans will continue to grow."

Perversely, the technology that promised to mitigate imbalances through improved productivity could have the effect of accelerating destabilization and contributing to a world-wide meltdown of the money markets should something bad happen. . . . According to Michael Mandel in *The Coming Internet Depression* (Basic Books, 2000), modern communications technology, combined with the shift of purchasing power to Europe and Asia that has made America a debtor nation, "could lead to a devastating run on the dollar, causing foreign investors to pull out their investments even more quickly than they put them in."

GROSSLY PADDED DATA, OR AS WE KNOW THEM, GDP NUMBERS

The comforting distortion: Increases in the gross domestic product (GDP) signify a healthy, growing economy.

The disturbing reality: The GDP is too full of fluff to be an accurate measure of economic health and growth.

When we're told our economy is growing (meaning healthy), reference is being made to quarterly reports showing increases in the gross domestic product (GDP), after adjusting for inflation, using a "deflator" based on the CPI (whose frailties were pointed out earlier).

The GDP started out as the GNP (gross national product) during World War II, when it was used to measure wartime production capacity. It was never intended to be used as a measure of the country's economic well-being, and its shortcomings are laughably numerous.

By definition, the GDP is the sum total of the monetary value of all final goods and services bought and sold within U.S. borders in a given year. The distinction between GDP and GNP, incidentally, is that GDP doesn't care about the nationality of the producer. It includes everything transacted within our borders, even BMWs manufactured in North Carolina. (GNP, which is almost never used, would exclude foreign manufacturers in the United States and include goods and services produced by U.S. firms operating abroad.) GDP thus includes the totality of consumer, investment, and government spending, plus the value of exports, minus the value of imports.

One big problem with GDP, although represented as a measure of economic health, is that it makes no effort to distinguish between transactions that benefit the nation's health and those that subtract from it. Destructive activities are included as well as productive activities. The GDP may not have been designed to measure economic well-being, but since it is used for that purpose, everything it includes—every monetary transaction that takes place anywhere and anytime within its time frame—is, by definition, progress and a contribution to the nation's economic health. Thus Hurricane Katrina added to the GDP despite tragic losses to the populace, as do other negative expenses, such as crime prevention costs, expenses incurred in divorces, medical costs, and national defense expenditures.

Another serious shortcoming is that it ignores everything that doesn't take place under the rubric of monetary trade. Money has to change hands. Functions performed in running a household, for example, are excluded because no money is paid. The same functions, such as child and elder care, if performed by a housekeeper rather than a family member, would add to the GDP because the housekeeper gets paid. Similarly, functions performed by volunteers, while worth money, are excluded because they do not involve money.

The depletion of natural resources used to produce goods adds to the GDP.

Income distribution is completely ignored. If one family had all the nation's income and the rest of the population had none, that one family's income would boost the GDP.

Money paid to clean up toxic waste adds to the GDP, as did the money spent to create the toxic waste in the first place. The *Exxon Valdez* oil spill increased the GDP because money was paid to clean it up.

Of direct relevance, money borrowed from foreign sources and spent here increases the GDP, even though repayment will be the responsibility of future generations.

Finally, GDP numbers are often the fabrications of statisticians. For example, the government assigns a value to free checking accounts and adds that value to the GDP. Another example provided by the hedonics experts we met when we discussed the productivity myth: If $10 billion worth of computers are purchased, but they have five times the computing power of computers previously purchased in some benchmark year, the government reports sales of $50 billion when it calculates GDP. That may be somebody's idea of realistic accounting, but it's my idea of manipulation.

Yet despite all this misrepresentation, manipulation, and fluff, the GDP is what everybody uses to gauge economic growth. Outrageous debt levels are considered justifiable because they are in line with historical percentage relationships to the GDP.

The real wealth-producing components of GDP (manufacturing, mining, et al.) have been shrinking in their percentages of the total. Our GDP is over 70 percent consumption, which could collapse at any time because it is financed by debt and not supported by domestic production.

CONSUMER CONFIDENCE: THE CRUELEST IRONY

The comforting distortion: Consumer confidence drives the healthy economy.

The disturbing reality: Consumer confidence drives it the wrong way. The consumer is misdirected and consumer confidence is an utterly useless statistic.

A skater, confident the ice is thick when in fact it's thin, has an excellent chance of getting very cold, very wet, and very drowned. Confidence by itself, unless it has a valid basis, can get us in trouble.

It is also true, getting back to our subject, that an economy in which consumers lacked confidence and were afraid to invest or spend money would be stagnant and unhealthy. Recessions start when people decide to stop spending money.

That is in no way to say, however, that consumer confidence is a synonym for economic health, although with more than a little help from the spinmeisters, it has virtually become so.

The problem, of course, is that consumer confidence is reinforced by the government's self-serving distortions of economic statistics. Represented as a self-contained dynamic with a life of its own, it feeds on itself and adds impetus to counterproductive trends. Thus consumers spend borrowed money because they are confident the economy is healthy, and in a healthy economy incomes can be expected to rise.

But the economy is not a net producer, the country and its citizens are overextended, and personal incomes are actually declining as high-paying manufacturing jobs are replaced by lower-paying retail and other service economy jobs. Because consumer confidence does not have a valid basis, a bad condition is worsening and disaster lies ahead.

What consumers need is less confidence. Instead of assuming perpetual sunshine, they should be planning for a rainy day. But Wall Street wants the opposite. It's happy when consumers recklessly borrow and spend like there is no tomorrow. Anything that smacks of a reality check causes Wall Street to panic.

As I write this, I am looking at an April 29, 2006, Associated Press release, reporting on economic results for the first quarter of 2006.

"Popping out of a year-end rut, the economy zipped ahead," it enthuses, noting that "consumers boosted spending at a brisk rate of 5.5 percent, compared with a paltry 0.9 percent in the fourth quarter."

Continuing the theme that the more consumers spend, the merrier becomes the economy, it quotes President Bush: "This rapid growth is another sign that our economy is on the fast track."

And then, still more good news: "Even with the economy motoring ahead, inflation moderated . . . *Core prices—excluding food and energy*—rose by 2 percent, down from 4 percent in the fourth quarter." (My italics.)

The only slightly sobering note was the mention that Federal Reserve Chairman Bernanke expected that the economy's growth would moderate in coming quarters, but still be strong enough to generate job growth. The risks to a mostly positive outlook, it quoted Bernanke as saying, would be a prolonged run-up in energy prices or a sharp decline in housing activity, neither scenario, for now, being envisioned.

Feeling better?

2009 UPDATE

Clearly, recent events have proven my point: Wall Street, the U.S. government, and the mass media have been using manipulated data to foster a falsely optimistic view of a fundamentally sick economy. Even more distressing, to my mind, is that the experts did not actually understand the problems threatening our economy.

What I could clearly see and they couldn't was the danger in their single focus on spending. They understood that the gross domestic product (GDP) was increasing because people were spending borrowed money, but that's where their analysis stopped. The debt didn't matter, they reasoned, because home and stock market values represented offsetting wealth. In their minds I was only looking at half the balance sheet and drawing alarmist conclusions. But I knew what they were calling wealth was just prices, and when those prices came down, the only thing staying up would be the debt, which would get more expensive when interest rates rose. That spelled trouble, but the public wasn't getting that message.

Now that the real estate bubble has burst and has become a global financial crisis, the messages being fed to us have transmogrified. But that is not to say they have become any less misleading.

The Obama administration's promises of new openness and transparency, the Treasury Department's new FinancialStability .gov web site, and the Congressional Oversight Panel (COP) mandated by the bill that created TARP are steps in the right direction, and it's nice to have an administration that acknowledges that the previous administration was playing with our heads. But if you think that means a fundamental improvement in the value of what's being communicated, don't bet on it. Some faces are new, but the same crowd that was telling us how great things were before is now telling us what went wrong and, more frighteningly, what should be done about it. They were wrong then and they are just as wrong now.

Their solution, needless to say, is more spending, more borrowing, and more regulation, meaning big government is about to get massively bigger, a giant step in the wrong direction and at the worst possible time.

The Current Spin

Here's how the national propaganda apparatus has decided to deal with this historic turn of events: Everything was just fine until the new millennium dawned. Then, coming out of left field without warning of any kind, a bunch of greedy capitalists had their way, contravening what flimsy remnants of regulation still survived after an era of deregulation. What was a buoyant and prosperous economy was thus thrown out of whack. Without the regulation necessary to catch the rascals who caused the trouble, how could anybody be expected to see a crisis coming? Former Fed Chairman Alan Greenspan said, "This is a hundred-year flood that nobody could have predicted." (Hey, c'mon, Al, some of us saw you blowing up the dam.) Well, I, for one, predicted it, and the government hasn't contacted me to ask how I could know what their Nobel Prize-winning economists didn't know. So I can only conclude that the financial establishment would prefer that the public not know the crisis was predictable. Adding insult to injury, the government is now forming a commission to look into the cause of the financial crisis. I wish they would just buy a copy of this book; it would save taxpayers a lot of money. Of course, by the time this version is published, that commission might have already reached its predetermined conclusion.

The solution, however, was obvious even to the Bush Republicans: Jump-start the stalled economy by stimulating consumer spending and home buying, and get us back to the good old days prior to the housing crash. To restore global confidence in the banking system, the government should arrange bailouts where necessary and get Congress to pass emergency legislation providing $700 billion of emergency backup funds. A sum that tidy would be analogous to having a bazooka in your pocket, as then Treasury Secretary Henry Paulson put it, since a heater like that would doubtless inspire the desired results without ever being actually used. (Half of it was quickly spent to shore up bank capital and encourage lending, but it produced no discernible result. Another chunk went to first forestall, and then under Obama to arrange, a bankruptcy at General Motors.

The Obama administration picked up where the Bush administration left off, but upped the ante, starting by steering a nearly $800 billion stimulus bill through Congress with the bipartisan help of three Republican senators. Accompanying the stimulus measures would be greatly expanded government regulation to prevent similar abuses of free-market capitalism in the future.

So score one for big government. Crises as great as this one are the stuff of politicians' dreams. The solution is always more government, and when that leads, as it almost inevitably does, to more problems, the answer is more regulation and even bigger government. In other words, since gasoline is the only way our politicians know to douse a fire, they will keep pouring more on as it gets bigger.

So while we all finally acknowledged that reckless borrowing and spending got us into this mess, we are now assured that even more reckless borrowing and spending are necessary to get us out. However, the current approach is not simply "a hair of the dog that bit us," as some maintain, but the dog's entire winter coat. Actually it's more like coaxing the errant dog back to maul us to death. When you are broke, the only true antidote is to be more productive and save your money. So it is with individuals; so it is with nations. But since this involves less borrowing and spending and thus some long-overdue self-sacrifice, our leaders want no part of it.

What Really Happened: The Dubious Magic of Government Stimulus

The economic crisis was not a failure of capitalism but rather a result of government efforts to interfere with free-market forces.

The real estate bubble had its genesis in Federal Reserve actions to stimulate an economy that was in a natural recession at the outset of the current decade as market forces tried to correct the excesses of the 1990s dot-com stock market bubble. The federal funds rate was at 6.5 percent when former Fed Chairman Alan Greenspan began a series of rate cuts that by mid-2003 brought fed funds down to 1 percent. That turbocharged a housing boom already well underway.

Without getting into the question of why the government has any more business deciding what interest rates should be than it does deciding what a latte at Starbucks should cost, it was clearly creating an environment in which excesses of various sorts were inevitable. With artificially low mortgage rates stimulating housing demand and forcing up home prices, growing home equity increased spending power and created a wealth effect encouraging extravagance and speculation. Fannie Mae and Freddie Mac were being pressured by the administration to lower their qualifying prime loan qualifications, and a budding Wall Street mortgage securitization industry was eager to buy subprime mortgage paper to satisfy the growing demand for higher yielding assets that existed only as a direct result of Fed policy. By keeping interest rates so low, hedge funds and homeowners were able to borrow cheaply. The former used the loot to speculate on mortgage-backed securities, while the latter used it to buy imported consumer goods, which resulted in large trade deficits that were recycled back into mortgage-backed securities. Swelling ranks of mortgage brokers solicited applications on an "originate to distribute" basis, meaning loans would immediately be sold off for securitization. Thus rewarded for volume and having no liability, they concocted the teaser rates and other gimmicks that seduced renters into becoming buyers and then they hired appraisers that would make valuations that supported prices. In Chapter 6, I covered all this chicanery and predicted the disaster it would cause. The point is that while the government didn't commit the sins, it created the environment that made them possible. The government, not capitalism, caused the real estate debacle.

Note, too, that a 1 percent fed funds rate provided the stimulus that sparked the housing bubble and made teaser rates so enticingly low. Now, in its efforts to revive the bubble, the Federal Reserve has dropped its funds rate to zero to ¼ percent and is pumping in trillions of dollars to boot. If the previous round of stimulus did all this damage, I can only imagine what the current round of stimulus will do. After all, it's not the economy that gets stimulated but the maladies that undermined it. When politicians say "stimulus," think poison, not antidote, and understand that an overdose will kill us.

A final thought before leaving the subject of stimulus. The word itself, as used in this connection, is something new. It appears designed to add fresh luster to the government's dog-eared old recipe for economic growth, "Just print money and stir."

Unfortunately, things don't work that way. If governments could stimulate economies, there would never be recessions. What they're calling "stimulus" should really be called "sedative." If the government truly wanted to stimulate the economy it would reduce the burden it places upon it. To stimulate a marathon runner already burdened by a heavy backpack, would you add or remove weight?

Stimulus Means Expanded Regulation. Why is that Bad?

Had rates been left to the free market, the housing bubble would never have happened, which makes a point about regulation.

Government activities require regulation, whereas private sector activities, operating freely, regulate themselves. For my money, forced regulation in the private sector provides little if any real protection for consumers, but it certainly makes for less efficiency and lower productivity. Looking again at the present crisis, the bailout money is going to banks and (before they adopted new charters and became commercial banks) broker/ dealer investment banks such as Morgan Stanley and Goldman Sachs. But there was no lack of regulation in those cases. Banks and brokers are the most regulated businesses in existence. In contrast, the hedge funds, where regulation is minimal, are not asking for bailout money—not yet anyway.

In the private sector, the operative forces of regulation, although unfortunately named, are fear and greed. The greed part evokes memories of Gordon Gekko, the role played by Michael Douglas in the 1987 film, *Wall Street,* and his repugnantly barbaric line, "Greed is good." As a practical matter, however, although greed always has and always will exist on Wall Street, we're really talking about two competing emotions, wanting to have and fearing to lose. The tension that exists between those powerful, universal emotions resolves the only way it can: in some acceptable compromise. The compromise may be in the form of a course of action or a free-market price.

Fannie Mae and Freddie Mac are cases where regulation should have existed but didn't. While they were technically private entities, the automatic regulation the free market normally provides was unavailable because fear, the downside control in the fear and greed equation, was replaced by implied government backing, leaving greed to run amok. The regulation would not have been necessary if the government backing hadn't been implied, meaning virtually guaranteed, in the first place.

Another example of government interference with free market regulation was the so-called Greenspan put. A put is an option contract guaranteeing its buyer the ability to sell an underlying stock at a certain price. If the price of the underlying stock drops precipitously, the put can be exercised and the stock sold at the higher exercise price, thus protecting the investor from serious loss. The Greenspan put refers to the intangible sense of safety that stock market investors felt during the Maestro's tenure because they had reason to believe that if the market were suddenly to tank, Greenspan would lower interest rates, causing money to flow into the market and put upward pressure on prices. The effect was analogous to the protection provided by a put option.

So our government overregulates a free market better left unfettered, and underregulates its own entities badly in need of restraint. In the end, although its own creations did most of the damage, it's the private sector that gets the blame—and the additional regulation to follow!

Where regulation belongs is in the government sector, and it's a sad irony that as the present crisis forces increased government involvement with *Wall Street*, Detroit, and elsewhere in the private sector, regulation comes with it.

A pet peeve of mine is the fair-weather conservative, who believes that in good times we don't need the government, but in bad times we do. Now is not the time for principle, these politicians protest, as they prepare to cast their votes for stimulus programs, with all the government regulation they would create. I say it's when times are tough that it's especially important to stick to your principles. During economic downturns is when we need capitalism the most. When times are good, we can at least afford government stupidity. If we ever needed free-market capitalism, it's now.

Lessons Not Learned from Japan's Lost Decade and the United States' Great Depression

The media tell us we must be guided now by the experience of Japan in the lost decade of the 1980s and this country in the Depression of the 1930s, but, tragically, we are about to ignore the lessons and wade into the same mistakes. In both cases there were bubbles similar to what we recently experienced here. But there were critical differences we are ignoring at our peril. Underlying those bubbles were fundamentally healthy economies that were thrown into imbalance by the misallocated investments causing the bubbles. When free-market forces tried to correct the imbalances and the governments got in their way, at least the structural economies were strong enough to withstand the bumbling. Recoveries were substantially delayed, but ultimately overcame the roadblocks.

That is not the case in the United States today, where our economy is fundamentally broken. The money we borrowed going into the 1930s and the money Japan borrowed leading up to its downturn went into factories and other productive investments, although not necessarily the right ones. But this time around we squandered our money on consumption and now it's gone. Sure, we spent a lot of money on houses and we still have them. But we spent an excessive amount of money on consumer goods with the result that we don't have the manufacturing bases enjoyed by Japan or this country in the 1930s, nor do we have the high savings rates or the exports those economies had.

So don't tell me we learned from these other experiences, because we learned nothing. Important lessons were there but we ignored them. History proves that what we're doing now to confront this historic economic crisis is the exact opposite of what we should be doing. When the problems predictably worsen, let's hope Washington finally learns the proper lesson.

3

For a Few Dollars More: Our Declining Currency

I talk with prospective brokerage clients all the time, and find it revealing, although not surprising, that while they'll lose sleep worrying about how many dollars their holdings are worth, it rarely occurs to them to worry about the worth of the dollars themselves.

That's an enigma that shouldn't be an enigma. In a well-managed economy, dependable purchasing power should not be a problem. Domestic investors shouldn't have to worry about the dollar.

The fact that the declining dollar is a domestic problem and people aren't generally aware of it shows how successfully the government has used the consumer price index (CPI) as a red herring to divert attention from the real cause and extent of inflation.

In the preceding chapter, I talked about how the public is being bamboozled, not just about inflation but about economic realities in general.

In the chapter that follows this one, I'll focus on inflation, how it's become the government's silent partner, and where it's leading us.

In this chapter, I talk about money and how the difference between real money and fiat money lies at the very root of our monetary crisis and the impending collapse that hangs like the sword of Damocles over our markets and our economy.

Americans are quickly running out of time to protect themselves. I can only hope that this book has found you while the economic clock is still ticking and that you have the good sense to implement the strategies outlined in later chapters before it stops.

But now let's talk about money.

FIAT MONEY: WHY IT IS THE ROOT OF OUR ECONOMIC PLIGHT

The American economy's grim predicament could not have developed if the U.S. dollar was still real money.

The present-day U.S. dollar is what is called fiat money. Fiat money is money in name only. It's money because a sovereign government says it's money. It has no intrinsic metallic or redemption value. Its nominal value is what the government engraves on its face. Its real value is what it will buy in the marketplace. In the international marketplace, its real value is what it is worth in exchange for another country's currency.

That has not always been the case. Until 1971, when the Nixon administration made the historic decision to abandon the gold standard, the dollar was backed by a percentage of the country's gold reserve. Without gold backing, the value of the dollar is nothing more than its purchasing power. How reliable that purchasing power is depends on how well the U.S. economy functions and how the supply of money is managed. The last point is key. *The abandonment of the gold standard in 1971 freed the Federal Reserve, which controls the supply of money, from its only restraint on printing money, by which we mean the various ways it has of increasing the amount of money in circulation.*

The dollar's declining value is thus more a symptom than a root cause of economic problems, although the problems we have today couldn't exist to the extent they do if the dollar represented real money instead of fiat money.

THE ORIGIN OF MONEY

Before the development of money as we know it, and going back to ancient times, trade was facilitated using the barter system. Like our friends from Chapter 1, Farmer Jones and Farmer Chang, one of whom grew oranges and needed apples while the other grew apples and needed oranges, they simply traded one product for the other.

However, the barter system was cumbersome and time-consuming. For example, if Farmer Chang wanted to buy a chair, he needed to find a chair maker who wanted oranges. As a result, people soon realized the practicality of finding one commodity in their particular culture that would be accepted in exchange for any other good or service. That became the first money, and it existed in such diverse forms as sheep and cattle in ancient times or beads made from seashells, called wampum, which the Indians took in exchange for the island of Manhattan. A more recent example was the use of cigarettes as money by American GIs in Europe following World War II.

What these different forms of money all had in common was that they represented an agreed-upon material value. As such, money facilitated the exchange of goods and services, made division of labor possible, and generally increased productivity and standards of living. The more easily exchanged the money was, the more vigorous the economy.

THE ECONOMIC FUNCTIONS OF MONEY

Money in any form should serve the following four functions:

1. *Unit of account.* Money provides one unit in which the values of various goods and services can be expressed and related to each other. It eliminates the obvious problems a barter system presents, such as how many watermelons would equal the value of one chair. By giving everything a price in money, we can easily relate one good or service to another.

2. *Medium of exchange.* Money facilitates the exchange of goods and services and expedites trade, making an economy more efficient and permitting a higher standard of living.

3. *Store of value.* Money that is not immediately spent can be saved and spent later, ideally at the same value. This encourages saving, hence capital creation, hence production.

4. *Unit of deferred payment.* Money not immediately needed can be lent to others, gaining interest and financing projects that provide a return to society.

All these functions and their benefits assume that money is sound, that is, that its purchasing power remains constant.

THE FIRST USES OF GOLD AS MONEY

As civilization advanced, societies narrowed down the varieties of money to types that worked best, and the commodities that were almost universally selected were gold and silver. In his book, *The Biggest Con* (Freedom Books, 1977), which is about the evils of paper money, my father Irwin Schiff describes how gold was desired because of its versatility and its unique properties:

> First of all, it had a rich and warm color and was capable of being highly polished. It was the only metal that neither tarnished nor rusted. It could be extruded to the fineness of a hair and beaten to the thinness of tissue paper. Since gold concentrated considerable value in a small area, it made transportation of one's wealth relatively simple. Imagine having to leave a country hurriedly when all of one's wealth was in cattle! Since gold was malleable, it was easily divisible and could accommodate exchanges of lesser value. Gold could be easily measured and its quality could be readily determined. These latter qualities, of course, made loaning money possible since it was easy to establish that the loan was repaid in the same type of money that had been loaned.

THE BEGINNING OF BANKING

Now that money could be lent, the early rudiments of banking developed, and with them the related concepts of "monetary reserves" and "money substitutes." Medieval merchants, traveling from city to city, would pay the local goldsmith a small fee to store their gold for them while they were doing business in the town. The warehouse receipt issued by the goldsmith became the forerunner of paper money and the first example of a money substitute.

The concept of a money substitute is key because as things developed, a distinction had to be made between money substitutes representing receipts for storage and money substitutes in the form of "bank notes" or promises to pay. The latter had intrinsic value only to the extent the goldsmith, now a banker and lending out the gold deposits not required to meet expected daily redemptions, had kept "gold reserves" on hand to meet the redemptions that were expected. A banker playing it too close ran the risk of arousing suspicion and causing a "run on the bank." That could ruin his business.

The fact that way back then the ratio of paper to reserves had to be kept conservative enough to maintain confidence and avoid anxiety provides a perfect historical parallel to why the U.S. economy, under the gold standard that prevailed until 1971, was more restrained and less prone to mismanagement than the fiat money economy that has existed since.

THE ORIGIN OF THE DOLLAR

A provision was included in the U.S. Constitution that "Congress shall have the power to coin money and regulate the value thereof," meaning it was empowered to take gold and silver, which the country then recognized as money, and put them in the form of coins. That is precisely why Article 1, Section 10, of the U.S. Constitution forbids the states from making anything other than gold and silver coin legal tender for payment of debts. It was intended that the metal value of the coin, which people in the business call "melt value," would equal the nominal value of the coin.

The dollar was first defined in the Mint Act of 1792 as 371.25 grains of fine silver, exactly the weight of the Spanish mill dollar, which was the most common coin in colonial America and which continued to circulate legally in the United States until 1857, 70 years after the signing of the Constitution.

The first U.S. currency was issued in 1863 as a gold certificate, essentially similar to the warehouse receipts of medieval goldsmiths. It read, "This certifies that there have been deposited in the Treasury of the United States ten dollars in gold payable to the bearer on demand." Gold certificates were circulated in the United States until 1934, when the Gold Reserve Act of 1934 made it illegal for Americans to own gold (with exceptions for jewelry, special collections, or gold needed for industrial or professional purposes).

Silver certificates, similar to gold certificates, were also issued and remained in circulation until 1963.

FEDERAL RESERVE ACT OF 1913 AND THE DEGENERATION OF THE DOLLAR

The first step away from full backing began with the Federal Reserve Act of 1913. That legislation, also called the Owen-Glass Act, established the politically independent Federal Reserve System for the principal purposes of supervising and regulating the banking system, managing the supply of money through the purchase and sale of government securities (called monetary policy), and acting as a clearinghouse for the transfer of funds throughout the banking system.

The Fed's role in monetary policy and inflation is something we'll get into later, but relevant here is that one primary reason it was established was to provide a "superior currency," a currency issued by one private national bank that would replace all the paper money being issued in the form of notes from individual private banks of varying credit quality.

One of the new Federal Reserve Bank's first actions was to introduce currency called Federal Reserve notes, which were redeemable "in gold or any lawful money" at any Federal Reserve Bank. Lawful money meant Treasury notes or gold, silver coins, and silver certificates.

These first Federal Reserve notes, although preserving the dollar's link to gold, introduced lawful alternatives in the form of silver coins and gold- and silver-backed Treasury paper, and thus set the stage for developments that would make the dollar/gold link weaker and eventually eliminate it completely.

THE END OF GOLD AND SILVER BACKING

The 1934 Gold Reserve Act removed the word gold from Federal Reserve notes and a new redemption clause read, "This note is legal tender for all debts, public and private, and is redeemable in lawful money at the United States Treasury, or at any Federal Reserve Bank."

It was only a change of wording, ominous in implication as we now know, but done then with enough subtlety to keep the public generally unawares.

On November 2, 1963, the redemption clause was eliminated completely, rendering all U.S. currency intrinsically worthless. On that date, our monetary system was transformed from the gold- and silver-based system specified in our Constitution to one of government fiat.

Whether the remaining language, "This note is legal tender for all debts, public and private," means anything other than that it is an acceptable form of payment for taxes and for such goods and services as are still produced in the United States can be argued.

The bottom line is that rather than representing legitimate IOUs redeemable in specified weights of gold or silver, U.S. Federal Reserve notes became IOU nothings, mere pieces of paper that bearers were free to circulate among themselves, but which did not constitute any liability on the part of the issuer.

What that meant was that any value the dollar had would depend purely on its purchasing power, which in turn would depend on the financial strength of the U.S. economy and how the supply of dollars was regulated.

BRETTON WOODS, THE INTERNATIONAL GOLD STANDARD, AND RESERVE CURRENCY STATUS

The dollar thus lost its gold backing domestically, but it was considered "as good as gold" internationally as a result of an agreement made at the United Nations Monetary and Financial Conference held at Bretton Woods, New Hampshire, in July of 1944.

Bretton Woods, as the conference and its agreements would be known, was a meeting of the financial heads of the allied countries, held to discuss the state of the international economy after World War II. It was a historic meeting, establishing, among other economic landmarks, the International Bank for Reconstruction and Development (World Bank) and the International Monetary Fund (IMF).

Of particular significance here, however, is that Bretton Woods established the U.S. dollar as the world's reserve currency and yielded a plan to fix the rate of exchange for all foreign currencies in Europe and Asia in relation to the U.S. dollar. The dollar, in turn, would be tied to gold to permit international settlement at a fixed price. Thus a foreign currency would always be worth a fixed number of dollars and a set number of dollars would always be exchangeable for an ounce of gold.

Having reserve currency status meant the dollar became the currency used by other governments and institutions as part of their foreign exchange reserves and as the international pricing currency for products traded on global markets, such as oil and gold. Being the reserve currency permits the United States to run significant trade deficits with limited economic impact as long as the major holders of reserve currencies do not issue statements suggesting otherwise. Needless to say, this protection from free-market forces that would otherwise cause current U.S. trade imbalances to have greater economic impact is a linchpin buying the dollar precious time. That could quickly change, however. The replacement of the dollar with the euro as the reserve currency is already being mentioned in international financial circles as a distinct possibility.

Between 1945 and the early 1960s, the free world enjoyed relative monetary stability thanks to the Bretton Woods accords, and the United States, enjoying postwar growth and prosperity, found a warm welcome abroad for excess dollars that would otherwise have caused inflation at home.

THE UNRAVELING OF BRETTON WOODS

During the 1960s, however, the guns and butter policies of the Johnson and Nixon administrations, with federal spending funding such things as the Great Society programs, fighting the War on Poverty at home and the real one in Vietnam, as well as the space race, resulted in significant budget deficits that were in large part monetized—financed by money supply increases—by the Federal Reserve.

The Federal Reserve's power to increase the supply of money was originally in its 1913 charter as the power to provide for an "elastic money supply." That meant that it could add to the money supply in times of economic expansion and reduce it in times of economic contraction, a traditional function of central banks consistent with classical economic theory that accepted business cycles as normal and regarded booms as artificial and problematical events to be corrected by salutary busts.

The Kennedy administration invoked the doctrine of the English economist John Maynard Keynes, which held that, contrary to the classical view and to the original intentions of the Federal Reserve, the money supply should be used to stimulate spending when the economy slowed, thus turning contractions into expansions.

As we will see later, what started as counteractive intervention became, in the Greenspan era of the 1990s and now, from all indications, in the Bernanke Fed, a policy of continuous monetary expansion with the inflation that goes with it. But that gets a little ahead of our story.

With the Federal Reserve thus expanding the money supply and creating inflation domestically in the later 1960s, countries abroad were forced to expand their money supplies at the same pace in order to maintain the agreed-upon ratios of their currencies to the dollar. The result of these expansions of foreign local currencies was inflation overseas that was, in effect, being exported by the United States.

As these patterns continued through the late 1960s, European and Asian countries, by then restored to economic robustness and aware that expansions of their domestic money supplies were creating inflation began returning excess dollars to the United States, demanding redemption in gold at the agreed-upon rate of exchange.

This drain on gold in the United States, which had accounted for some 60 percent of official world gold reserves at the end of World War II, caused U.S. holdings to fall to dangerously low levels.

THE CLOSING OF THE GOLD WINDOW

By 1971, President Nixon was forced to close the "gold window" by no longer exchanging dollars for gold at the agreed-upon rate. Since that time, exchange rates have been allowed to float, with rates determined by the supply of and demand for currencies.

The significance of that repudiation cannot be minimized. It was the national equivalent of declaring bankruptcy.

In the Introduction to his book, *The Demise of the Dollar* (John Wiley & Sons, 2005), Addison Wiggin comments:

The power and influence of the United States in 1971 should not be ignored. It was the decision to go off the gold standard that, in effect, destroyed the orderly economic policies that had been possible though Bretton Woods. There were bound to be periods of inflation, unemployment, and currency instability, just as part of the natural economic cycle. The period of the early 1970s was the start of a very unsettled time, based on both economic and political strife. In hindsight, it seems obvious that the decision to go off the gold standard was devastating. It didn't lead to the fall of capitalism, but now—more than 30 years later—it has brought us to the precipice—and perhaps the decline in the long-running U.S. domination of the world economy.

THE BALANCE OF TRADE AND THE VALUE OF THE DOLLAR

With international currencies allowed to float and to establish their exchange values through supply and demand, the concept of strong and weak currencies became relevant; but here it is important to understand the precise meaning of terms that could otherwise be hopelessly confusing in a discussion of the declining dollar.

Efficient economies export what they produce and import what they don't produce, so under ideal conditions, trade accounts overall should balance. At any given time, however, a country will have a unilateral or aggregate trade deficit or surplus depending on its relationship between imports and exports. That, along with other factors, such as a country's political and economic stability and the returns its securities pay to foreign investors, contributes to a supply/demand relationship between currencies. But weak and strong refer to one currency's rate of exchange with another's and not to a currency's domestic purchasing power. When the U.S. dollar exchanges for more units of the Japanese yen today than yesterday, the dollar has strengthened and the yen weakened in relationship to each other (and vice versa).

In international commerce, strong and weak currencies are both good and bad. For example, on the one hand a strong currency is good for consumers in the home country because it makes imported goods cheaper to buy and traveling abroad less expensive. Being strong means the currency buys more units of another country's currency. On the other hand, a strong currency is bad news for companies that export, because it makes their products more expensive and harder to sell. The reverse is true for a weak currency.

So a weak currency doesn't necessarily signify a moribund currency, although in the case of the U.S. dollar, it has come to mean exactly that. Its persistent and increasing weakness in world markets (measured against the currencies of our trading partners, such as China and Japan, or against an index of major foreign currencies) has dangerous implications for the American economy. That is so because our economy has serious fundamental problems.

The dollar lost 24 percent of its value against other currencies between 2002 and 2004, had a technical bear market rally in 2005 that only worsened its long-term outlook, then resumed its decline in 2006, losing nearly 12 percent between mid-March and mid-May. It corrected until mid-October before plunging again, finally breaching its May lows by late November. Notwithstanding occasional bear market rallies, the dollar seems certain to be headed for historic lows.

Our current account deficit, which is somewhere around $800 billion and growing and is mainly a trade deficit, is being financed by borrowings from foreign countries like China and Japan that export to us. This is debt we cannot repay because we have become a nation of borrowers and consumers instead of savers and producers.

Countries, like people, have to live within their means, but the United States is not doing that. Our savings rate has steadily declined in recent years and is now negative. At the same time, personal indebtedness in the form of credit card debt and borrowing against inflated home values has reached record levels.

The national economy has shifted from a production (manufacturing) orientation to a service economy providing fewer goods to export and paying lower incomes. Yet we continue to spend like drunken sailors on imports from foreign countries that do save and produce, in the process building massive trade

THE POLITICS OF THE CHINESE CURRENCY PEG

Hardly a month goes by without another U.S. government official or elected politician calling on the Chinese government to appreciate the yuan, which is currently pegged to the U.S. dollar. Such public browbeating is pure political grandstanding. It's all a bluff. Privately, I am sure, we are begging the Chinese not to float their currency.

China is the biggest buyer of U.S. Treasury securities, and the Chinese do it to defend the currency peg. They are also the biggest suppliers of low-priced consumer goods to Americans. Why on earth would American officials and politicians demand that China increase both consumer prices and interest rates in America? The result would surely be a severe recession. This could also be a giant exercise in reverse psychology. Since what worries American politicians the most, other than their own reelection, is China dropping its peg, why not demand China do just that? That way, the Chinese would lose face if they complied and appeared to be bowing to U.S. pressure. If America were demanding that the Chinese keep the peg, they would likely have dropped it already.

deficits that we finance with money borrowed from our trading partners, money we can't repay because of huge budget deficits and mounting national debt.

We have gotten away with this so far because the dollar is the world's reserve currency and because our inability to repay has been camouflaged by reckless consumer spending reported and thus perceived as economic growth.

The looming dollar crisis cannot be prevented, only delayed, and only at the cost of exacerbating the collapse (see Figure 3.1).

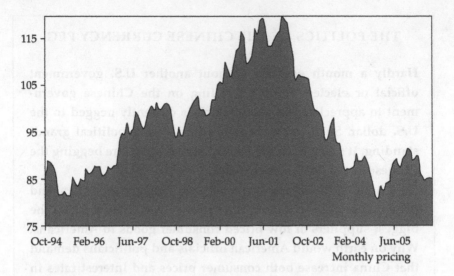

FIGURE 3.1 *U.S. dollar index, 1994–2006.* As the stock market bubble inflated and the world bought into the new economy and budget surplus myths, the dollar rose. When both myths proved false, the dollar quickly fell back to earth. Once this index decisively breaks below the 80 support level, the next leg of the dollar's long-term bear market will begin.

Source: Reprinted by permission from David L. Tice and Associates (www.prudentbear.com).

THE FEDERAL RESERVE AND INFLATION

President Nixon's closing of the gold window was forced by what was, in effect, an imminent run on the bank by foreign countries presenting their dollars for redemption in gold. But Nixon also believed that desirable economic growth was being limited by the gold standard, which required, in effect, that expansions of the money supply be accompanied by proportionate increases in the gold reserves.

Although Nixon chose to deal with his stagflation problems not by tampering with the money supply, but rather by a disastrous effort to control wages and prices, the Fed's power to expand the money supply would in later administrations be used, contrary to its intended purpose, like an economic amphetamine.

In the 1990s and 2000s, expansions of the money supply have been used to create permanent inflation in order to relieve the symptoms of inefficient government. As new money stimulates consumer spending and increases the gross domestic product (GDP), it creates an illusion of healthy economic growth. By diluting the dollar's value, it artificially reduces the costs of social programs, the massive national debt and budget deficit, and our huge current account deficit. Reflected mainly in asset bubbles (stocks, bonds, and real estate) and being exported to buy consumer products from Europe and Asia, this inflation is not reflected in official figures, such as the consumer price index (CPI). But inflation it is, and it is diminishing the purchasing power of the dollar as this is written. What is now high, if largely invisible, inflation will become acutely felt hyperinflation as dollars being accumulated abroad come home to roost.

Chapter 4 is devoted entirely to inflation, a word that literally means expansion and is defined by economists as too many dollars pursuing too few goods, another way of saying that the purchasing power of the dollar is declining.

RISING GOLD PRICES—A VOTE OF "NO CONFIDENCE" IN THE U.S. DOLLAR

The fact, of course, is that the government should be and no doubt is worried about its debt and current account imbalances, its declining productivity, and its consumer debt and consumer spending. Instead of acting early with the required financial discipline, however, it has let conditions reach a point of no return.

Trapped between a choice of higher interest rates that would precipitate recession and lower rates that would lead to hyperinflation, the powers that be have opted to present an appearance of well-being that is ultimately untenable and allowing fundamental weaknesses to worsen.

Because our trading partners, who also happen to be our financiers, are enjoying our trade, and their complacent central bankers have thus far been willing to throw good money after bad and to finance our imbalances, we have to this point managed to stay the execution.

But not everybody is being fooled. A sort of reverse flight to quality is taking place as investors desert what was so long the safe haven of the American dollar and bid up the price of gold and other commodities having intrinsic value.

Although dismissed by many as a reflection of Iraq war and other Middle Eastern tensions, the bull market in gold, which rose from the below $300s to a recent close above $700 in only six years, is, I am firmly convinced, a vote of "no confidence" in the dollar and a trend still in its early stages.

The fact that gold pulled back in mid-2006 from a spring high of $725 an ounce and is trading around $600 as this is being written in November is a temporary development caused by leveraged speculators and a supreme buying opportunity.

THE GOVERNMENT'S CURIOUS COMPLACENCY

Despite all this negativity surrounding the U.S. dollar, the folks managing our economy stand like miners around a comatose canary, wondering what's bothering it and concluding maybe it's taking a nap.

In a way that would be funny if it weren't so serious, we occasionally have what I like to call "strong dollar sightings," in the form of utterances by Treasury officials to the effect that "the United States favors a strong dollar." Reminiscent of the mythical "strong dollar policy" of the Clinton-Rubin years, such claims and policies are about as real as Bigfoot or the Loch Ness monster. Things have gone too far.

The administration would surely prefer a strong dollar but it's stuck with a weakening dollar and there is really nothing it can do about it. The desire is similar to a student's stated intention to make the dean's list. Surely making the dean's list is in the student's best interest, and it is certainly preferable to flunking out. But merely saying that one has a straight A policy while simultaneously cutting class, smoking dope, and partying all night will hardly produce the desired result.

The declining dollar is the result of an American economy characterized by declining production, inadequate savings, reckless consumption, soaring household debt, ballooning federal budget deficits, and an overly accommodating Fed.

HOW IT IS LIKELY TO PLAY OUT

What is going to happen, be it sooner or later, is that foreigners are not going to want our dollars anymore, so they will stop sending us goods and will begin spending hoarded dollars over here on goods that we have.

So it's going to be the present situation in reverse. All those dollars that are on deposit in China and Japan and elsewhere are going to come flooding back to the United States bidding up the prices of whatever isn't nailed down.

And when that happens, even if the Fed were to start restricting the money supply, prices are going to go through the roof. *The Fed is now trapped between inflation and recession and it's too late to stop the consequences of either.*

All of that inflation we've created for 20 years that the Japanese and Chinese have kept at bay by hoarding our dollars will come back at us like a tsunami. Foreigners will start spending dollars here, and the domestic money supply will shoot up and prices with it.

Right now, of course, our trading partners have our money in our bonds. They're not taking it to the Wal-Mart. They're not trying to buy pots and pans or TVs—actual stuff. But that will change.

When they don't want to hold our financial assets anymore, they're going to want to buy our consumer goods and those prices are going to go sky-high. We're talking about stuff like used cars, furniture, and appliances. We don't have the factories to make new things. And goods are going to stop being shipped into this country. All those container ships are going to stay in China.

FAIR WARNING

Those of you still holding dollars had better do some serious reflection and ignore the talk about a mythical strong dollar policy. The alternative is to go down with a sinking ship, as the captain stands atop the bridge saluting, waist-deep in water, assuring all aboard that "a strong ship is in its passengers' interest."

And don't buy either the argument that private foreign investment will step in to replace the foreign central banks when they stop lending to us. Private lenders account for a small portion of present loans and for us to try to attract more private capital by raising interest rates would surely prick the housing bubble and send already overburdened consumers into the bankruptcy courts.

Once the dollar loses its reserve currency status and the collapse ensues, the process of returning to economic viability will be a painful one, requiring substantial austerity from both the government and its citizens. Whether the United States is up to the task remains to be seen. Although I am skeptical, I nonetheless remain hopeful.

In any event, you can protect yourself from the collapse and prepare yourself to profit in the reconstruction of economic health. I'm going to show you how.

2009 UPDATE

Those of us who toil in the minefields of money and markets learn to expect surprises. Long-term trends are interrupted from time to time by short-term dynamics we dismiss as noise. Bear market rallies and bull market corrections, as such countercyclical movements are called, are temporary, although they may give impetus to the more rationally based, longer-range trends that overarch them.

In the chapter you just read, I noted how the dollar lost 24 percent of its value against other currencies between 2002 and 2004, had a technical bear market rally in 2005, then resumed its decline in 2006.

In midsummer of that year, as I was writing *Crash Proof*, the Dollar Index, which measures variances in the U.S. dollar's value relative to 100, was around 85 and I was predicting that once it broke decisively below the 80 support level, the next leg of the dollar's long-term bear market would begin. (The Dollar Index [USDX] compares the dollar with a basket of currencies that includes the euro, the yen, the British pound sterling, the Canadian dollar, the Swedish krona, and the Swiss franc.)

As I expected, the dollar broke 80 late in 2007, then continued its downward drift, falling to a fraction over 70 in mid-March 2008.

That same month, the deteriorating economic picture in the United States entered a new phase. The Federal Reserve held the first emergency weekend meeting in 30 years to decide what to do about Bear Stearns, the first in a series of too-big-to-fail investment banks and other financial services behemoths threatened with bankruptcy because of their heavy investment in mortgage-backed securities and collateralized debt obligations (CDOs).

The escalation of a domestic mortgage meltdown into a credit crunch and an economic crisis that, following the bankruptcy of Lehman Brothers, quickly became global in scale, did not, however, cause a further plunge in the dollar, as would have been logical. Instead, it marked the beginning of a significant bear market rally in the dollar that persists as this is written in Spring 2009.

The strength of this latest dollar rally illustrates how ironic and perverse the behavior of markets can be, and it's causing a lot of people to draw some very erroneous conclusions. But don't be fooled into thinking it is anything but temporary. The decline will resume, and where I had predicted earlier that the Dollar Index would likely bottom out at around 40, I now see a bottom closer to 20 or maybe even lower. The difference will be the vast devaluations that will result from the government's decision to stimulate the economy rather than face the pain required to restore solid fundamentals such as those that already underlie the temporarily depressed economies of our trading partners.

Why the Dollar Rallied

Let's not forget that when we speak of ups and downs in the dollar, we refer to valuations relative to other world currencies rather than to the store of value represented by gold. The fact is that all the major world currencies, including the U.S. dollar, are losing value when measured in gold. Relative to the basket of currencies used in the Dollar Index, the dollar is falling along with other fiat currencies but not at as rapid a rate, making it appear to be rising. When two cars are backing up at different speeds and you're sitting in the slower one, you have the sensation your car is going forward. The same analogy explains the dollar rally and also the seeming enigma that the price of gold and the Dollar Index are both rising, when normally gold rises as the dollar falls. Relative to gold, the dollar is falling.

The question nonetheless remains: How can the dollar rally against other currencies when economic conditions here are fundamentally much worse than they are abroad? The U.S. dollar is the currency of the world's biggest debtor nation and that nation is broke. The dollar should be falling faster in value than other currencies, not more slowly.

Part of the answer is found in something I touched upon in the update to Chapter 1, when discussing the issue of decoupling. As our trading partners see it, they were watching their best customer go down the tubes, and their first reaction was to come to its rescue. One form that took was what in American commerce is called vendor financing, where the seller of goods gives the buyer extended payment terms, in effect lending it money so it can continue buying.

Even when the dollar was falling, the rest of the developed world was propping it up through currency pegs or central bank interventions. Had all that dollar buying not been going on, the dollar would have lost much more value than it did leading up to the present crisis. The fact that foreign countries had to create a lot of their own money to buy up surplus dollars produced inflationary problems in other parts of the world along with attempts to control prices, all of which distorted the global economy but gave artificial support to the dollar.

Foreign governments also finance our deficits, and every time they buy our Treasury securities they support the dollar. We already owe them more than we can repay, and our borrowing needs are growing by leaps and bounds with the trillions needed to fund programs to artificially stimulate our economy. Foreign governments, despite some recent indications of reluctance, are still buying our Treasury securities; but obviously this can't go on forever, as the world simply cannot afford it.

Meanwhile, other developments were putting wind under the wings of the dollar. Americans were experiencing something analogous to a margin call. With troubled financial institutions demanding the repayment of loans, and with investment funds being faced with redemptions, assets were being liquidated in markets around the world. Hedge funds, to meet redemptions, were forced to sell assets that were highly valued but could be readily liquidated, meaning hard commodities such as gold and other precious metals. As prices dropped, their lenders wanted their money back, causing more asset sales. Asset liquidation around the world meant more demand for dollars.

Another significant factor increasing dollar demand was the unwinding of the yen carry trade. People had borrowed several hundred billion dollars in Japanese yen at near zero interest rates and invested the proceeds in U.S. Treasury bonds at a spread of more than 3 percent plus a profit on conversion. In 2008 the dollar's appreciation against the yen was 12.7 percent. In addition, yen carry trades also financed the leveraged purchases of other higher-yielding assets around the world. As asset prices fell, those loans had to be repaid, putting additional downward pressure on asset prices.

As the American economy sank deeper into recession, costing foreign exporters lost sales, troubles in foreign economies were compounding. They were already hurting from bad loans they had made to American borrowers and now they were experiencing additional losses on loans made to other borrowers adversely affected by the U.S. financial crisis. With credit drying up here, America turned increasingly to foreign sources to meet its borrowing requirements, thereby crowding out private investment abroad and expanding the credit crunch globally.

Now facing recession themselves, foreign countries were lowering rates and taking measures to stimulate their own economies, creating further inflationary pressures that undermined their own currencies and sent people looking for a safe haven. With the U.S. dollar on the rise from a relatively low level, it seemed like a better bet than the euro, the ruble, the Australian dollar, and other currencies that were losing value. As a result, more money flowed into the dollar and U.S. Treasury securities, counteracting countries' stimulus efforts for their own economies. Of course the best stimulus would be to abandon their support of the U.S. economy, stop buying, or even start selling U.S. Treasuries and allow the dollar to fall. Higher local interest rates and stronger local currencies would unleash domestic demand, reward local savers, and free up credit for local businesses.

From the Frying Pan into the Fire

Switching money from other currencies into the dollar was, in reality, jumping from the frying pan into the fire. However bad the problems are in other countries, the problems here are worse. But the propagandists of the American media and financial establishment preferred to see it differently. If the dollar is rising, they say, it must be because as bad as things are here, they must be that much worse everywhere else. They simply won't let themselves admit that the dollar's strength is irrational noise and just another bubble. In fact, the dollar is rising only because people are buying it, plain and simple, the same way they bought overvalued dot-com stocks and condos in Miami.

As with the previous bubbles, the dollar is rallying not because the fundamentals are good, but despite the fact that the fundamentals are horrible. The problem is that too many people lack the sophistication to understand why.

Others are buying dollars along with Treasury securities and other U.S. government–guaranteed debt, because they want a temporary safe haven. They are in dollars not for the long term, but as a place to wait out the financial storm at home so they can get back into their own currencies and assets when the coast is clear. What these folks don't realize is that they have entered a currency roach motel—easy to get in but with no way out. Buying dollars now is easy. Demand for dollars is high and easily satisfied even as the biggest seller, the Federal Reserve, is running its printing press and flooding the world with them. But selling those dollars at a later time, when foreign governments have decided to stop throwing good money after bad, when other asset prices are rising, and when safe-haven demand is no longer there, is going to be a huge problem. When you also factor in the increase in supply as the Fed revs up its presses even faster to monetize greater quantities of unwanted U.S. government debt, the dollar will go into free fall.

Nowhere is the speculative nature of dollar buying more evident than in the U.S. Treasury market. No one is buying long-term U.S. government bonds to clip 3.5 percent coupons for the next 30 years. Every buyer is looking to trade out of his position long before maturity. Of course, when speculators try to sell, actually finding buyers is no easy task—just ask any condo flipper in Las Vegas. To get real investors (those willing to hold to maturity) to buy, bond prices would have to plunge.

Part of the demand for Treasuries has to do with their reputation for safety from default risk. With so many corporate bonds now suspect, nobody wants to take any chances. However, once worry about return of purchasing power trumps worry about

return of principal, default risk will take a backseat to inflation risk. When that happens, even if U.S. Treasuries manage to
hold on to their specious AAA rating like many exotic subprime
mortgage-backed securities did, there will be few takers.

All the reasons the dollar was falling before its latest rally are
still there, and now more reasons have been added. The government will only get bigger and have to borrow even more money.
Ironically, the only people in a position to end the madness are
the foreign governments subsidizing us at the cost of depriving
their own citizens and sabotaging their own economies. We've
created all these new dollars to fund the stimulus and bailouts
and in the process have further undermined the economy by
turning over more resources and more companies to government control rather than the private sector. So our economy is
becoming inherently less efficient and less productive at the
same time that we are increasing the amount of dollars in circulation. A far greater economic collapse will now result from the
currency crisis our government is in the process of setting up.

So do not be fooled by those with vested interests rational-
izing the dollar's rise. We heard similar nonsense from the same
crowd with respect to stocks and real estate. Again, these are the
same folks who confidently assured us that all was well as late as
mid-2008. When this rally ends, the bottom is going to fall out of
the dollar. This is its last gasp. For all I know, the final breath may
have already been drawn by the time you finish this chapter.

4

Inflation Nation: The Federal Reserve Fallacy

Like the shill in a game of three-card monte, official inflation numbers are decoys designed to distract you from what's really happening with inflation, which is the invisible expansion of the money supply by the Federal Reserve and the consequent diminishment of your dollar's purchasing power.

At best, the consumer price index (CPI) and producer price index (PPI), by tracking prices, measure the effects of inflation and not inflation itself. The significance of that distinction, which I'll elaborate upon presently, is that inflation can exist before its effects are experienced. This allows for an element of secrecy that is of no small importance to our government, which needs inflation to advance its agenda, but for other reasons cannot afford to have the real extent of inflation officially recognized (see Figure 4.1).

As we saw in Chapter 2, both the CPI and the PPI are engineered to represent a level of price inflation that the public will find acceptable. Contrived figures that appear to represent

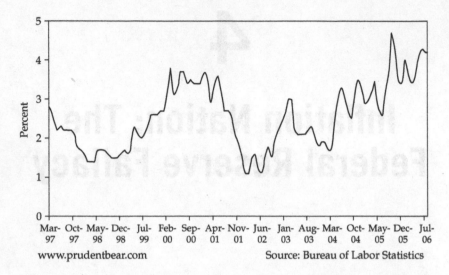

FIGURE 4.1 *Consumer price index, year-over-year change, 1997–2006.*
Even the government's own highly flawed and greatly manipulated
index revealed inflation was accelerating even as the government
and Wall Street claimed that it was well contained. By the time the
problem was partially acknowledged, the government's response was
too little and too late.
Source: Reprinted by permission from David L. Tice and Associates
(www.prudentbear.com).

relative price stability can keep the public naive about what is
really happening to the purchasing power of the U.S. dollar.

In this chapter, I explain what inflation is and why it is generally misunderstood; why our government, through the Federal Reserve, both creates inflation and conceals it; the devices
the government uses to keep the public misinformed about
inflation; the historical background of Federal Reserve monetary
policy and how its powers have been abused; why our misguided monetary policy has gotten us into a mess; and how our
economic mismanagement will affect you personally.

WHAT INFLATION IS AND ISN'T

Inflation means expansion, in the same sense that a balloon expands when you blow air into it. In economics, inflation refers to expansion of the amount of dollars in circulation, called the money supply. When new money or credit is added to an economy, thus diluting the existing supply, the general level of prices (aggregate prices) will rise, assuming the amount of goods and services within the system stays the same. But understand the distinction: The money supply expands and contracts. Prices go up and down. Inflation and price increases are not the same thing. One is cause. The other is effect.

The reason that expansion of the money supply causes aggregate prices to rise is simple. As the supply of dollars grows relative to the supply of goods, more dollars are needed to buy a given quantity of goods. In other words, the dollar's value is diminished relative to the goods available for sale. It's basic supply, represented by sellers, and demand, represented by buyers. Any kid who collects baseball cards understands it. The more a particular card is in circulation, the less it is worth. The value of a card is a function of its scarcity. The more abundant the supply, the less something is worth. The same holds true for money.

HOW INFLATION CREATES ARTIFICIAL DEMAND

So inflation is monetary expansion or, in other words, more money chasing a constant or diminishing supply of goods and services. It doesn't have to be physical dollars added to the supply of money. It can just as well be expanded credit. Anything that artificially increases aggregate demand for goods and services is inflation. *Printing money* is a figurative term referring to the different ways the Fed adds liquidity to the economy.

(Since the word *demand* in noneconomic terms connotes want and need, it is less confusing to think of it here as referring collectively to buyers or users, absent the element of incentive.)

The demand is artificial because it does not result from increased productivity, but from inflation. For example, in a basic barter economy, a shoemaker's demand is determined by how many shoes he produces. The more shoes he makes, the greater is his ability to exchange them for other products, which is a long-winded way of saying the greater is the demand for his shoes (up to a point). Demand is created by shoes that the shoemaker actually produces. The shoes are real goods that satisfy the demands of anyone needing a pair.

Contrast that with an expansion of the money supply, which adds no real goods to the economy. Demand created by inflation, therefore, is artificial, as no tangible goods are produced. The result is simply an increase in prices—not all prices, but prices in the aggregate—to reflect the new equilibrium between the increased money supply and the constant supply of goods available for sale.

The underlying economic principle is known as Say's Law or Say's Law of Markets, which is attributed to the French economist Jean-Baptiste Say. Although Say's Law is commonly summarized as "supply creates demand," the element of production is essential; expressed more accurately, he was saying "production creates consumption" or, even better, "the supply of each producer creates his demand for the supplies of other producers." This way, equilibrium between supply and demand always exists on an aggregate basis. (Say acknowledged that there could be gluts and shortages with respect to individual products.) Another way of putting it: You want some of my apples? What have you got to trade for them? To the immediate point, Say believed the creation of more money simply creates inflation; more money pursuing the same amount of goods does not create an increase in real demand.

WHY INFLATION IS THE GOVERNMENT'S SILENT PARTNER

Governments love inflation. It's a way for them to take money from the people without the people realizing they took it.

Why would the government secretly want to confiscate your money, which is what it does when the Fed expands the supply of money, thereby creating inflation and diminishing your purchasing power?

Do you think I'm being a little shrill, using words like *secretly* and *confiscate*? None other than former Federal Reserve chairman Alan Greenspan, in a 1966 essay, "Gold and Economic Freedom," called inflation "a scheme for the hidden confiscation of wealth." On August 16, 2006, Federal Reserve Governor Richard W. Fisher, in a speech titled "An Update on the Status of the Economy and Its Implications for Monetary Policy" and reprinted on the Federal Reserve Bank of Dallas web site, said "[Inflation] is a sinister force that has the capacity to charm and romance the heck out of you, but in the end wreaks only havoc."

There are five reasons for creating inflation:

1. Inflation makes the national debt more manageable because it can be repaid with cheaper dollars.

2. In a democracy full of personally indebted voters, the government will pursue monetary policies hospitable to debtors even as it accommodates the special interests that lend to them.

3. Inflation finances social programs that voters demand but avoids the politically unpopular alternative of higher taxes, allowing Uncle Sam to play Santa Claus.

4. Inflationary spending is confused with economic growth, which is confused with economic health. (Of course, GDP numbers are theoretically adjusted for inflation, but that doesn't mean much if the inflation figures are misrepresented.)

5. Inflation causes nominal asset prices to rise, such as those of stocks and real estate, instilling in the minds of voters the illusion of wealth creation even as the real purchasing power of their assets falls.

WHY THE GOVERNMENT WANTS ITS SILENT PARTNER SILENT

The government also has five reasons for hiding inflation:

1. It keeps the interest on national borrowings lower because conspicuous inflation would cause lenders to require an inflation premium in the form of higher interest rates.

2. Social Security payments and other government benefits are indexed to inflation as measured by the understated CPI and thus cost less.

3. Income tax brackets and personal exemptions are indexed for inflation using CPI as the benchmark.

4. Lower inflation premiums (the portion of a long-term interest rate designed to offset the erosion of value by future inflation) keep interest rates lower for everyone, allowing our consumer debt–dependent economy to continue its phony expansion.

5. The introduction of Treasury inflation protected securities (TIPS) requires the government to adjust interest and principal payments upward to reflect changes in the CPI. Talk about the fox being hired to guard the henhouse!

So the government has an interest in creating inflation and also has an interest in having it underreported in the official statistics.

BUT DOESN'T INFLATION THIS PERVASIVE HAVE TO SHOW UP IN THE CPI AT SOME POINT?

The reason inflation created by expanding the money supply can remain largely invisible has to do with the fact that prices rise in various stages. Much depends on how the new money enters the system and where it is spent first. Inflation can show up more markedly in financial assets than in consumer prices, such as during the stock market bubble in the 1990s or the more recent real estate boom. Some of it goes overseas in the form of dollars our trading partners convert to their local currencies, but that remain on deposit in central banks, thus deferring their impact on domestic prices.

So I don't know when, or even if, an expansion of the money supply will cause CPI prices to rise more rapidly. I do know the government calculates the CPI and the government doesn't want it to accurately reveal how bad inflation really is. Maybe the government will decide to reduce the CPI market basket to one microchip or something else that won't go up in price, thereby ensuring there's never any official inflation.

But the fact remains that inflation is causing some prices to rise. We may not be able to measure it, but we can see much of it just by opening our eyes.

HOW THE GOVERNMENT OBFUSCATES
THE REALITY OF INFLATION

The Scapegoats: Cost-Push, Demand-Pull, and the Wage-Price Spiral

Rising prices got labeled as inflation because the government wanted to divert the public's attention from what caused prices to rise in the first place. If the public realized the Fed was creating inflation instead of fighting it, they would scream bloody murder. To place the blame for inflation elsewhere, the government and the Fed simply redefined the term.

The result was a bunch of gobbledygook in the form of "cost-push inflation," "demand-pull inflation," and the dreaded "wage-price spiral." All this jargon was designed to portray inflation as an economic inevitability, arising from factors like economic growth, speculators, aggressive labor unions, profit-seeking (read greedy) businesspeople—anything or anybody but the government itself.

Think about the concept of "cost-push inflation" for a moment. For an automobile manufacturer, the cost of steel is the price the steel manufacturer sells it for. Cost and price are, in reality, two words that describe the same thing, only from different perspectives.

The same thing applies to wages, which are merely the prices at which workers sell their labor. The "wage-price spiral" therefore is nothing more than a portentous metaphor for the same nonsense. One might as well argue that prices rise because prices rise. On the surface, however, citing other names for certain types of prices, such as costs and wages, allows the government to make a circular argument seem logical.

It's the same thing with so-called "demand-pull inflation." A stable economy has a balanced relationship between the supply of money and the amount of goods and services. Certainly, within that framework, demand for individual goods and services can rise and fall and cause prices to rise and fall. By definition, however, there will be offsetting changes in demand and prices elsewhere in the system. General (the economic word is *aggregate*) demand and prices would remain the same, however.

The only things that could cause aggregate prices to rise would be an expansion of the supply of money or a contraction of the supply of goods and services, two parts of the same dynamic. By blaming rising prices on demand, the government tries to convey a false message that inflation is merely an acceptable trade-off for economic growth, that in a sense we are victims of our own success. The reality, of course, is that true economic growth causes consumer prices to fall, as increased productive output raises the supply of goods relative to the supply of money.

Another Scapegoat: Inflation Expectations

Another attempt to shift the blame for inflation from the government to the market is the concept that inflation is a function of expectations. The assumption is that if businesses expect inflation they will raise prices, thereby creating it. The false conclusion is that inflation can be controlled by dampening expectations. This is analogous to blaming the rain on people having the foresight to carry umbrellas. Convincing the public to leave their umbrellas at home will not stop the rain, but it will certainly result in a whole lot of people getting soaked!

The Misuse of Core Inflation

Core inflation figures, as earlier noted, exclude the most volatile components of the CPI, food and energy, on the reasoning that their inclusion would distort extrapolations based on short-term data. That is a valid argument, but to feature core inflation as the primary indicator of price inflation is where the chicanery comes in. Because food and energy are such major components of the CPI, a number that excludes them is usually going to be lower than a figure that includes them. So guess which figure the government highlights when it releases inflation data. Core inflation, of course, despite the fact that the prices that impact us the most are not counted. The "headline number," the one that includes food and energy, is mentioned second, if at all.

The exclusion of food and energy from annualized presentations, which is done virtually all the time, is an even more flagrant deception since the time period automatically eliminates the distortions short-term figures might cause. When such price increases occur on an annual basis it's not volatility, it's a trend.

More egregious even than that are presentations by the news media that use core CPI numbers in multiyear comparisons. In many cases the media report only the core numbers, without so much as mentioning the headline numbers. Indeed, you could make a plausible argument that food and energy are so vitally important that if their prices got high enough they could bring other prices down. Consumers, once fed and warm, couldn't afford anything else. As a matter of fact, if any of the prices in the CPI can truly be considered core, they would be food and energy.

Oil Prices and Core Inflation: The Elephant in the Living Room

The absurdity of the Fed's use of core CPI figures to distract attention from real inflation couldn't be more dramatically illustrated than it is right now with oil prices at historic highs.

Oil, of course, is energy and one of the prices excluded from core figures, although it is a price that directly or indirectly impacts every American in major and unavoidable ways.

The historic vulnerability of oil prices to political tensions in the Middle East, combined with price volatility in recent months, makes it easy for the government to blame recent spikes in crude oil on such events, which is particularly unfortunate since recent price trends are in fact the result of inflation.

I was, in fact, one of the first on Wall Street to predict back in 2003 that oil would move above the $70 per barrel level. As I write this in September 2006, oil and gas prices have fallen sharply, explained, I believe, by technical factors temporary in nature.

There are two reasons primarily that I believe oil prices will resume their long-term ascent. First, years of cheap oil and the false perception that prices would stay low indefinitely led producers to underinvest in exploration and development and consumers to overutilize energy resources. Second, I expect Asian demand to surge as purchasing power shifts from the United States to Asia and the appreciated Asian currencies make oil cheaper to buy.

Rising oil prices are a direct result of inflation, not a cause of it, and should be recognized as such.

The PCE and the Mischief of Substitutions

The PCE, short for (believe this or not) the Chain-Type Price Index (or Deflator) of Personal Consumption Expenditures (CTPIPCE), is put out by the Bureau of Economic Analysis of the Department of Commerce and was adopted in 2002 by the Federal Open Market Committee of the Federal Reserve as its primary measure of inflation.

The Fed reportedly feels that the PCE, which tracks the part of the GDP representing expenditures by individuals, is better than the CPI because it better accounts for the fact that, as prices of goods and services change, consumer spending habits change.

In other words, whereas the CPI, taking many liberties as we've observed, tries to track a fixed basket of goods and services, the PCE makes constant substitutions. The theory is that if one item gets too expensive, you'll simply substitute another.

I like to make the analogy of a person sitting in a comfortably heated room under a chandelier eating filet mignon. Now fast-forward a few inflationary years. The same person sits in the same room; but having no heat, he is wrapped in blankets; having no electricity, he is using candlelight; and unable to afford filet mignon, he is eating cat food. However, since the individual spends the same amount of money in either circumstance, according to the PCE there is no inflation. After all, he is still warm, still has light, and is still eating.

If you really want to see the effects of inflation, just look around you. The prices are rising wherever you look, yet the CPI, the PPI, and the PCE say otherwise. That is because the indexes do not measure how much prices actually rise, but how much the government wants us to think they rise. Paying attention to the CPI and the others is like leaving your house on a rainy day without carrying an umbrella because a government weather report told you it was sunny.

Bogus Deflation Threat

The government says that an increase in official inflation is okay because it shows we're successfully avoiding deflation. They've got to be kidding.

I've touched on it before, but the use of a bogus deflation threat to advance the inflation disinformation campaign is something I find especially galling. It's one thing to make a bad thing seem less bad, but it's another to make a bad thing out of a good thing.

And that is exactly what our government, with some help from Wall Street, is doing by representing positive inflation figures as somehow being salutary because they militate against deflation.

Look at Japan, they say. Japan has falling prices and a weak economy so therefore the weak economy is the result of the falling prices. That is faulty logic. It is true that Japan's economy is weak and that prices are falling, but it's wrong to suggest the two go hand in hand.

Without getting into a lot of detail about Japan's economic problems (although there is no lack of relevance), what happened there in the late 1990s was a boom-bust cycle that wasn't allowed to play out naturally. Repeated attempts to stimulate Japan's economy with spending programs only succeeded in increasing its debt. And corporate restructurings, although attracting foreign investment, haven't addressed the basic problem of government deficits.

But falling prices are not among Japan's problems. In fact, falling consumer prices were one of the bright spots in the Japanese economy, which would have been a whole lot worse had prices been rising instead.

Deflation, which we technically define as the opposite of inflation, meaning that in deflation the supply of money contracts, is erroneously defined by government and Wall Street as falling consumer prices. Using that false definition, what is wrong with falling consumer prices? Aren't lower prices, in general, beneficial and conducive to better living standards? Why would it be a problem if food became less expensive, or if education or medical care became more affordable? What is so bad about being able to buy things at cheaper prices? Why does the government have to save us from the supposed scourge of lower prices?

Furthermore, contrary to popular belief, falling prices are actually a more natural phenomenon in a healthy economy than are rising prices. Manufacturers recover their costs and gain economies of scale that result in lower consumer prices, which lead to greater sales, higher profits, and rising living standards. In fact, it is the natural tendency of market economies to lower prices that makes them so successful.

The best example of what I'm talking about is the U.S. industrial revolution, a period of unequaled economic growth when our country was transformed from an agrarian society to an industrial society, when people started driving cars instead of riding horses, and they traded their candles for electricity. For more than 100 of the most prosperous years in American history we had falling prices, sometimes sharply falling prices.

The only time during the period from 1780 to 1913 when we saw rising consumer prices was during the Civil War, when the introduction of paper money expanded the money supply. When the war was over, the paper money was taken out of circulation and prices came back down.

The usual fears about falling prices, as we saw in Chapter 2, simply don't make sense. Unless an economy is in a total free fall, people don't stop buying in anticipation of lower prices, as we illustrated with the example of flat-screen TVs. Sure, sets didn't sell well at $10,000, but when prices dropped into affordable ranges, instant gratification kicked in and people paid the price the TV was worth to them.

Nor does the argument that corporate profits suffer from falling prices hold water. Profits represent margins, which exist independent of prices, and what is lost in dollar sales is gained in volume.

Yet under the guise of "price stability," generally defined as annual price rises of 2 to 3 percent, the government robs its citizens of all the benefits of falling prices and uses the loot to buy votes, thereby trading the rising living standards of their constituents for their own reelection. In addition, the natural tendency of prices to fall makes inflation far less obvious to the public, as it requires a certain amount of inflation each year just to stop them from falling.

Real deflation, or credit contraction, can actually lead to inflation as the Fed creates additional money to replace credit lost due to defaults. The new money will not reflate the bubbles just burst, thereby increasing asset values such as stocks and real estate, but will go straight into commodity and consumer prices, thus increasing the cost of living.

The Government's Decision to Stop Releasing Money Supply Figures

As though it weren't bad enough that the government goes to extraordinary lengths to distract us from the serious inflation being created by increases in the money supply, in 2006 it did something even more brazen. In an apparent effort to make it harder for those of us of analytical bent to gauge increases in the money supply, it announced it would no longer release the figures comprising M3 (see Figure 4.2).

M3 is the most informative of several categories the Federal Reserve uses to classify the total stock of money in the economy, in other words, the money supply. Components of the money supply range from currency in circulation, the monetary base, to what is known as "near-money," meaning Treasury bills, savings bonds, commercial paper, and other assets readily convertible into cash. M3 includes everything but certain types of near-money and is the money supply total one would use to track increases and decreases.

Now we can't even see that.

And We Don't Feel the Inflation We're Exporting

Another factor that has been muting the inflationary impact on consumer prices is the fact that so much of the money we

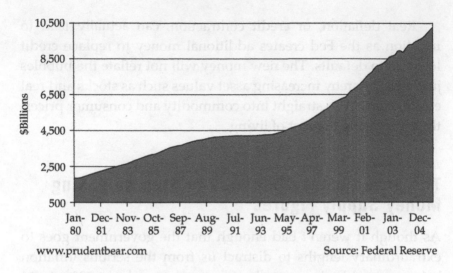

Source: Federal Reserve

FIGURE 4.2 *Money supply (M3), 1980–2005.* The nearly 20-fold increase in M3 since 1980 reveals the true extent of government-created inflation. Is it any wonder that the Fed decided to stop reporting actual inflation while focusing attention on far less revealing government measures of inflation?

Source: Reprinted by permission from David L. Tice and Associates (www.prudentbear.com).

created has been going abroad instead of bidding up prices domestically. If we didn't have China, if we were a closed system and we were printing money the way we are, not producing, and spending it all here, consumer prices would already be off the charts.

But our trading partners, by accumulating dollars, haven't stopped inflation; they have only delayed its effects. One day the flows will reverse, with the Chinese and others using their dollars to buy consumer goods as well as properties in the United States. When that happens, prices will rocket upward, as Americans compete with foreigners for a scarcer supply of goods. With our lack of productive capacity, most of those goods will be secondhand. In effect, the Chinese will merely repossess all those goods they sold us on credit!

Actually, in the case of China, the yuan-dollar peg has artificially kept U.S. import prices low, temporarily suppressing U.S. consumer prices. Most economists think that China's exporting "deflation" is part of a new era that will continue indefinitely. The reality is that this is a temporary fluke. China, sooner rather than later, will allow its currency to rise and Chinese exports will become more expensive, reflecting that and higher raw material and labor costs.

So real inflation, thanks to a deliberate government misinformation effort, is pretty hard to follow, harder than ever now that we can't see M3, and while it's taking its toll, the politicians stand tall. But it's still inflation, pure and simple, meaning that aggregate prices go up and the purchasing power of the dollar goes down.

And that bodes ill for your standard of living unless you take measures to protect yourself. So keep reading.

HOW GOVERNMENT-CREATED INFLATION BECAME POLICY

The process of dumbing people down so they'll buy official figures showing inflation "under control" at levels of 1 to 2 percent or so (when it is actually more like 8 to 9 percent) is actually a fairly recent development.

Back in the early 1970s, the market basket of consumer prices tracked by the CPI, although not a perfect indicator, was at least relied on by the government itself as a guide. We were still on the gold standard, meaning the money supply had to be managed conservatively. When inflation then reached 4 percent, it was considered a serious enough problem to warrant wage and price controls, a misguided policy to be sure, but at least a recognition that a problem existed. Today real inflation is much higher and we're told it's virtually nonexistent.

The Ford administration was the first to face real problems with government-created inflation, and its strategy, inspired by a young Alan Greenspan serving then as chairman of the Council of Economic Advisors, was to blame the inflation problem on the public. Remember the WIN buttons, standing for "Whip Inflation Now"? As though individual businesspersons could beat inflation by simply refraining from raising prices.

It wasn't until after inflation's effects on consumer prices went out of control during the Carter years that the then Fed chairman Paul Volcker took inflation on directly with high interest rates during the Reagan years. His successor, Alan Greenspan, began using inflation first as a means of financing the enormous federal debt built up during the Reagan administration, and then to postpone the consequences associated with any economic crises and to prolong phony expansions and thereby spare incumbent politicians the unpleasant task of dealing with severe recessions.

Contrary to conventional wisdom, the inflation of the 1970s was not caused by rising oil prices. Instead, rising oil prices were rooted in the inflation produced by the monetary and fiscal policies of the 1960s. The guns-and-butter spending of the Johnson and Nixon administrations created budget deficits that were eagerly financed (monetized) by William McChesney Martin Jr., the Alan Greenspan of his era. (His near-19-year term slightly exceeded Greenspan's, making him the longest-serving Fed chairman to date.) Today, of course, our current inflation problem is firmly rooted in the irresponsible monetary policies of maestro Greenspan.

At first the policies of the 1960s produced a speculative bubble in the stock market that eventually spilled over into consumer prices. Similarly, our current inflation problem had its roots in monetary and fiscal policies of the 1990s and 2000s. Here too the initial effect was to produce speculative bubbles in both stocks and real estate, with the inflation only now moving into consumer prices (despite the government's efforts to keep this fact hidden from the public with phony numbers). As was the case in the 1970s, the big increase in oil prices we are currently experiencing is an effect, not a cause, of the inflation that preceded it.

With Greenspan's help, the government discovered it could finance entitlement programs with inflation and simultaneously eliminate it as a problem by simply denying its existence. In other words, by playing with the numbers that purported to measure inflation, the government could convince the public that it wasn't a problem. How can you have your cake and eat it? Lie.

HOW THE FEDERAL RESERVE DEFIED THE CONSTITUTION

As I discussed in Chapter 3, the original reasons the Federal Reserve System was established in 1913, namely to provide a superior currency and an elastic money supply, ultimately paved the way to the financial hell into which we are about to enter. The Federal Reserve notes that replaced gold and silver certificates became IOU nothings ("Greenies," as my dad called them in The Biggest Con), and the creation of a central bank enabled the government camel to get its nose under the monetary tent, where it now permanently resides.

This was all contrary to the intention of the founding fathers, who in their wisdom specially wrote the Constitution to prohibit the monetary fraud currently being perpetrated. The Constitution denies the states the power to make anything other than gold or silver coins legal tender in payment of debts. The Constitution confers no power on the federal government to make anything legal tender, nor does it authorize the government to issue bills of credit, which was a term for paper money. In fact, in the original draft of the Constitution that power was included but it was struck down. So it was clear that the government doesn't have the power to print money. The government does not have the power to do anything but coin gold and silver, which the states can then declare to be legal tender in payment of debts.

And the reason the federal government wasn't given that power was because the framers didn't want it to have the power to create inflation. They had just experienced it firsthand with the Continental dollar, which ended up being worth around 10 cents and gave rise to the expression "not worth a Continental."

So the founding fathers knew what they were doing. They knew inflation was a problem in the Greek city-states and in the Roman Empire and wanted a limited government without the power to issue paper money.

But the government over the years decided it wanted more power than the Constitution allowed, and the establishment of the Federal Reserve with its power to print money allowed the government to usurp powers not authorized by the Constitution.

THE NATURAL RELATIONSHIP OF BUSINESS CYCLES AND MONEY SUPPLY

As discussed earlier, the concept of an elastic money supply meant a money supply that would expand and contract along with the economy. Thus, in times of economic expansion the Fed would expand the money supply, and in times of contraction it would contract the money supply. The theory was that by expanding and contracting the money supply with economic activity, the economy would function more smoothly and credit would be allocated more efficiently. The idea was not to prevent economic contractions from taking place, but to streamline the process.

That sounds odd to modern Americans accustomed to the (Keynesian) idea that just the reverse is true and that it is a function of monetary policy to fight off recessions by increasing the money supply even faster when the economy contracts than when it expands.

The Classical and Correct View of Business Cycles

According to the classical economists, like Ludwig von Mises and Friedrich A. von Hayek of the Austrian school, recessions should not be resisted but embraced. Not that recessions are any fun, but they are necessary to correct conditions caused by the real problem, which is the artificial booms that precede them.

Such booms, created by inflation, send false signals to the capital markets that there are additional savings in the economy to support higher levels of investment. These higher levels of investment, however, are not authentically funded because there has been no actual increase in savings. Ultimately, when the mistakes are revealed, the malinvestments, as Mises called them, are liquidated, creating the bust. Legitimate economic expansions, financed by actual savings, do not need busts. It is only the inflation-induced varieties that sow the seeds of their own destruction.

This flies in the face of modern economic thinking that regards the business cycle as the inevitable result of some flaw in the capitalist system and sees the government's role as mitigating or preventing recessions. Nothing could be further from the truth. *Boom/bust cycles are not inevitable and would not occur were it not for the inflationary monetary policies that always precede recessions.*

Economists today view the apparent overinvestment occurring during booms as mistakes made by businesses, but they don't examine why those mistakes were made. As Mises saw it, businesses were not recklessly overinvesting, but were simply responding to false economic signals being sent as a result of inflation. For that reason Mises called such mistakes malinvestments rather than overinvestments. One of my pet anecdotes makes the point clearly.

The Circus Comes to Town: How Inflation Causes Business Cycles

Let's suppose a circus comes to a small town, temporarily increasing the population and bringing a surge of business to local merchants. One restaurant owner, however, mistakes the upturn in his business for a permanent increase in demand and proceeds to hire more workers and add a new wing. This is the boom.

All is well until the circus pulls up stakes and moves to another town, leaving our restaurant owner with surplus staff and capacity and exposing a malinvestment that must now be unwound. This is the bust.

So the bust had to occur to correct for the malinvestments of the false boom that preceded it. Had the increased patronage been the result of a real increase in the town's population, the expansion would have been economically justified and the bust unnecessary. It is only because the owner misinterpreted the economic signals that there had to be a false boom and a corrective bust. Had the owner tried to prevent the recession by keeping the additional workers on and the new wing open, he would have been looking at bankruptcy. The recession was necessary to restore balance and maintain the viability of the business.

This analogy describes perfectly the false boom of the 1990s; just put the circus in place of the dot-com bubble. As a result of the inflation of the 1990s, start-ups flush with cash from their initial public offerings (IPOs) spent money without regard to profitability. This sent false economic signals to technology and telecommunications companies with respect to demand for their products. A wave of malinvestments ensued, which needed to be liquidated once the dot-com boom went bust.

Absent inflation, it is still possible for individual entrepreneurs to misread economic signals and make bad investments that need subsequently to be liquidated. But it is only with inflation that malinvestments are made on a national scale and result in economy-wide recessions. *That is why inflation is such a destructive force in a market economy, even if its effects are not immediately reflected in rising consumer prices.*

THE MODERN FEDERAL RESERVE: AN ENGINE OF INFLATION AND A CREATOR OF BOOMS AND BUSTS

The Federal Reserve turned the concept of the elastic money supply on its head by expanding the money supply indefinitely. When the economy expands, the Fed expands the money supply, and then when the economy contracts, it expands the money supply even faster, in an effort to stimulate spending to offset those contractions. It's like a heroin addict trying to kick the habit who shoots up each time any withdrawal symptoms set in. It is a painless way to go, but one unlikely to produce a healthy outcome.

So the Federal Reserve ultimately became nothing more than an engine of perpetual inflation, the precise opposite of what it was originally intended to be. Today the money supply is anything but elastic, as it always expands and never contracts. Had such a harebrained scheme been proposed at its inception, the concept of the Fed never would have seen the light of day and its proponents would have been laughed out of Washington.

WHEN IS PAYBACK TIME FOR OUR MONETARY MANAGEMENT?

Inflation is the unhappy result of our monetary mismanagement and the ultimate cause of the coming economic collapse. When will the collapse happen?

Unfortunately, it's not the kind of question we can answer with any degree of precision. We've got cynical forces playing to a gullible public. We've been buying time and may be able to buy some more. The weaknesses in our domestic economy, and the role inflation plays, are not generally well understood. Our inflation problem has largely been successfully concealed. Our trade imbalances are allowed to exist and grow because having reserve currency status, however tentative, we are exempt from restraints that would otherwise apply. Our national debt, now $8.5 trillion and mounting, is being financed through foreign borrowings. Counting Social Security, Medicare, and other unfunded government obligations, our debt is estimated at some $50 trillion. Our budget deficits persist, the administration jawbones ambitious deficit reduction goals, but there is no real plan to support them.

Who knows when the breaking point will come? All I know for sure is that it will come and when it does it will be calamitous. For all I know, it may have already happened by the time this book is published. If not, then you're in luck, as there is still time to implement the strategies outlined in later chapters. Do not press your luck by procrastinating. It's okay to be too early, as it is far better than the alternative of being too late.

AN UNWELCOME IMPETUS: THE VELOCITY OF MONEY

Compounding the problem when it does happen will be the factor of velocity of money and how that's going to further impact prices. Velocity refers to the rate at which money changes hands, and nobody's going to want to hold money that's losing value at such a rapid pace. They'll want to get rid of it as soon as they get their hands on it. Such spikes in velocity signal the terminal stage of a currency, where nobody will keep it.

Then the government will have to make it illegal not to take it. That will cause black markets because you can't really buy anything with a currency nobody wants. That black market hasn't happened yet in the United States, but it's a real possibility.

THE BIG ROUNDUP: WHEN THE INFLATION WE'VE BEEN EXPORTING COMES HOME

So we're ultimately going to have to suffer all the results of this inflation that we've been exporting.

So far, this huge buildup of dollars abroad has been bidding up the values of our financial assets, such as stocks and bonds, which has been welcomed and misinterpreted as legitimate wealth creation. Recently, however, inflation's effects have been increasingly evident in rising commodity prices, such as oil, lead, zinc, steel, gold, silver, corn, wheat, and sugar prices.

By buying our bonds, foreign investors have helped lower interest rates, causing our housing sales to rise and giving impetus to our rampant consumption. A lot of that money went into mortgage-backed securities or other forms of real estate financing, which blew the bubble bigger and allowed us to borrow even more money to send overseas in payment for more products we couldn't afford and lacked the industrial capacity to produce ourselves. That put more dollars in foreign hands and resulted in foreigners buying even more of our debt, perpetuating what appeared to be a virtuous circle of prosperity. Ultimately the truth will be revealed, as the "virtuous" circle turns into a vicious one, and prosperity turns into poverty.

Bottom Line

While we've been buying time, things have gone from bad to worse. We have debased our currency so much it is already beyond control. We just haven't felt the full impact yet because we have had massive artificial support from abroad.

But once those artificial supports from abroad disappear, look out. Waves of dollars will be flowing back in and stuff will be flowing out that we will need and want.

We'll be awash in dollars of greatly diminished value and, in the final analysis, looking at goods that will be too expensive to buy.

As I will detail in Chapters 8 through 10, there are several ways you can safeguard you own wealth and avoid the inflation tax by getting out of dollar-denominated assets and investing in foreign securities and gold. The United States has only the dollar to debase. It can only create one currency. Foreign central banks are debasing their currencies too, but to a lesser extent than we are, and given the dynamics of their economies they will be debasing less going forward 10 or 20 years.

But an economy that lives by inflation will die by it as well.

SLOWER GROWTH WILL NOT
CONTAIN INFLATION

When Ben Bernanke told Congress in July of 2006 that moderating economic growth will likely contain inflationary pressures, Wall Street responded with its biggest one-day rally in nearly two years. Unfortunately for the Wall Street party boys, the Fed chairman is likely wrong on both counts. In the first place, the U.S. economy will not merely slow, but tumble in the coming months/years, and rather than quelling inflation's fire, the inevitable recession will actually stoke its flames.

Bernanke's faulty logic assumes that inflation is somehow a by-product of economic growth. However, real economic growth emanates from increased productivity, which tends to hold prices down. Bernanke also dramatically underestimates the strength of the economic headwinds that will quash consumption and crush GDP growth. The rising costs of energy, adjustable-rate mortgage payments, rents, insurance, food, and local taxes, combined with the reverse wealth effects associated with collapsing real estate prices will produce a recession much worse than those seen in the past 30 years.

The argument that weaker growth will somehow cause consumer prices to rise more slowly focuses on the demand side of the price equation and ignores the supply side. Prices are a function of both supply and demand, and while slower growth, or an outright recession, would certainly reduce demand, it would also work to reduce supply. The result could well be equilibrium prices that are higher during a recession than during an expansion.

As the U.S. economy contracts, the federal budget deficit will grow and the perceived appeal of U.S. financial assets will be lost.

(Continued)

SLOWER GROWTH WILL NOT
CONTAIN INFLATION (Continued)

As a result, foreign capital will flee at precisely the time it is needed the most. This will put additional upward pressure on interest rates, further increasing mortgage rates, suppressing real estate prices and consumer spending.

More importantly, it will also cause the dollar to fall, making imports more expensive and pushing up raw material prices, thereby increasing production costs for domestic manufactures as well. As the dollar loses value relative to other currencies, foreigners will be able to outbid Americans for scarce consumer goods. As a result, fewer products will be imported into the United States and more of America's domestic production will be exported. Therefore, despite the fact that financially strapped Americans will be consuming much less, they will be paying much higher prices for the privilege of doing so.

2009 UPDATE

A few pages back, I used the metaphor of a circus coming to town to illustrate how surges in business activity and spending, when they are caused by temporary factors but misread as permanent, can cause artificial booms followed by proportionate busts. The bust phase involves the liquidation of unprofitable investments, called "malinvestments" in the parlance of Austrian economics, along with lost jobs, lost wealth, and other related dislocations. Assuming the boom/bust cycle is allowed to play out, however, free-market forces will thereby restore the potential of affected economies to enjoy optimal prosperity in the future.

But governments, which are politically driven, are loath to let free-market forces work in such situations, preferring to hide busts behind new booms they have been able to create by putting new money and credit into the economy. The inflation they create this way can be hard to detect, at least initially, so the public unwittingly allows them to defer the consequences, which continue to compound in severity, to a time when others are in office.

As I was writing *Crash Proof* in 2006, the real estate boom (or bubble), which the Greenspan Fed created to mitigate the recession that would have corrected the excesses of the dot-com boom of the 1990s, was approaching a bursting point. The bubble burst a few months thereafter and we are at present living with the consequences.

At the risk of overworking my circus metaphor, you could say the first circus was simply replaced by a larger one, which has now folded its big top and departed. In a mind's eye admittedly jaundiced by recent news coverage of the Obama stimulus plan, I have a picture of townspeople milling around the village green carrying shovels. Maybe the shovels are for cleaning up what the elephants left behind and getting things back to normal, but that's not what I'm seeing.

In my picture, these folks are the ranks of the unemployed, and they are looking for taxpayer-financed "shovel ready" projects to keep themselves busy. Be assured, I know there are infrastructure projects that are worthy and necessary, if only we could afford them. But unless I miss my bet, the result of these and other recovery programs will be a money hole of mind-boggling proportions. The stimulus value will be minimal and the inflationary consequences unthinkable. Of course, a hole deep enough to reach China would at least connect us to the source of much of the money we intend to borrow to finance the next circus. All of which brings this exercise in circular logic back to square one, which is exactly the point of it. What it boils down to is a metaphorical microcosm of what's about to happen to our national economy.

Inflation and Economic Recovery

If expanding the money supply in an economy that would otherwise be contracting causes inflation, and if inflation causes false
economic booms followed by proportionate busts, why would
our government have committed itself to borrowing or printing open-ended trillions of dollars to stimulate an economy that
free-market forces are working to bring into balance?

Obviously, after listening to a range of economic opinion
that did not include my own, President Obama has reason to
believe his stimulus program will succeed in restoring economic
viability; that the inflation genie can somehow be put back in the
bottle at a future time when the nation is better able to tolerate
contraction; and that if fundamental economic imbalances and
bad personal finance habits can be put on a long-term corrective
track, other nations will work with us until our economy regains
solid footing.

The problem, as I've said before, is that our economic leaders
are essentially the same people who misread the situation leading up to the present crisis and who don't seem to be looking at
things realistically now. They all admit they are in "uncharted
waters," which is a way of admitting they are winging it. The
only thing they are sure of is that doing nothing—letting free-
market forces work freely—is an unacceptable alternative,
although nobody to my knowledge has described the scenario
that would demonstrate why that is so.

In fact, for all his talk of change, President Obama is merely
repeating the mistakes of his predecessor. When Bush came
to office he inherited a busted stock market bubble and recession from Clinton. Instead of allowing market forces to correct
the imbalances, his response was to artificially stimulate the
economy with deficit spending in conjunction with a highly
accommodative Fed. Obama/Bernanke is merely following the

Bush/Greenspan playbook, only with larger deficits and easier money. Given how much damage we are now suffering from the first duo, imagine what horrors await as a result of the second!

I did see this crisis coming—saw it clearly, as you will appreciate the more you read of *Crash Proof*—and I am very confident of my predictions going forward. And while I know I sound immodest putting it that way, my conviction is not arrogance. I, along with a small handful of others using the same lens, am simply applying the basic laws of classical Austrian economics. The Austrian school is not considered mainstream these days, so guys like me are few and far between. But my predictions based on the fundamental laws of economics have been dead-on accurate. I don't consider myself prescient, but the success of my analysis speaks for itself. For your own sake, I hope you'll hear me out.

Inflation and Deflation

At this stage of the crisis, key economic variables waft around in all directions like the snowflakes in those glass globes we pick up and shake. There are forces pushing prices up and forces pushing prices down. But inflation is really the problem, and to understand why that is true, we have to distinguish between forces that are temporary and those that are long-term.

As I noted several times in *Crash Proof*, the specter of deflation has been used repeatedly by the government and Wall Street, both of which furtively consider inflation an indispensable tool of the trade, as a straw man representing the greater evil to which inflation is the antidote. That at least secures inflation's public acceptability, in controlled dosages, as a fact of life.

In the present environment, however, deflation has moved to center stage, being perceived both as a problem in itself and as a countervailing reality that makes inflation a manageable element in the risk analysis of massive government stimulation. Both views are dead wrong.

To begin with, as pointed out in the chapter, deflation is monetary contraction just as inflation is monetary expansion, but the popular understanding of deflation is falling prices. While it's possible to construct scenarios in which falling prices present problems, generally speaking they are a good thing and, in free-market economies, a natural thing. Of course, the word *deflation* is used capriciously, depending on the circumstances of the person talking. Falling stock market, house, and other asset prices are deflationary and must be stopped, say the same folks who wouldn't have thought of using the word *inflationary* to describe prices when they were rising. You don't hear complaints about deflated oil and gas prices. Everybody drives a car and has a heating bill, so nobody's arguing that oil prices should be higher.

Credit destruction and wealth that is being destroyed because of bankruptcies and bad loans are deflationary forces because they reduce the quantity of money in the economy and cause downward pressure on prices. Still, we don't have the net contraction that would define economy-wide deflation because the government is adding to the money supply at a rate that more than compensates. Absent such government-created inflation, yes, we would have deflation, but then we would want and expect prices to come down. And if everything comprising the cost of living dropped in price, nobody would be any the worse off. In the real world, there is no evidence we have anything to fear from falling prices, and in a down economy they provide a needed cushion.

If we were still on a gold standard, as was the case during the 1930s, the government wouldn't be able to counteract deflation with more inflation so easily. However, if we measure prices in gold instead of paper dollars, they are falling through the floor.

But the problem for most Americans is that they have no gold, only paper, so they will not see any benefit from falling prices. Those who forecast deflation fail to make this key distinction. What they forget is that while prices will be falling, the value of paper dollars will be falling even faster. So they will be correct in that prices will indeed fall in terms of gold, but they will totally miss the mark in that prices will skyrocket in terms of paper dollars being run off the printing presses at warp speed.

It is also important to point out that in terms of gold, asset prices are falling even faster than consumer prices. As consumer prices rise relative to asset prices, purchasing power is destroyed for average Americans who counted their wealth in terms of unrealized stock market gains or home equity. In addition, the realignment of asset and consumer prices is an essential adjustment of the bust, as during the boom asset prices rose much too high relative to consumer prices. As painful as this realignment might be, it is absolutely necessary for the restoration of future prosperity, and government attempts to interfere with it run the risk of turning inflation into hyperinflation.

So we had inflation when the boom was underway, and now that we are in a downturn, we have even more inflation because the money supply is growing even faster. Instead of letting deflation happen, the government is doing all it can to stop it by printing money and buying up assets to keep prices up, to keep debts from going bad, and to make sure everybody is kept whole. Not a dime has been lost by people with money in bank accounts or even in money market mutual funds. Everything the government is doing is the opposite of what it should do. Many argue that all this money printing is not inflationary as it merely replaces the money lost due to debt defaults. However, this naive view fails to account for the loss of output represented by defaulted loans. Money supply must contract to maintain an equilibrium. If money supply is held constant while real output falls, prices still rise. What you have is the same amount of money chasing a diminished supply of goods. If governments could offset real losses by simply printing money, there would be no need to allocate credit based on risk, as any defaulted loans could be made good at no cost by a government printing press.

People cannot afford 20 percent down payments and 30-year amortized mortgages, and nobody will lend against home values at today's levels unless the government guarantees the loan. So prices should adjust downward, an idea not easily accepted by baby boomers who saw home values rise steadily as a function of demographics for nearly 30 years. But the notion that real estate should appreciate in value as a function of time, although reasonable in the case of property bought for investment purposes, is fundamentally mistaken. Unlike stocks, which should increase with value as companies grow and prosper, a home, assuming the supply/demand relationship doesn't change, would lose value with time unless an effort is made to maintain its condition. So it's not in the holy writ that housing prices should increase, and when they do for whatever reason, the owner realizes a profit only when the property is sold, at which time the seller's gain is offset by the buyer's higher cost. Society itself doesn't benefit from high home prices. And the recent experience we had with reliance on home equity as a borrowing source has shown clearly the fallacy of confusing paper real estate appreciation with real wealth.

Why Deflationary Pressures are Temporary

If the government wasn't creating all this inflation, consumer prices would be falling instead of slowly rising, and falling consumer prices would be a stabilizing element, as noted earlier. The fact that with all the bankruptcies happening around us prices are simply declining and not totally collapsing is a telling comment on the excessive inflation the government is creating.

Even so, the deflationary pressures existing now, however temporary, are substantial enough to have persuaded many people that deflation, not inflation, is our economy's dominant threat. Deflationary forces causing the most confusion stem from deleveraging and related issues, and I discussed them in some detail in my update to Chapter 3. In summary, the major deflationary forces are:

- Investors and speculators being forced to sell assets and positions in commodities held on margin, thus depressing prices.
- Retailers overestimated the seasonal holiday demand and got stuck with inventory, forcing them to slash prices and cause competition to slash prices. Bankruptcies and going-out-of-business sales added to the downward price pressure.
- The stronger dollar helps hold down prices for Americans. More dollars are being created, but the dollars are buying more. Increases in the money supply that would normally elevate prices are being soaked up by the increased global demand for dollars as investors seek a safe haven in Treasury securities.

But the big point here is that these deflationary factors are temporary.

Why Inflationary Pressures Will Prevail

At some point the demand for dollars as a safe haven will wane because buyers will realize that dollars are not safe. Most of the dollar buyers are speculators who, like the condo flippers, will soon be looking to sell.

Also, there is a supply/demand adjustment in the works. What's going to happen is that ultimately the supply of consumer goods and commodities will contract even faster than demand. Tighter budgets are shrinking demand while the credit crunch is impacting businesses, including commodity producers such as farms and mines, many of which are shutting down or canceling expansion plans.

Right now there's a glut of raw materials and other commodities because speculators are dumping stuff on the market. But that will end and net demand will eventually return, albeit substantially diminished at home and greatly expanded abroad. When demand returns, however, supply will be inadequate because expansion capital has been hard to come by, and in some cases capacity was taken off-line in the ill-founded belief that prices will remain low indefinitely.

In the meantime and despite these factors, supply exceeds demand, mainly due to inventory liquidation. But seeing demand shrinking, retailers will not replenish the excess inventory they have been liquidating. Instead, they will reduce capacity. Retailers like The Gap will close stores. Price adjustments as a way of staying in business will give way to a new, smaller-scale retailing model where profits will be made with fewer items on fewer shelves selling at higher prices. The big markdowns and bankruptcy sales we are seeing now will disappear. A smaller group of surviving retailers enjoying increased pricing power because of less competition will make it on fewer sales and higher margins.

The Real Game Changer

The real game changer will be the resumption of the dollar's decline. With a weaker dollar, all the prices on all the shelves will go up. For the moment, shelves are being stocked with stuff bought at low prices with strong dollars and the higher margins are being passed on to customers in the form of lower prices. But when the dollar starts to implode and imports go up in price, it's going to be the other way around.

Also, when the dollar falls, so too will the prices of goods for foreign consumers, who buy with appreciated currencies. Increased foreign demand will mean fewer foreign products showing up on our shelves, and more of our stuff being shipped over there. This will drive up prices for Americans as they compete for scarce goods with wealthier foreign consumers.

Up to now the counterbalancing pressures on prices have been like a person who eats high-carb foods but works out furiously at the gym so manages to stay thin. In the economic arena, we similarly have inflationary forces pushing prices up and counter-vailing forces pushing prices down, leaving the public somewhat confused. There's slightly more of the former than the latter, but not a dramatic enough difference for people to make judgments as to what policies are obviously wrong or obviously right. But that will change. When our friend stops showing up at the gym, his waistline will give him away.

When the Inflation Danger Will Reach Full Flower

Inflation will be recognized for the problem it potentially is, I believe, when the temporary flurry of worldwide demand for our government securities dries up and buyers change their focus from default risk to inflation risk. Investors around the world will soon stop worrying about whether havens are safe or unsafe and begin saying, "The guarantee that the U.S. government is going to pay me my money back means less to me than the fact that the money itself will be worth less when I get it." When the focus is on inflation and Uncle Sam is printing the next trillion of stimulus money, demand for our debt will implode and the only buyer left will be the Federal Reserve. At that point there will be an increase in the velocity of money, as in, "I'd better spend this dollar today because it's going to buy less tomorrow." High velocity marks the terminal phase of a currency, and we are setting the stage for the stampede right now.

5

My Kingdom for a Buyer: Stock Market Chaos

The American stock market resembles an inebriate, reeling off walls but somehow still standing. It has the earmarks of a bear market, but it's a bear on its hind legs on roller skates.

Unlike the bear market of the 1930s, when the dollar's increased purchasing power somewhat offset the nominal collapse of stock prices, the bear market now looming will be more similar to the 1970s variety, where a collapsing dollar exacerbates the nominal decline in stock prices, making the real decline that much more devastating even as it is harder for most to detect.

In fact, with valuations more extreme this time, and with the acute problems the dollar has, this bear market could make the 1970s version look like a bull by comparison.

Just for openers, nominal stock prices, as the Dow registers record highs at the end of 2006, will have to fall much lower, some 30 percent from where they are, just to return to historical levels. On top of that, the real value of shares and the dividend income they throw off will reflect the greatly reduced purchasing power of the dollar. If you're planning to retire on your stock market wealth, forget it. It's the market that's going to do the retiring (unless, of course, you're talking about foreign stocks, about which much more later).

I'm going to get into some parallels between previous market collapses and the impending one. I'll also show you why the "this time it's different" mantra, while alive and well, has an ugly element of truth to it. Not only will the collapse be different this time—it's probably going to be worse.

The double message: Get out of the domestic stock market and get out of the U.S. dollar. I'm going to get into some strategies for doing this later in the book.

HOW WALL STREET HAS MISLEAD THE AVERAGE INVESTOR

What really roils me is that so many Americans have their necks overexposed to the risks of common stocks to start with. By that I do not mean that stocks are generically too risky, although I do recommend staying out of the overpriced U.S. stock market and dollar-denominated stocks. Stocks that are selected conservatively and pay high cash dividends are, in fact, my favorite investment alternative, especially where there is the prospect of currency profits, as I'm going to discuss later in detail.

But Wall Street has led the American public to think stocks have the safety of bonds. There's a huge difference, of course. Stocks carry all the risks inherent in business ownership. Bonds are contractual loan obligations that must be paid before owners get anything. Because stockholders have all that risk, they should naturally expect a higher rate of return than bondholders. But Wall Street has fostered a myth that because shareholders enjoy unlimited upside (capital gain) potential, they should settle for a dividend return that, if it exists at all, is often far lower than the interest rate on comparable bonds.

I also feel Wall Street puts an unhealthy value on potential capital gains. Just look at the widely used formula for setting up an individual's investment program. You take 100 and subtract the investor's age. That determines the basic asset allocation. If the customer is 20 years old, you recommend 80 percent stocks and 20 percent bonds, and then adjust the proportions as the investor gets older on the reasoning that youth justifies risk and advancing age requires safety and income.

My problem with that kind of thinking is that it assumes stocks rise in value as a function of time, that they are always a good buy regardless of valuation, and that there's always going to be a pool of people that you can sell out to so you can buy bonds and retire on the interest. As we'll see, though, the market has a well-earned reputation for perversity and there have been long periods when prices remained flat or declined.

Call me old-school, but I've seen enough of self-serving corporate management to make me want cash on the barrelhead. I want stocks that pay cash dividends and provide a higher yield than bonds do.

Neither stocks nor bonds can be depended upon to adjust themselves to anyone's life cycle. An investment approach that depends on future market values is another Ponzi scheme that assumes there's always going to be somebody there to bail you out.

Wall Street has also muddled the distinction between investing and speculating. The argument that growth stocks of companies that plow all their net earnings back into the business reward shareholders with future capital gains assumes that the objectives of corporate managers and shareholders are the same—that the two interests are in alignment, to use more elegant language.

Now I'll grant that there have been many companies over the years where this has been true, and where investors profited handsomely from capital gains that, until recently, were taxed at a more favorable rate than dividends.

But to overpay for stocks that don't produce income and derive their attractiveness from the promise of future capital gains that may or may not materialize to my mind smacks more of speculation than investment. Some stocks will gain, of course, but only at the expense of other companies, whose earnings shrink. If the market is trading at a given multiple, there have to be stocks whose earnings go up and stocks whose earnings go down. They can't all be winners.

Conflicts of interest are rampant on Wall Street and in corporate America, and the victim is the little guy. I started out as a broker with one of the big investment banks, and know from firsthand experience how Wall Street's symbiotic relationship with corporate America has operated to the disadvantage of retail investors. Year in and year out, the risks of common stocks are played down by firms that make their real money from advisory or underwriting services performed for client corporations.

Brokers are paid extra commissions to push certain stocks as favors to corporate clients or to move positions held by their firms acting as dealers. "Suitability rules" designed to protect investors from undue risk are treated perfunctorily as brokers pass spoon-fed recommendations off to trusting customers who think they're getting thoughtful advice.

On the research side, although stricter regulation has resulted from recent scandals, analysts are under pressure to favor existing or potential corporate clients by assigning higher ratings than their shares warrant or failing to assign negative ratings to inferior stocks that retail investors might otherwise avoid.

Lately, the interests of corporate executives and shareholders have diverged to a point bordering on or actually constituting scandal. The most infamous example, of course, was Enron, where shareholders walked away with nothing after criminal activities by top executives that were so complex and extensive they are being analyzed to this day. Here's the point, though, and it's a big one: *If Enron had been forced to pay cash dividends, it could never have pulled that caper off!*

There were so many other examples of corporate skulduggery at the expense of shareholders—WorldCom, Global Crossing, Adelphia, et al.—in the early 2000s that it really serves no purpose to go into them.

More significant than the laundry list of major scandals are practices we read about every day. Executive stock options that are timed and structured in ways that give managers incentives to make corporate planning decisions designed to maximize their personal profits at the expense of shareholder values are now commonplace. Just the salaries of top corporate executives have become so outsized as to penalize shareholder returns. Stock repurchase plans are often timed to create capital gains to benefit managers.

As this is written, a scandal seems to be breaking that involved the back-dating of executive stock options to capitalize on favorable stock price movements.

It can be argued that the U.S. brokerage and investment banking industry has transformed the modern American stock market into nothing more than a mechanism for transferring wealth from shareholders to management. Instead of paying out earnings to shareholders in the form of dividends, the cash is used to buy back the shares issued to management as a result of either option grants or stock compensation packages.

Wall Street has conditioned the public to think about stocks simply in terms of their prices. According to Wall Street, prices can only go up if one simply holds them for the long term. Most investors regard low-priced stocks as being cheap and high-priced ones as being expensive. The real fundamental value of the business those shares represent seldom comes up. This general misconception concerning stocks is evident even among my own clients. Whenever I call one to recommend a stock, the first question that I am usually asked is "What's its price?" My typical response is "What difference does price make?"

By itself, the share price confers no real information about the underlying value of the stock. Price is meaningful only when related to other factors, such as earnings, sales, book value, and shares outstanding. When such factors are considered, a stock selling for $5 per share can be expensive while another selling for $100 per share can be cheap.

That's why the public is so confused about stock splits, where a stock's perceived value is enhanced simply by reducing its price, with investors ignoring the increased number of shares outstanding. Stock splits originated because under the old system of trading and commissions odd lots (increments under 100 shares) were expensive to trade, so splits made it easier for small investors to trade in round lots.

For similar and equally foolish reasons, investors believe that it is easier for a stock selling at a low share price to double than for one selling at a high price. However, price is meaningless, as a company's earnings would have to double for the real value of its shares to double, which of course has nothing to do with price. If it were really easier for low-priced shares to rise, perpetual stock splits would rule the day.

The only reason low-priced stocks tend to move faster is that most are less liquid and often manipulated. If it were true that low prices meant faster appreciation, all high-priced shares would split, not at $50 or $100, but at $10, $5, or even a dollar. In most Asian markets, share prices below $1 are the norm, even for billion-dollar companies. However, their prices appreciate no faster as a result of prices being lower.

Wall Street's failure of responsibility is glaring even where clear conflict of interest isn't the issue. I strongly believe Wall Street deserves much more opprobrium than it got for its failure to discourage in a proactive way the naive investor behavior that drove the dot-com bubble. Sure, brokers were only giving customers what they wanted, but I strongly feel they had an implicit fiduciary responsibility to make investors aware of the insanity they knew they were witnessing.

At the risk of sounding unctuous, I don't mind saying that I personally sleep at night with a clear conscience. When other brokers were riding the tech-stock wave, I spent many hours persuading my clients to avoid the foolish risk of buying stocks without earnings. "But it's a long-term investment," I'd hear. "Sure, in a company that will not even be around in the long term," I'd tell them, and more often than not I was right. At Euro Pacific Capital, I do no investment banking. I don't make markets or act as a dealer. I am purely a retail broker specializing in stocks that pay cash dividends, and I plan to keep it that way.

But Wall Street, I'll say again, is rigged against the little guy and I see no signs of that changing, either.

Mutual funds are an overrated investment heavily promoted by Wall Street. During the latter 1990s, as I was still cold-calling prospective clients, a typical question I would ask those who professed to be invested in mutual funds was "What is the yield you are earning?" Of course it was a loaded question, as dividend yields at that time were next to nothing, if not zero itself. Even if the stocks that the funds owned paid some minimal dividend, they were not high enough to offset the fees charged by the funds. However, the typical answer to my question was "My funds are yielding about 20 percent per year." What my prospects were doing, of course, was confusing yield with past performance. How much a fund's share price had risen over the years has nothing to do with its dividend yield. However, shareholders typically confused illusory price appreciation with actual dividend yield.

Another major problem with mutual funds, and one rarely understood or seldom discussed, is the concept of relative versus absolute performance. Investors of course should be concerned with the latter; however, managers are far more concerned about the former. That often overlooked conflict of interest is vitally important and is the principal reason that most mutual funds will underperform the market in the long run.

This conflict arises from the way fund managers are paid and the way funds themselves are marketed. It's all about short-term quarterly performance, relative to either a benchmark or competitive funds with similar objectives. Therefore, no manager wants to underperform and no fund wants its recent performance to compare unfavorably to the performances of its competitors. This reinforces speculative behavior and causes fund managers to chase performance by buying overvalued stocks, the prices of which keep rising as more funds buy.

Then those funds buying such overpriced shares post impressive relative performance numbers, which results in increased inflows from performance-chasing investors. Those funds need to be invested in those same overvalued shares that goosed the performance in the first place, and it is a self-reinforcing cycle. When it ends, of course, the share prices collapse, and long-term investors lose big. However, the managers already earned their bonuses, and since all the funds collapse together, no one cares as no one's relative performance suffers.

Assume a diligent fund manager, with the good sense not to buy the overvalued shares, who instead invests in undervalued companies. The prices of such shares could languish for years before finally rising to reflect the true value of the companies they represent. While such a strategy is fine for investors, it could be disastrous for fund managers, who would likely lose their jobs long before such investments paid off.

In the final analysis it does mutual fund investors no good to pay managers big-time fees for impressive short-term performance when by the time investors need their money it's all gone. What is important to investors is absolute, long-term performance, which is the furthest thing from the minds of most fund managers.

If you think mutual funds aren't a flagrant enough example of conflict of interest, try hedge funds. Once relatively obscure bastions for the superrich, hedge funds, which are largely unregulated and exempt from disclosure requirements, have become the current rage, now numbering around 9,000 and holding over $1 trillion in assets. Their managers, the latest crop of gazillionaires, conventionally charge a 1 to 2 percent annual management fee plus 20 percent or more of the quarterly profits. You heard right: 20 percent or more of quarterly profits.

Since "hedge" means to protect against risk, it's ironic that the conflict of interest in hedge funds exists because of heightened risk taking, the very thing hedging was supposed to minimize.

Although, to be sure, the hedge fund universe has its share of exceptional managers, too many of the impressive returns boasted by the industry are produced not by outperforming investments, but by investments with ordinary returns that excessive leverage has turned into huge dollar windfalls on which managers base their 20 percent performance fees. There's actually very little hedging being done. Most hedge funds would be more accurately termed "risk funds" or "ultraleveraged funds."

For example, a yield of 8 percent might be achieved by buying junk bonds. But leverage it up 10 times by borrowing money at 4 percent, and you magnify the return over fivefold. In other words, simply by assuming additional risk, an 8 percent return is transformed into a 40-plus percent return through the magic of leverage. If a $1 billion hedge fund specializing in junk bonds merely leverages up 10 times, an 8 percent return becomes a windfall of more than $400 million. That gives the manager a payday of $80 million.

Hedge fund investors, trusting the expertise of hedge fund managers, are accepting risks they would never assume on their own and giving away 20 percent into the bargain. The hedge fund managers are taking a ton of risk, but with other people's money, not their own. When the risks pay off, the manager gets 20 percent. If the risk goes bad, the manager doesn't lose anything; he just doesn't gain anything. The investors take the hit. Heads, the manager wins. Tails, the investor loses.

Sure, when losses occur the fund managers have to get back to the last high-water mark before they can start collecting performance fees again. But the effect of this is a moral hazard even greater than existed before the loss: Now they have an even stronger incentive to push the risk envelope.

So that 20 percent performance fee creates a powerful incentive to use leverage and, since hedge funds tend to pursue similar strategies, they create short-term market momentum in the direction money is flowing. This tends to increase the paper gains for funds already positioned in those strategies, creating a lot of performance fees in the process.

The problems will arise when everyone tries to get out. The big paper profits will quickly evaporate when the momentum reverses, but that's the investor's problem. While the managers were raking in their 20 percent of profits each quarter on the way up, it's not as though they'll have anything to lose on the way down. They will gain as long as there's a profit. Managers can press a trend until it ends. There's no need to get out early, because there's no way they can lose. They can have their cake and eat yours, too.

Take the recent example of Amaranth, the $10 billion hedge fund that blew up in September of 2006. It lost better than 60 percent of its capital in a few short weeks as some highly leveraged natural gas bets went south. As those bets were paying off the managers made millions, but when they finally blew up, it was their investors who got creamed.

Did the Amaranth managers really earn their fat incentive fees for strategies that ultimately caused their investors to lose lots of money? Do you think they're going to reach into their personal pockets to help cushion the blow for their shell-shocked investors? Don't hold your breath.

BACK TO BASICS

Because the risks of common stocks have a way of getting forgotten amid the dazzle of Wall Street's aggressive marketing, I think it's useful to take a minute to revisit the basics. If it sounds like baby talk, forgive me. I meet a lot of intelligent grown-ups who cry like babies when they bring in their stock portfolios.

Common stock is simply corporate ownership broken down into units that can be bought and sold. When companies become publicly traded, which happens by way of a highly lucrative investment banking process called underwriting, the shares, which are traded on organized stock exchanges (like the New York Stock Exchange) or electronic stock exchanges (such as NASDAQ), acquire a market value. That market value is based not just on what the shares are worth as a portion of the company's equity, but on what investors in general think they should be worth, anticipating corporate and economic developments still in the future. The more assured future profits seem to be, the more investors are willing to pay for the shares.

In a nutshell, that's what the stock market is basically about, except for one all-important thing, which is the risk that stock investors assume.

Why Common Stockholders Bear the Greatest Corporate Risk

The fact that common stock represents ownership, whether it's ownership of General Motors or ownership of a lemonade stand, means that shareholders assume all the risk of business failure. Except for what they may have received from the business in the form of dividends, which are cash distributions made from profits, the owners (including common stockholders) in the event of liquidation rank last in terms of their claim on assets. Only after every bill is paid, all lenders and bondholders are made whole, and preferred stockholders take their share are common shareholders legally allowed in to rake the rubble.

In a going concern, common stockholders likewise stand at the end of the line when profits are paid out. Lenders, including bondholders, get paid their contractual interest before preferred dividends are paid, and whatever is left is either paid out as dividends on common stock or retained in the business as ownership equity.

The only acceptable reward for taking the risk of ownership is dividend yield. A cash dividend policy is the only insurance an investor has that a business will be operated for the benefit of shareholders. Non-dividend-paying growth stocks can be attractive but should be viewed as speculation rather than investing.

How Stocks are Valued

Stocks, of course, come in all shapes, sizes, and degrees of quality, but their prices tend to be a function of what the underlying companies are expected to earn.

If you were to try to buy a corner cigar store from the retiring owner, for example, you might agree to pay a price of, say, 10 times the store's annual earnings. That would be typical for a business that has an established and reliable customer base and is mature in the sense that it is not likely to see any marked increase in sales (in which case you might pay a higher multiple). In the case of large, publicly traded companies, a stock's value—whether it's overpriced, underpriced, or fully valued—is usually measured by its price-earnings ratio, called its P/E or its multiple.

Price-Earnings Ratio

By itself, the dollar share price carries no information with respect to value. The P/E, however, which can be expressed as "trailing" (meaning the current market price is divided by the average earnings per share over the prior 12 months, or as "forward," meaning the current market price is divided by estimated average earnings for the next 12 months), provides an indication of whether a stock is cheap or expensive, particularly when compared to its industry peers.

As we will see when we look at the history of market cycles in the next section, the overall market P/E, based on an index such as the Standard & Poor's 500 index (S&P 500), gives an indication as to whether stocks in general are over- or undervalued by historical standards.

Other Valuation Ratios

The P/E, although the most widely used valuation tool, is not the only one. Among the others are the price-to-sales ratio, which has the advantage that sales are less subject to short-term variability than earnings, and the price–to–book value ratio, which relates the stock price to value of the company's net assets and is a very rough indication (because assets are depreciated, valued at the lower of cost or market, or otherwise not reflective of liquidation value) of how the stock value relates to the net asset value.

Dividend Yield

The P/E's main limitation, however, is that by relating price to earnings, it ignores dividends. Thus, for our purposes in comparing individual stocks, we would want to look at the stock's dividend yield. The dividend yield, called simply yield, is the annual dividend divided by the market price (i.e., the latest quarterly dividend multiplied by four). Like the P/E ratio, yield is most meaningful when a company is compared with industry peers. Public utilities, for example, have higher yields as a group than stocks in other industries, where earnings are less predictable.

Like P/E, the overall market yield, as represented by an index like the S&P 500, is a useful tool for determining whether stocks in general are over- or undervalued by historical standards.

A Caveat Regarding Dividend Yield

One caveat regarding yield: American companies place a high value on the consistency with which they pay out dividends. This is in contrast with companies in the United Kingdom, which routinely raise and lower dividends as earnings vary. An American company would lower or eliminate its quarterly dividend only as a last resort to conserve cash. What this means, ironically, is that a higher than average yield can be a sign of financial problems.

Say, for example, XYZ company sells at $100 a share and pays an annual dividend of $3, giving it a yield of 3 percent. Then something happens that will affect corporate earnings adversely, and in reaction to publicity the stock drops to $50. The company, confident the problem can be solved and wishing to preserve its history of consistent dividend payments, keeps the dividend at $3, which has the effect of raising the yield to 6 percent. An investor attracted to the higher yield would be well advised to investigate the earnings problem and make sure it's not going to result in a lowering of the dividend if the company is forced to conserve cash.

Obviously, the point here is that no investment decision is made on the basis of one ratio. The fundamentals of every investment should be analyzed and the company's financial strength and earnings prospects confirmed.

MARKETS AND CYCLES

Stocks, with the exception of those combining strong fundamentals and high cash dividends, are a long-term investment. There will always be companies that fail, but viable companies, the overwhelming majority of stocks listed on exchanges, grow and become more valuable with time. Economies, markets, and companies, however, are subject to inevitable business cycles, and that is why stocks are inappropriate investments for your short-term goals. If you're going to need your money in five years, there's an excellent chance that stocks will be in a down cycle or market correction when you need it. And if you're depending on capital gains, you should be aware of how long some bear markets have historically lasted.

The severest market downturn or bear market in history lasted 10-odd years between the start of the Great Depression and the early 1940s. The second-worst bear market spanned the years 1966 until 1982, during which time the Dow Jones Industrial Average traded between 600 and 1,000 with inflation eating away at its real value all the while. The worst correction of that period began in 1973 and lasted through 1974, when the Dow dropped 45 percent in nominal terms from peak to trough. It then took 10 years for prices to get back to their previous peak (see Figure 5.1).

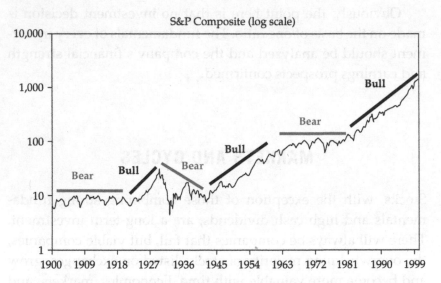

FIGURE 5.1 *Secular markets in 100 years of stock market history, 1900–2000.* Six years into the current secular bear market, we can see that during the prior century there were three secular bull and three secular bear markets. Remaining invested during each bear market, particularly when adjusted for inflation, was very costly. The current bear market will be no exception.

Source: Reprinted by permission from David L. Tice and Associates (www.prudentbear.com).

Since the early 1980s and up until 2000, stock prices followed a steep upward trend, but—stocks being stocks—there was a ratchet pattern to the rise. In 1987, a 36 percent correction lasted just under three months. Adjusting for inflation, if you had bought the Dow Jones Industrial Average in 1966, you would have waited until 1995, nearly 30 years, to get your money back. Since 2000, stocks have traded sideways to lower, in some cases sharply lower, as inflation, once again, eats away at their real values. On average, we have had a market setback once every two years in the past 100 years. See why I prefer stocks that provide a return on investment immediately—and in cash?

Past Bull Markets and the Bear Markets that Followed Them

It is interesting to look back at the bull markets of the 1920s and 1960s and the bear markets that followed in the 1930s and 1970s and make comparisons to the bull market of the 1990s and the bear market that is currently underway as this is book is being written in late 2006.

In each case, there was supposedly dawning a new era of eternal market gains: the Roaring Twenties, the go-go 1960s with the " 'tronics" boom and then the (all-weather, one-decision) Nifty Fifty, and recently the so-called new paradigm in the high-tech 1990s. Each featured astronomical multiples having absolutely nothing to do with reality.

The 1929 Crash and 1930s bear market saw a 90 percent drop in the Dow Jones Industrial Average in nominal terms. In 1973–1974 the Dow, as previously noted, dropped 45 percent in nominal terms, but with high inflation factored in, the decline in terms of gold or even consumer prices was also about 90 percent.

AVOID THE CURRENT U.S. STOCK MARKET

By historical standards and given the gloomy corporate profits outlook in an environment of high corporate debt and rising interest rates, the Dow Jones Industrial Average is considerably overvalued at late-2006 levels and should be avoided. I say that, even setting aside the imminent prospect of a collapsed dollar and the recession and hyperinflation that would accompany it.

Rising interest rates have potential impact on stock prices for a number of reasons. They increase the carrying costs of corporate debt, reducing earnings. Because other companies are experiencing the same pressure on profits, interest rates have the additional effect of lowering sales and revenues. Large corporations with underfunded pension plans are forced by declining stock prices to make additional contributions, thereby impacting profits. So rising interest rates cause multiple contractions.

SHORT THE MARKET?

It's not everybody's cup of tea, but an investor of above-average sophistication might reasonably ask, "If the U.S. stock market is a train wreck waiting to happen, why not just sell it short?" Selling short means selling an asset borrowed from a broker with the anticipation that it be subsequently purchased at a cheaper price and the profit taken to the bank.

The asset in this case would be an exchange-traded security representing a market index, such as a Diamond representing the Dow Jones Industrial Average, a Spider representing the Standard & Poor's 500 index, or a Qube (so-named because its symbol is QQQQ), representing the NASDAQ 100 Index.

Here's why I would recommend against doing this.

Retail brokers normally require investors to hold any short-sale proceeds in U.S. dollars, usually earning no interest. The dollar, seen through my famously jaundiced eye, could lose more purchasing power than the security you sold short lost value. Example: If the dollar loses 90 percent of its value and the security you shorted at $50 went down to $10, you'd earn $40 per share. If the margin on the short sale was $25, you would have earned a profit of 160 percent. But you'd need a profit of 1,000 percent just to offset the loss of the dollar's value.

I've got a much better idea, which is to borrow dollars and spend them to acquire foreign income-producing assets, using the income to pay the interest. Short selling accomplishes the opposite, as you end up borrowing assets, which will probably have some intrinsic value, and acquiring dollars, which may have none. Doing it my way, if the dollar collapses you can sell a small percentage of your appreciated foreign assets, repay your entire debt, and hold the remainder free and clear. Beats having to buy back "appreciated assets" with near-worthless dollars, no?

More in Chapter 8.

Valuation Factors and the Market Outlook

Just as individual stocks are deemed over- or undervalued based on their price-earnings ratios or their dividend yields, the overall market, as measured by a stock average such as the Dow Jones Industrials or a stock index such as the S&P 500, can be valued using the same ratios. For example, the 30 stocks in the Dow have, as this is written, an overall Dow P/E of 21.07. Compared with a historical Dow P/E of around 15, the market—as the Dow represents it—is overvalued by the difference. A regression to the mean, to use a popular statistical device, would entail a correction in nominal terms of 25 to 30 percent. Similarly, the Dow's dividend yield at 2.28 percent is down from 2.47 a year ago this July 7, 2006. The lower the yield, the greater the overvaluation, and prior to the start of the latest market bubble a Dow yield under 3 percent signaled danger.

Factor in an estimated 8 to 10 percent inflation level, and the prospect of a more severe real, as opposed to nominal, drop in the Dow-measured market would appear a distinct possibility.

In the perspective of previous bear markets, notably those of the 1930s and the 1970s, the prospects look even worse. Economic conditions now are as bad as or worse than what existed then. Historically, the length and intensity of booms have tended to be matched by busts of similar length and intensity. The bull market just ending was the longest and strongest on record, with valuations stretched to unprecedented levels.

So can we rule out a market drop of 90 percent? In nominal terms perhaps, but not in real terms meaning priced in gold or in relation to consumer prices.

Oh, I knew I was forgetting something. There's the imminent collapse of the U.S. dollar as Asians wise up to our trade and budget deficits, invest elsewhere, and spend all those surplus dollars buying back their own goods in our markets.

If I have raised anxieties with the foregoing, let me remind you that salvation will be found in later chapters.

2009 UPDATE

The inebriated bear on roller skates to which I compared the 2006 stock market at the outset of Chapter 5 is still tippling, high as a kite one day and in a nosedive the next, but generally fighting a losing battle in a sick economy. We may see a sustained

bear market rally or two before it's over, but all signs point ultimately to a stay in rehab. The only question is when.

Could a Market that's Lost Nearly Half its Value Be Overpriced?

As I was writing the chapter at the end of 2006, the Dow Jones
Industrial Average was hitting what were then record highs
above 12,000 and would go on to an all-time high of over 14,000
in October 2007. As I write now in March 2009, it's below 7,000.
Of course, we're talking nominal rather than inflation-adjusted
figures. In reality, neither peak, when adjusted for inflation,
eclipsed the Dow's nominal high of 11,750 reached way back in
January 2000.

But on a valuation basis, despite a 53 percent decline in the
Dow Jones Industrial Average from the 2006 high, the trailing
price-earnings (P/E) ratio is about 22. That's on the high side by
normal standards, never mind the single-digit multiples typically
seen at bear market bottoms. The forward P/E, which relates
price to projected earnings for the year ahead, is also above bear
market lows and reflects far more optimism than is warranted,
especially given the ever worsening economic signals.

That the market is still overvalued on a price-to-earnings
basis despite huge price declines, widespread dividend cuts,
and sharply reduced earnings is not as enigmatic as it may seem,
however. When prices and earnings both fall proportionately,
the P/E ratio stays the same. Thanks to enough die-hard opti-
mists, earnings are falling somewhat faster than prices, which
raises the ratio. The point, though, is that the market has further downside, although bear market rallies will likely delay the
adjustment process. However, despite any counter-trend rallies,
corporate profits will continue declining and there will be more
announcements of corporate debt defaults and write-offs of

collateralized loan obligations (CLOs, the corporate loan equivalent of collateralized debt obligations [CDOs]), all of which will increase downward pressure on stock prices.

Where will the Dow Go from Here?

Eventually the Dow will stop falling because inflation is going to be so high that prices of everything will rise. If I had to guess, the Dow could drop as low as 4,000 or 5,000 in nominal terms. In 1994 and 1995, 4,000 was a resistance level (a price ceiling it was hitting, then bouncing back from), and once we broke through that we started the huge leg up. So that would be a logical place for the Dow to bottom out, although enough inflation could raise the level higher.

As I said earlier, I would not be surprised to see a few sustained rallies, some spectacular, before the downside of this market runs its course, so its low point in nominal terms could still be years away. However, it is even possible that given enough inflation, the March 2008 low of 6470 will hold. But in real terms—that is, adjusted for inflation or priced in gold or foreign currencies—this bear market could easily be with us for another five to 10 years, perhaps longer.

A Double Whammy: Stocks of Industrial Companies Take a Surprising Hit

As is hardly news, the stock market drop was led by the banks and other stocks in the highly leveraged financial sector. But as Warren Buffett observed, when the tide goes out we discover who's been swimming naked. In March 2008, breathtaking plunges in the prices of two of the country's most iconic industrial companies, General Electric (which collapsed to a low of $5.72 per share in ealry March 2009 a share from a 2001 high of just under $60) and General Motors (which dropped from close to $100 per share at its peak in April 2000 to just above $1.50 per share by March 2009), revealed dramatically how dependent those companies were on the earnings of their own finance activities and how extensive the "financialization" of the American economy had become.

In the cases of these and a host of other companies representing the country's diminishing manufacturing base, captive finance companies, set up originally to finance customer purchases of what the core companies were producing, expanded and diversified into financial services behemoths. They were heavy borrowers in the capital markets and had become the main contributors to the consolidated earnings of their parent companies.

General Electric and General Motors are startling examples of a flaw in the American business model that mirrors and matches in significance the shift from manufacturing to services in the American economy at large.

Until 2008, General Electric, a household name and one of the 12 original components of the Dow Jones Industrial Average, was considered the American paragon of corporate enlightenment. Under the stewardship of former CEO Jack Welch, who retired in 2004, GE gained a reputation as a model of innovative and uniquely successful management strategies.

General Electric is classified as a conglomerate by stock analysts, with its widely diversified activities grouped as technology, media, and financial services. The genesis of financial services, as with so many other industrial companies having captive finance companies, was financing customer purchases of its many products. In GE's case, customer financing was expanded and broadened to include, in addition to capital and consumer finance, insurance, investment banking (Kidder Peabody between 1986 and 1994), and a diversified range of other financial services, including a heavy investment in credit cards used by department stores and other vendors. GE's financial activities eventually became the company's primary source of profits, overshadowing everything else. Yet, despite the transition, the company maintained its identity as an industrial bulwark. When the credit markets ground to a halt, problems initially impacting financial services naturally spread throughout the company.

General Motors has suffered manufacturing losses so gigantic it has filed for bankruptcy. Like the other Detroit automakers, GM has been unable to make cars profitably for a number of reasons, but its day of reckoning would have come much sooner had its financial services activities not been its real profit center. During the 1990s and 2000s GM derived the bulk of its earnings not from manufacturing, but from finance, with all the leverage, financial gimmickry, and specialized accounting that went along with it. It even got heavily involved in residential mortgage financing through Ditech ("Lost another loan to Ditech") and other companies.

I'd be willing to bet that the liabilities of companies like GM and GE now exceed the value of the productive assets that used to comprise their core businesses (While I won my GM bet prior to publication of this edition, my GE bet is still in play). Therefore, much of the big profits earned by such industrial companies through their financial activities from the 1990s on, and from which executives were paid huge bonuses, were phony. Managers were being paid outrageous sums of money as they were busily laying the foundation for the future destruction of their companies.

Conflicts of Interest as a Contributor to Stock Market Chaos

As a general observation, customer financing, which is a vital part of many companies we think of as industrial, is now increasingly viewed as a flawed business model because there is an inherent conflict of interest between sales goals and credit standards, with sales usually prevailing.

Conflicts of interest involving corporate executives, hedge fund managers, and other Wall Street powers at the expense of customers and shareholders were themes I stressed when I wrote Chapter 5, and it has been a source of some satisfaction that so much of that conflict was exposed by the events of 2008.

It's ironic (or maybe it isn't) that 2008 set the record for executive bonuses and stock options, when you look at all that happened in that very year. Lehman Brothers went bankrupt. Bear Stearns was effectively bankrupt when JPMorgan Chase took it over with the help of the Federal Reserve. Merrill Lynch had to be saved by Bank of America (in what was apparently a shotgun wedding with Henry Paulson and Ben Bernanke pointing all four barrels at a very reluctant Bank of America CEO, Ken Lewis). Citigroup trades as this is written for $1 a share and change, after former Treasury Secretary Robert Rubin walked away with more than $126 million in cash and stock received in compensation during the eight years he served as director and senior counselor. American International Group (AIG) executives received generous bonuses after the government began bailing them out. In addition, those major Wall Street investment banks that survived, albeit in different forms, only did so as recipients of massive government bailout money and because the Fed loaded up its balance sheet with hundred of billions of dollars' worth of toxic paper that otherwise would have poisoned them to death.

Anyway, my statement in Chapter 5 that "the U.S. brokerage and investment banking industry has transformed the modern American stock market into nothing more than a mechanism for transferring wealth from shareholders to management" may have seemed a bit shrill at the time, but it was obviously validated by everything that happened. The people who brought down those

Wall Street firms left with fortunes, while their shareholders left broke. Sadly, now that in many cases the shareholders have been wiped out, the government has picked up the slack and is transferring taxpayer money to management instead.

The same was true with a lot of the hedge funds that collapsed in 2008. They had huge losses, but the investors took the hit, not the managers. Hedge fund managers are not required to give back the incentive fees they charged before their bad bets went bad. While everyone was leveraging up and piling into bad trades, paper profits soared, allowing managers to rake in their 20 percent incentive fees. Now that the bottom has dropped out the paper profits have been replaced by real losses; while investor gains were merely on paper, the managers walk away with real money. The only downside is that they simply can't take additional incentive fees until account deficits, which the managers call high-water marks, are made up. Of course many managers have a solution for this problem: Fold their funds and launch new ones, without the high-water marks! Nice work if you can get it!

Conflicts of interest persist even with all the bailout money flying around. For example, look at who's benefiting from the bailouts. It's not the common shareholders, whose stock is being zeroed out or whose dividends are being slashed. It's the executives, high-level employees who get to keep their cushy jobs and lavish bonuses. If nobody cares about the shareholders, one wonders why anybody would want to buy stock in U.S. companies. So far, at least, the government has been respecting the legal status of bondholders (at least until the sham Chrysler bankruptcy in which secured creditors had their claims dismissed in favor of politically connected labor unions), but they'll take their lumps in the end when inflation ultimately takes away the purchasing power of bond principal in addition to its steady erosion of interest. In the meantime, by bailing out bondholders who made bad decisions, the government creates a moral hazard that circumvents normal market vigilance on the part of lenders. In addition, those companies perceived to be too big to fail now get access to credit that otherwise would have gone to smaller, more creditworthy borrowers. In effect, small companies that have viable uses for funds face higher capital costs to subsidize lower capital costs for the larger companies that are wasting resources. The end result is that fewer profitable investments get funded, while those that lose money receive additional funds. Ironically, the only reason companies become too big to fail is that government interferes with free-market forces that would otherwise have limited their growth! To make matter worse, the Obama administration has proposed making the Fed the systemic risk regulator specifically to oversea firms that it deems "too big to fail" that only exist due to moral hazard supplied by the government itself. Rather then further empowering an agency that has already wreaked havoc on our financial system, we should reign it in, allowing market forces to prevent firms from becoming too big to fail in the first place.

The Protectors of Our Wealth

"Thank heaven for the Securities and Exchange Commission, the Financial Industry Regulatory Authority (FINRA), and the other regulatory bodies that keep our money safe." Those words could have been uttered by Bernie Madoff, who, I am convinced, could never have fleeced so many smart people out of so much money for so long if it weren't for the SEC and the false sense of security it gives investors who would otherwise do their own due diligence. Leaving aside evidence that in Madoff's case whistles were reportedly blown by SEC staffers and not acted upon by their superiors, the fact that an SEC exists as a guardian of the public interest and routinely performs audits confers, in the absence of negative information, an implicit seal of approval, which is disarming to the public it is supposed to be protecting. In the case of Madoff, it had the effect of legitimizing and protecting him.

With all that has happened recently to the detriment of investors, one has to wonder if they wouldn't have been better off without the government's involvement in securities regulation. Right under the nose of the SEC and FINRA we've recently seen investors victimized by two huge Ponzi schemes, with more probably to surface. With the Dow down 80 percent in eight years measured in gold, imagine how much wealth has been lost and how many investors have been wiped out as the result of bad advice. Add to that the money people paid for that advice.

And look who was doing the advising. Bastions of investment wisdom such as Merrill Lynch, Bear Stearns, Lehman Brothers, Goldman Sachs, and Morgan Stanley followed their own advice and wound up either bankrupt or seeking government bailouts. Other Wall Street firms have seen their stocks collapse, and many have lost more money in the past two years than they made in their histories. Investment banks no longer exist as a form of organization, and those that reincarnated themselves by adopting commercial bank charters would not have survived without the intervention of alumni well placed in the Bush and Obama administrations. So we're looking at a group of Wall Street's best and brightest who borrowed a lot of money, took tremendous risks, were lucky long enough to amass staggering profits, then blew themselves up and landed in the waiting arms of their bailout buddies in Washington.

Buy-and-Hold Gets a Bad Name

A sad consequence of vanishing brokers, falling markets, and Wall Street's misadventures is that long-term, buy-and-hold investing has been discredited because it is seen as having failed in the United States. Mainstream American brokers were urging people to buy, buy, buy because stocks for the long term were a good bet. Investors did what they were told, got into the market, and were disappointed when the market declined.

What the mainstream brokers were doing was recommending a good strategy in a bad market that was overvalued and low-yielding. Brokers go to work to sell stocks, and they bring along a mind-set that every market is either a bull market with upward potential or a bear market about to enter a bull phase. Since good companies grow and their stocks gain value as they do, stocks are always a good long-term investment, or so they are trained to persuade unwary investors.

The fact, of course, is that even the best companies, when they are overvalued and low-yielding, are bad investments, whatever the merits of the investment strategy. Price means nothing absent the context of valuation. You have to know not to overpay. But a quality stock backed by a strong balance sheet, paying a good dividend, and bought at a favorable price is an ideal candidate for a buy-and-hold strategy. It will pay dividends in markets that are up or down, and if the dividends are reinvested and allowed to compound, your wealth will grow.

What has been discredited is not the long-term, buy-and-hold stock strategy, but the Wall Street institutions, their investment advice, and their misunderstanding of the economy. How many strikes do they get? I say they're out.

The Future of Wall Street as the Financial Capital of the World

As Detroit yielded its status as the automotive capital of the world, I predict New York by the end of the next decade will be replaced as the world's financial capital, probably by a group of centers such as Shanghai, Hong Kong, Singapore, Tokyo, London, Stockholm, Frankfurt, and perhaps others. When the United States became the center of the world's capital markets, we were its richest country. We were the one investing our surplus savings all around the world. We had a lot of capital to allocate and it was done in New York. People who wanted to list their companies came to our markets because that's where the investors with money could be found. Capital should be allocated where it's being accumulated.

Also, the Wall Street debacle has besmirched our reputation and brought our credibility into question. The world has watched our companies turn their backs on shareholders and our brokers misguide their customers. By making shoddy merchandise and selling poor quality securities backed by substandard mortgage, credit card, and auto loan paper all over the world, we've created ill will nearly everywhere.

If burdensome regulation made the United States less competitive in the past, imagine how much less competitive we'll be with all the new regulation being drafted supposedly to prevent disasters like those that led to our present predicament.

Why should other countries outsource their capital allocations to the United States, especially given prior results, or American companies try to raise money here when we're all broke and they could raise it more easily in Shanghai or Tokyo?

6

They Burst Bubbles, Don't They?: The Coming Real Estate Debacle

The July 31, 2006, *New York Times* had an article accompanied by a picture that might have been captioned "The Life of Riley."

It showed a smiling, well-coiffed, 53-year-old former steelworker and sometime math teacher, relaxing in his jeans on a chaise lounge. The article title was "Men Not Working, and Not Wanting Just Any Job."

The article explained that the man's life of leisure was being financed by home equity extractions. But that was not the article's angle. That part seemed to be okay with the Gray Lady. The point was that our friend could afford to be idle and planned to stay that way until something befitting his dignity came his way.

To me, it was a telling example of how the idea that home equity is a modern form of wealth is routinely accepted.

If the dot-com mania was a warm-up, the main act is the real estate bubble. Stock market collapses are bloody, but their damage is pretty well limited to those who bought overvalued stocks. Real estate, though, is all about leverage, and that debacle, already well under way, is going to affect virtually every American.

You can be an exception, if you read on and follow the steps I outline in this book's later chapters.

THE AMERICAN ECONOMY HAS NEVER SEEN ANYTHING LIKE THIS

The real estate bubble, easily the worst speculative episode in American history, has been artificially propping up the entire national economy. The unwinding will cause havoc reaching well beyond the stakeholders directly involved.

According to a Northern Trust Company report, a stunning 43 percent of the increase in private sector jobs between 2001 and April 2005 were housing related, and these jobholders are themselves homeowners and consumers. But furniture, landscaping, appliances, municipal governments, and nearly everything else depend, directly or indirectly, in one way or another, on real estate. The amount of consumption related to home ownership is almost without limit.

Ironically, the worst-case, and most likely, scenario would not be a bust proportionate to the boom. That would be devastating, but natural and ultimately salutary. The worst case would be politically inspired re-inflation aimed at preventing a crash landing. That would mean winding up Helicopter Ben

Bernanke's money printer to keep nominal home prices artificially high. If foreign central banks, suddenly awakened to reality by mortgage-backed security investments gone bad, reacted to U.S. economic woes by backing away from Treasury securities or by releasing a flood of dollars in our consumer markets, hyperinflation would compound the problem, causing an economic coup de grâce, with hell to pay.

So how did this impending disaster come about?

HOW PUNCTURING ONE BUBBLE SET US UP FOR ANOTHER

Following the bursting of the dot-com bubble in 2000 and the World Trade Center tragedy in September of 2001, the newly inaugurated Bush administration and Republican-controlled Congress made a bad choice. Instead of using the bully pulpit to appeal for national sacrifice to see us through a corrective recession, they swept everything under the rug and bought some costly time.

For starters, they enacted a $1.35 trillion tax cut and passed a series of irresponsible spending increases in the name of stimulation. Then, an accommodative Federal Reserve dropped interest rates to levels unprecedented in the postwar United States, ignoring the fact that the national savings rate was about to go from low to negative.

Those actions quieted recessionary forces for the time being. Now flush with renewed spending power, Boobus Americanus looked around for places to put money. Much was spent on consumption, mostly of goods imported from the Far East, but where to put the rest? Recent stock market performance had been a chastening experience, so that was out.

But enticingly low mortgage rates were drawing attention to real estate, initially encouraging mortgage refinancing, which was adding further to spending power. Renters were discovering that low rates made it feasible to own, and so they began buying. A $500,000 capital gains tax exemption existed on home sales for couples who had been in their homes for two years, so real estate became an obvious investment opportunity. Growing housing demand began to show up in rising home prices, validating the seeming wisdom of speculation. *In short, a recession was being postponed, while a stock market bubble was being replaced by a much larger one in real estate.*

SOME PERSPECTIVE: THE GOOD OLD DAYS OF A DECADE AGO

To fully appreciate what went awry with the real estate market, it is useful, I think, to take a look back at how homes were bought in the old days, meaning roughly 10 years ago, before the effects of monetary mismanagement began spilling over from the stock market into real estate.

Traditionally, a bank or savings and loan institution would make a 30-year mortgage loan that would be an asset on its books. Because the lenders wanted to be repaid, they were very careful about the persons they were lending money to and about the value of the collateral.

The process of securitization, the purchase of prime residential mortgage paper from originating lenders by government-sponsored entities that pool and repackage it in the form of high-yielding mortgage-backed securities, had been an important part of the real estate industry since the early 1980s, but the function of entities doing it, such as Fannie Mae, Freddie Mac, and Ginnie Mae, was to provide a national secondary market for mortgage securities, thus expanding the service of local mortgage lenders. How securitization became a bugaboo rather than a boon to responsible home ownership is something I'll get to in a minute.

So the lender traditionally had a vested interest in the creditworthiness of local borrowers and in the validity and accuracy of appraisals. Appraisers earned their living from banks, and their reputations for honesty and integrity were their lifeblood.

Lenders also required a down payment, usually 20 percent, and that was because they wanted to feel that the borrowers had something to lose, that they weren't going to walk away from the mortgage at the first sign of trouble or fail to make mortgage payments on time.

Also, the ability to save a down payment was a confirmation of good character. Solid citizens knew how to manage their money, and that meant being able to save. It also meant people would make sure that the mortgage payment didn't represent too big a burden on their income.

One rule of thumb was that a bank would lend about twice one's annual income. If you made $100,000, the most they would lend was $200,000. Another was that the total of mortgage payments, interest, and taxes should amount to no more than a third of pretax income, which was something people could comfortably handle. They didn't want people to be stretching. And they wanted an honest appraisal of the property for the obvious reason that they wanted good collateral if the borrower defaulted.

The fact that so many households are now dependent on two paychecks to meet mortgage payments adds to the volume of new home purchases. Without sufficient savings, the loss of one of those paychecks means default is inevitable, especially if the mortgage has an adjustable interest rate. The coming deluge of foreclosures will only exacerbate the real estate downturn and the severity of the price declines.

This recession will differ substantially from those of the past, where sufficient savings existed to bridge the gap between jobs, and mortgage payments were fixed. In addition, if the primary breadwinner required more time to find a job, the nonworking spouse might take a part-time job during his search. Or he might work part time himself until he could find a better, full-time job. The result of having a spare worker at home was that a family had the ability to weather a financial storm, should circumstances temporarily require it. However, with two full-time paychecks already committed to a mortgage, this safety net no longer exists. Now one pink slip for either spouse means a foreclosure notice likely will soon follow.

Then, as now, homeowners borrowed against their homes, but they did it then to make home improvements, realizing they couldn't expect their full investment to translate into appreciation, unless, of course, they did the improvement themselves and the value equaled their labor and time (see Figure 6.1). When you were paying, though, you figured on getting back a percentage of what you put in if you sold, depending on what the improvement was. On a fancy new bathroom, for example, you could probably expect to get 80 percent or so back, at most. Swimming pool investments were typically worth something like 40 percent of their cost. During the recent mania, however, people figured an investment of $50,000 in a remodeled kitchen, complete with granite countertops and Viking appliances, would add $150,000 to the value of the house. It was crazy.

From the homeowner's standpoint, buying a house was traditionally a good investment because once the mortgage was repaid, one could retire and live rent-free. These days, you pay $500,000 for a house and when you retire you owe $1.5 million because you kept refinancing or kept trading up into bigger properties.

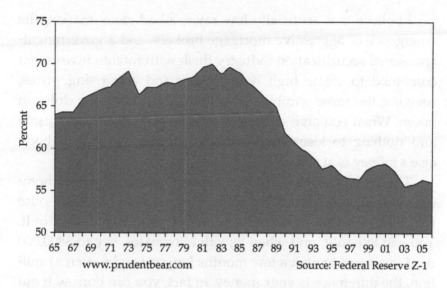

FIGURE 6.1   *Home equity as percent of home market value, 1965–2006.*
In recent years American homeowners have borrowed so much
money against their homes to finance consumption that despite
record price appreciation home equity now represents the smallest
percentage of home values in U.S. history. Imagine how much worse
the situation becomes when real estate prices decline!
Source: Reprinted by permission from David L. Tice and Associates
(www.prudentbear.com).

*The economic effect of the prudent lending policy was that it put
a natural limit on the extent to which home prices could rise. Houses
couldn't appreciate faster than down payments could be saved or faster
than household incomes could rise.*

What Caused Lending Standards to Suddenly Deteriorate

How did things so quickly reach a point where somebody can
walk into a bank without a job, with a bankruptcy, and with
credit card debt, and walk out with a zero-down, interest-only
mortgage for half a million dollars?

I believe that artificially low rates, a bad stock market, the emergence of aggressive mortgage brokers, and a government-sponsored securitization industry flush with foreign investment combined to create high housing demand and rising prices, reviving the same gambling mentality that drove the dot-com boom. When you give somebody a situation with tons of upside and nothing to lose, who wouldn't gamble when somebody else's money is at stake?

Things had finally reached a point where potential homeowners were in effect being told, "Hey, you can buy this house for $500,000 without putting a penny of your own money in it. You can live in it, and when its value increases, say to $800,000 or, if you want to wait a few months longer, maybe even $1 million, the difference is your money. In fact, you can borrow it out tax free in a cash-out refinancing. So you've got all the upside and no downside because you didn't put anything in."

In the meantime you could enjoy artificially low monthly payments by making the minimum required payment on an interest-only negative amortization, adjustable-rate mortgage (ARM). Who cares how much higher the payments would ultimately become? You would have all that equity to extract or you could sell the house at a profit. Worst case, you could simply walk away from your zero-down mortgage no worse for wear, having saved a few bucks on rent, as your teaser rate may have been less expensive than what you might otherwise have paid in rent.

It actually reached a point where there were reported cases of college students who, instead of living in a dorm, would buy a house and figure the appreciation would cover four years of tuition and expenses.

There's quite a difference between a situation like that and one where a banker was judiciously extending credit to borrowers with established creditworthiness.

SECURITIZATION: THE ROOT CAUSE OF THE REAL ESTATE BUBBLE

If mortgage lenders had had to worry about defaults, the sudden explosion in home buying would have been tempered. But Uncle Sam wanted economic growth and Fannie Mae and Freddie Mac, by relieving banks of credit risk, became a moral hazard.

Securitization, when housing demand is abnormally high, creates a conflict of interest. On one side are the mortgage originators, the banks and mortgage brokers that represent 80 percent of them. They do the marketing and the paperwork and collect hefty commissions and fees. With no risk of default, they want mortgages. On the other side are mortgage-buying entities that take on the risk, package loans, and issue mortgage-backed securities. They want prime loans that won't default.

The result: collusion between originators and appraisers resulting in faulty documentation, phony appraisals, and lax credit screening practices that have gotten many people in over their heads, caused speculative home buying to be rampant, and discouraged the kind of saving that an economy needs to be productive and healthy.

THE GOVERNMENT-SPONSORED ENTITIES THAT BUY PRIME LOANS

In the way of a more formal introduction, the two biggest buyers of qualifying home mortgages are the government-sponsored Federal National Mortgage Association (Fannie Mae) and the Federal Home Loan Mortgage Corporation (Freddie Mac). It is to these publicly held corporations with implied (but yet untested) government backing that mortgage lenders sell their prime or conforming loans, meaning the loans must meet certain qualifications, such as dollar maximums and proof of income. The Government National Mortgage Association (Ginnie Mae) is government-owned and operates as a guarantor of paper that remains with the originating lender. Payments are passed through via Ginnie Mae to investors holding Ginnie Mae pass-through certificates.

It was these organizations that gave the housing boom its thrust and momentum (see Figure 6.2). Homeowners discovered sudden wealth in the form of appreciated home value, which banks were eager to convert to cash in the form of home equity loans, often under home equity lines of credit (HELOCs) granted at the time of purchase, so assured was the upward direction of prices. On the theory that such loans served the human need

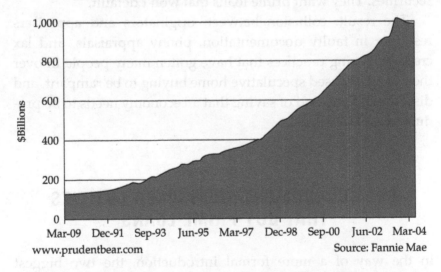

www.prudentbear.com   Source: Fannie Mae

FIGURE 6.2 *Fannie Mae total assets, 1990–2004.* The explosive growth of Fannie Mae and the moral hazards it created helped inflate the biggest housing bubble of all time. Now that it has burst, the phony economy it helped prop up will deflate as well.

Source: Reprinted by permission from David L. Tice and Associates (www.prudentbear.com).

for shelter, an incentive to borrow was added when the banking lobby got into the new tax bill a $100,000 tax exclusion on the interest paid.

But in an exquisite example of a self-feeding process, the homeowners took the home equity extractions over to Wal-Mart, figuratively speaking, and spent them on imported consumer products, sending more dollars to the Far East. When the dollars made the return trip in quest of seemingly safe investments paying somewhat more than artificially low-yielding Treasury securities, who should be ready with a double handshake? You guessed it: two old friends with ravenous appetites for investment funds—Fannie Mae and Freddie Mac.

WALL STREET JOINS THE FRAY

But Fannie Mae and Freddie Mac were restricted to prime conforming paper, and with housing demand expanding by leaps and bounds, a growing population of nonconforming, sub prime mortgage applicants remained unserved. What to do about them?

Here, Wall Street came to the rescue with sophisticated securitized mortgage products called collateralized mortgage obligations (CMOs) and real estate mortgage investment conduits (REMICs) that split huge mortgage pools into different risk, rate, and maturity classes called tranches, Wall Street-ese for separately marketed bonds. These products are complex, and a technical understanding of them is not necessary to appreciate their significance. Essentially what they do is eliminate specific risk through the diversification provided by huge pools of mortgages and then, by relegating the likeliest defaults to one or more specialized high-risk tranches, qualify the majority of the bonds for AAA credit ratings. (The high-risk tranches are sold typically to hedge funds, which are legally restricted to high-net-worth investors, at yields sufficiently rich that defaults can be factored in.)

Wall Street's entry into the mortgage market was a signal development for five reasons:

1. Wall Street was eager to seize this sub prime market because its institutional clients, like mutual funds and hedge funds, were desperately looking for high yields in a low-yield environment. Anything that would juice up their performance in a market competitive on the basis of quarterly returns mattered more to them than long-run safety.

2. By making it possible for just about any warm body to own a home, Wall Street encouraged high-pressure cold-calling by brokers who often engaged in corrupt practices.

3. Although the size and diversity of their mortgage pools are bound to eliminate some risk (for example, to the extent that "all real estate is local," geographic diversification would afford some protection against defaults), macroeconomic factors bear on local markets and massive defaults would impact Wall Street's sub prime mortgage pools more than their prime counterparts at Fannie Mae and Freddie Mac, where it is estimated a default rate as low as 5 percent would precipitate insolvency.

4. Wall Street's appetite for sub prime mortgages, commonly with zero down payment, added substantially to the moral hazard already existing thanks to Fannie Mae and Freddie Mac. The conflicting interests of mortgage originators and mortgage holders virtually guarantee corruption at the contract level, auguring gloomily for the unqualified homeowner, the entity holding the mortgages, and the investors in mortgage-backed securities, a large constituency of

which is made up of the foreign central banks on which
we rely unduly to finance our national debt.

5. A related Wall Street contribution was the no-documentation or "stated income" mortgage loan, whereby one could
avoid documenting income by paying a higher rate. Since
a person of sane mind having income that could be docu-
mented would do that to get the lower rate, these loans were
aptly dubbed "liar's loans." But many have been made and
the general quality of mortgage paper was not improved.

Bottom Line

*By creating a conflict of interest between the real estate market and
the mortgage market, securitization has corrupted an industry in which
the availability and cost of credit are of central economic importance. It
is the root cause of a speculative episode unprecedented in American history,
the resolution of which will cause severe stagflation and possible hyperinflation and profoundly affect Americans with assets in U.S. dollars.*

NONTRADITIONAL MORTGAGES

A myriad of elements fueled the real estate bubble. As it loses
air, many of the shenanigans that caused it are being exposed in
news articles, but that doesn't mean they are history. As this is
written, zero down payments and other gimmicks designed to
make mortgages affordable are alive and well and, in a morbid
sense, are "gifts that will keep on giving." Adjustable-rate mortgages and variations thereupon are a prime example.

Adjustable-rate mortgages (ARMs) transfer the risk of rising interest rates, which in a traditional fixed-rate mortgage is a
risk the lender takes, to the home buyer. What the homeowner

gets in exchange for taking this risk is a rate initially lower than the going fixed rate. Thereafter, at intervals ranging from one to 10 years, the rate is reset to reflect prevailing levels, measured by some indicator or index, such as the Treasury bill or the average national (fixed) mortgage rate. The initial rate, which has been as low as 1 percent, is sometimes called a "teaser" rate, the implication being obvious: When a person is aiming to get the biggest house possible for the lowest monthly payment, the house appears affordable. (Oh, sure, all the terms are spelled out in black and white, but who's going to be bothered with that stuff when what it boils down to is "What's the monthly payment and can I swing it?")

I take a dim view of ARMs as a so-called affordability tool for the simple reason that people who need the initially lower monthly payments, by definition, are likely to have trouble making monthly payments that get higher as the rate is adjusted to reflect market levels. And remember, these deals got popular at a time when market rates were at historic lows. It's pretty safe to say there's nowhere for interest rates to go but up.

Compounding the problem is that our country's lack of domestic savings forces it to rely on foreign financing. When foreign lenders finally lose confidence in the dollar, interest rates will skyrocket, sending ARM payments to the moon as well. For a nation so vulnerable to higher interest rates to further compound its predicament through overexposure to ARMs is reckless beyond belief. It's analogous to a cheating husband, caught red-handed in the act, putting a noose around his neck, throwing the other end over a tree limb into the waiting arms of his jealous, enraged, soon-to-be ex-wife, and hoping she decides not to pull.

Variations on basic ARMs are available with **option ARMs**, which come to the rescue when the monthly payment is too steep.

Interest-only loans, as the name implies, require payments consisting only of interest for the first few years. That minimizes the payment initially, but when the initial period is up, let's say in five years, for example, there are some unpleasant realities. The rate, of course, is reset, presumably higher, but now you have to start repaying principal. And what started as a 30-year period of amortization has become a 25-year period with higher monthly payments.

Because you made no down payment and made no payments on principal, you have no home equity unless, of course, the home appreciated in value. But what if it didn't, or it decreased in value as happens when rates rise? You've got payments you can't afford and no borrowing power. So you're forced to sell. And if it's a recourse loan, you'll be liable for any balance.

Closely related to the interest-only option is the **negative amortization ARM.** In this case, you make a minimum monthly payment with the difference between what you pay and the scheduled payment added to the balance of the mortgage, which is allowed to build to a specified limit at which automatic reset is triggered.

The rascals purveying these products to ordinary folks argue that the months of lower payments will more than offset the months of higher payments. What do they think a young couple is going to do, salt away the difference so they'll be sure to have the money to make the higher payments later on? Give me a break. The money they've saved is already off to Wal-Mart en route to China.

The other argument you hear for ARMs is that the owner is planning to sell and move out after two or three years. That doesn't make any sense, either. Why would anybody incur the costs of ownership for a period that short? The only reasons could be to sell and buy a bigger house or to sell and rent. Both alternatives assume that the house would appreciate in the interim. Where I come from, they call that speculation. There's a lot of that around, but it isn't counted as speculation when the owners occupy the house. But wait until all those properties come onto the market (when interest rates will be higher and, we hope, lending standards stricter).

Since none of the monthly payments on such loans reduce the principal of the mortgages, buyers utilizing them are no better off than renters. Since they also must pay property taxes, insurance, and maintenance, interest-only buyers actually get the worst of both worlds. They rent property from lenders, yet get stuck with all the headaches associated with ownership. The only way interest-only buyers build equity is through price appreciation. In other words, they are the ultimate speculators.

ARMs and their variations are a not-so-tender trap to lure people into commitments they can't afford, thus adding impetus to the bubble and accelerating selling pressure on the way down. Unfortunately, the Fed's patience in not raising rates to discourage speculation meant more homeowners were lured into the ARM time bomb.

HOW HOME BUILDERS HELPED EXPAND THE BUBBLE

Developers and home builders contributed their part to the cynical dynamics driving the real estate bubble. Reminiscent of the incubator companies that nursed Internet ventures in their early stages and made killings for investors in initial public offerings when the dot-com market was hot, real estate operators would plan communities that they would roll out in stages.

Marketed in lotteries, with buyers committed to contracts that locked them up for one- or two-year periods, the properties in each succeeding stage would be priced higher than the last. Creating artificial scarcity by keeping supply off the market and then progressively setting prices higher, the developers effected the illusion of a rising market, making themselves fortunes and encouraging other developers to follow.

INDUSTRY LEADERS EXPLAIN PRICE RISES

For anyone suspecting that a speculative episode was under way, real estate industry spokespersons have a number of reasons why the whole thing has been a natural function of supply and demand.

In fact, since much of the demand, of course, was simply a function of low interest rates, lax lending standards, and speculation, its effect on prices could only be temporary. Once interest rates rose, lending standards tightened, and speculative buyers became sellers, excess demand would be replaced by excess supply, causing prices to reverse course.

This simple fact always seems to escape the notice of the real estate boosters. The rhetoric is reminiscent of the Internet bubble, where analysts assured investors that sky-high stock prices were actually fundamentally justified based on new-economy valuation matrixes called by such names as "page views" and "click-throughs."

A March 2006 report published by Bankrate.com and titled "Real Estate Review 2006" offers a sampling of industry wisdom. Commenting on the fourth quarter of 2005, the report says:

"The modest dip in appreciation is an early sign of a market adjustment," says David Lereah, the National Association of Realtors' chief economist. "These historically high home-price gains are the simple result of more buyers than sellers in the market," says Lereah. "The good news is that the supply of

homes on the market has been trending up and we are enter-
ing a period of more normal balance in supply and demand."
[See Figure 6.3.]

The softening of the housing market doesn't mean home
values will plummet. NAR president Thomas M. Stevens pre-
dicts housing values will keep at a high plateau because of con-
sumer demands for housing.

(I hate to be a wet blanket, but the "plateau" metaphor rings
a bell. In 1929, while the good times were still rolling, stocks
were said to have reached a "permanent plateau.") As to the frequent pronouncements of NAR's chief economist and wishful
thinker, David Lereah, I can't resist sharing a quote of my own

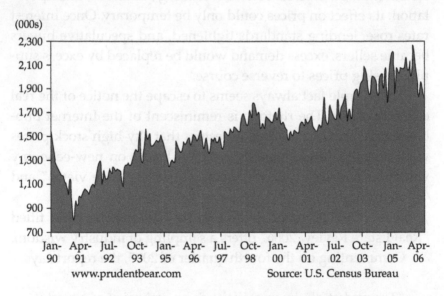

FIGURE 6.3 *Housing starts, 1990–2006.* Rising real estate prices result
in an ever-increasing supply of newly constructed homes. Now that
demand has collapsed, the new supply has turned into a glut. Prices
will now have to collapse as well to alleviate the imbalance.

Source: Reprinted by permission from David L. Tice and Associates
(www.prudentbear.com).

that was picked up in an October 2006 issue of BusinessWeek: I said, "If the National Association of Realtors chief economist David Lereah had covered the arrival of the Hindenburg in New Jersey in 1937 (instead of Herb "Oh the humanity" Morrison), it too may have been described as a 'soft landing.'"

Anyway, back to the report I was citing and a final quote of NAR president Stevens:

"The children of the baby boom generation, often called the 'echo-boomers,' are the second largest generation in United States history and are just entering the period in which people typically buy their first home. Along with a strong immigrant impact, and the boomers themselves who remain in peak earnings years, this means the need for housing will stay strong over the next decade and long-term prices will continue to rise," Stevens says.

My own opinion is that while there is undoubtedly validity to the observation that demographic factors have contributed to housing demand, they in no way explain the real estate bubble and certainly don't represent evidence suggesting anything like current price levels will persist. For one thing, having read many analyses of the real estate market, I would point out that demographic factors like echo-boomers and immigrants are simplistic elements of a complex subject. For example, a much longer-standing and more significant demographic phenomenon has been fewer occupants per household. That has been largely a function of affluence and could reverse in an economic heartbeat, shrinking housing demand substantially.

The real point, however, is that at the heart of the real estate bubble has been speculation, pure and simple, caused by all the factors we've been discussing, which can be collected under the rubric of monetary mismanagement.

Let's, then, look at the reasons why an unwinding of this horren-
dous malinvestment is inevitable, what form it is likely to take, and
what the financial consequences will be for Americans.

WHY COLLAPSE IS INEVITABLE

As is clear by now, I'm fond of analogies and would compare the real estate bubble to a beach ball I'm holding up in the air with my hand. My hand represents the collective speculative forces we've discussed, and when I pull that prop away, the ball will drop.

To assume that the ball will remain levitated in midair despite the absence of my hand would be absurd. However, that is precisely what real estate promoters would have us believe—that the props of record low interest rates and lax lending standards could be removed, yet the high home prices they supported could remain. In fact, we are told that not only will prices stay high, but they also will continue to rise, albeit at a slower pace. How could that possibly happen? Who could afford to pay such inflated prices were traditional financing and lending standards to return?

Anybody who thinks the real estate bubble can have a soft landing simply can't be aware of the overbuilding, the number of properties bought by people unable to afford them who were planning on flipping them, and the second and third and vacation homes bought with money borrowed against inflated home equity. All of these properties are going to come on the market. Whether that causes the recession or the recession causes that doesn't matter. There's going to be a recession combined with inflation and it's going to be an extremely bad situation.

I wrote earlier of all the consumption related directly or indirectly to real estate and how much of that was financed by home equity extractions or made possible by temporarily low mortgage rates. With interest rates headed higher and home prices headed lower, all of that consumption will stop.

As spending cuts back, people lose jobs, which means they can't make payments even on fixed-rate mortgages, never mind the nontraditional mortgages that will have turned "upside down," to use a trade term meaning a loan balance higher than the home's value.

To understand why prices have to drop, consider this example: Let's say there is an upscale community made up of 100 similarly opulent, owned and occupied houses. One of them goes on the market and sells for $1 million. By the popular logic of real estate valuation, the value of the other 99 homes becomes $1 million.

But could everybody put their houses on the market and get $1 million? Of course not. The only reason the first house sold for $1 million is that 99 of the houses weren't for sale. The price in a normal market would shift according to supply and demand. If suddenly there were 10 homes for sale, prices might drop sharply as sellers competed against each other to attract buyers.

But the buyer in this case was a real estate investor who was willing to pay $1 million because he thought he could turn around and sell it for $2 million, even though he knew he was going to lose $3,000 a month in negative cash flow, representing rental income less expenses. Without the expectation that the value would double, the amount the investor would be willing to pay would be limited to the amount required to produce a positive cash flow sufficiently above the risk-free rate to justify the risks inherent in property ownership. Let's assume that amount would be $500,000.

Removing the speculative element, then, the price of the home has to go to $500,000. So it goes with real estate prices. The fact that at one time one speculator who misread the market was willing to pay $1 million means nothing.

The only thing permanent about a loan collateralized by home value is the loan. Unless you happen to live in a state where loans are made on a nonrecourse basis, the loan balance has to be repaid, whatever the value of the collateral.

THE ECONOMIC EFFECTS OF THE REAL ESTATE DEBACLE

So the importance of real estate to the economy, based on related jobs and related consumption, is such that as one goes, so goes the other.

A dynamic that has a built-in multiplier is the wealth effect. As people saw their property values appreciating, their perceived need to save was diminished. Their houses were doing their saving for them, and their retirement was a simple matter of downsizing their houses and moving to Florida. The money that would otherwise have gone into savings was freed up for consumption, providing an artificial, short-term boost for the economy.

Now, of course, with real estate prices falling and homeowners realizing how much they've undersaved and need to make up, the effect on consumption will be reversed.

So there were many ways that the real estate bubble artificially pumped up our economy. And as we consumed more and produced less, the result was an exacerbation of the trade deficit and a huge increase in the amount of U.S. dollars in global circulation.

So as real estate continues to decline and the U.S. economy goes further into recession, the dollar really will come under increasing pressure as foreigners, recognizing the relative weakness of our economy, begin bailing out of U.S. assets. The declining purchasing power of the dollar will cause consumer prices to pick up and the Fed will ultimately be forced to raise rates. Rising interest rates will accelerate the collapse of the real estate market and the economy generally. Foreigners will want to get even more money out of the United States, sending interest rates and consumer prices even higher.

It's a spiral that will feed on itself and ultimately cause the American economy to implode.

Of course, as I mentioned at the outset, there is bound to be political pressure to reinflate real estate prices in order to engineer a soft landing. Experience tells us, however, that once market forces are let loose, efforts to reverse them seldom succeed. Once popped, bubbles don't inflate again. The added liquidity simply flows into something else. Just as the 1990s stock market bubble became a bubble in real estate, any effort to reinflate the housing bubble will likely produce one someplace else, such as in commodities, precious metals, or increased consumer prices. Under present conditions, any added inflation would likely exacerbate the stagflation that is already inevitable.

But we can't underestimate the consequences that could result from the real estate collapse.

What will happen when Fannie Mae and Freddie Mac go bankrupt? Will the federal government, with its implied backing of these corporations, step in and bail them out? With what money? At what cost to the purchasing power of the U.S. dollar?

However, if the government lets them fail, what happens to the U.S. government's credibility as an implied guarantor of other indirect government agency or government-sponsored entity obligations? Or, to put the question another way, what happens to the U.S. government if its agencies can no longer attract financing? What happens to you?

One thing that would surely happen is that the real weaknesses of the U.S. economy would be exposed, raising legitimate questions about its ability to meet direct Treasury obligations.

Will that precipitate the withdrawal of foreign investment and reverse the flow of dollars to the domestic economy, creating hyperinflated prices and shortages of goods? It's something to worry about.

LIFE AFTER THE BUBBLE

This past June, in one of the commentaries I write regularly for clients and friends of Euro Pacific Capital, I talked about the paradox of housing.

I noted, in the way of review, that as real estate prices spiraled upward over the past 10 years, artificially low interest rates and lax lending standards were not the only factors helping to maintain housing affordability. Equally important was the hallucination that the only way to lose money in real estate was to not own any, and the suppression of the rental market as investors willingly accepted low rental returns or even negative cash flows as trade-offs for expected appreciation. Flat rents anchored a rock-bottom core CPI, which allowed the Fed to keep rates artificially low and the cheap mortgage money flowing.

As appreciation now slows or reverses, buying paradoxically becomes more expensive, as the following example illustrates:

Assume a home buyer purchased a condominium for $500,000 using a zero-down, no-documentation, interest-only ARM at a rate of 4 percent, with taxes, insurance, and maintenance adding another 1 percent a year. The annual cash cost would be $25,000, or just over $2,000 a month.

However, if the buyer figured on annual appreciation of 10 percent (only half last year's expected appreciation rate of 20 percent, according to a Los Angeles survey), creating a potential $4,000 a month in extractable equity, the buyer would be "earning" $2,000 a month instead of paying $2,000 a month. So even though she had monthly income of only $3,000, she would have no qualms about stating a higher income to qualify for a loan representing nearly 70 percent of what she actually earned on a pretax basis.

Now suppose that rate on her ARM is reset at 7 percent. Assuming taxes, insurance, and maintenance still add 1 percent, her annual cost rises to $40,000, or $3,300 a month. That's a 65 percent increase, but is really the tip of an iceberg. If the borrower, now reading the economic tea leaves, cuts her appreciation expectation in half to 5 percent, her expected annual cost is now $15,000. Instead of "earning" $2,000 a month in extractable equity, she has an actual cost of $1,250 a month to own.

The true increase in cost is not 65 percent but 3,250 percent.

And that's just for starters. If housing prices stabilize and expected appreciation goes to zero, the real cost becomes much higher. Even the $1,250, which now represents over 40 percent of her pretax income, means she's going to have to struggle. *Without any appreciation to cash out, she simply wouldn't be able to afford to live there.*

THE REVIVAL OF THE RENTAL MARKET AND THE FED'S DILEMMA

As the perceived cost of buying increases due to the slowing housing market, renting becomes a far more compelling option. But the supply of rental housing has been shrinking with the recent wave of condo conversions. And with interest rates going up, landlords, particularly those who financed with ARMs themselves, will have to raise rents to cover their increased debt service expenses and won't have any trouble getting away with it.

Recent data, in fact, show national rents increasing at a rate not seen in more than five years. Since rents, as observed, represent 40 percent of the core CPI, the paradox of rising home prices suppressing the core CPI is being replaced by the paradox of falling home prices increasing it.

A revived rental market puts the Fed in an interesting predicament. It can add rents to food and energy as prices it excludes from the CPI, so it can point to low inflation, or it can respond to high core inflation by raising rates. The hypocrisy revealed by the former will destroy what little faith remains in the Fed, prompting a run on the dollar and more inflation. Raising rates would add to the downward spiral of home prices and surely tip the economy into recession. It's a Hobson's choice.

THE FINAL PLAYING OUT

In the final analysis, the temporary factors artificially elevating real estate prices will subside. Rising interest rates and inflation, and a resumption of savings as home equity disappears, will combine to suppress consumer spending, leading to recession, job losses, and reduced housing demand.

A glut of unsold houses will continue to grow as higher interest rates, tighter lending standards, and higher down payments price more potential buyers out of the market. Absent the expectation of routine cash-out refinancing, home buyers will no longer be willing to devote staggering percentages of their incomes to mortgage payments. In addition, the expectation of lower prices will bring more sellers to the market, just as buyers are backing away.

Once the trend reverses, falling prices will purge speculative demand from the market. Once speculators become sellers, supply will overwhelm demand. As lenders see housing prices fall and inventories of homes rise, increased risk of default will result in a return to traditional conservative lending standards, further restricting access to mortgage credit.

As more mortgages go into default, the secondary market for mortgage-backed securities will dry up as well. This will begin a self-perpetuating vicious cycle, as tighter lending standards reduce housing demand, leading to lower home prices, more defaults, fewer qualified buyers, lower prices, and even tighter standards, ad infinitum.

The collapse of consumer spending, associated with higher mortgage payments and vanishing home equity, will plunge the economy into severe recession, further exacerbating the collapse in real estate prices, worsening the recession, and continuing the vicious cycle.

The housing mania, like all manias that have preceded it, is finally coming to an end long overdue. Time-tested principles of prudent mortgage lending will inevitably return and houses will once again be regarded merely as places to live.

Still, the country will be a lot poorer as a result of the unprecedented dissipation of wealth and accumulation of consumer and mortgage debt that occurred during the bubble years. Before real estate prices can return to normal levels, they will first have to get dirt cheap.

It has been a wild party, and it has left us with a gigantic hangover, although, one hopes, with some lessons learned and a resolve to mend our ways.

THE IMPORTANCE OF LIQUIDITY

I am convinced that the real estate bubble will burst; it will cause severe financial losses and will be followed by a period of painful sacrifice and adjustment.

I have every confidence, however, that we will ultimately look back on this experience as the nadir of a long period of economic and monetary mismanagement marking the beginning of a revived American economy in which people once again save, produce, and live happily with the anticipation of a rising standard of living.

For my own part, I can say in all humility that I have seen it all coming for many years, and have been professionally engaged in investment strategies that will enable those who follow my advice to avoid personal losses and position themselves to profit personally and contribute constructively to the reconstruction of national economic health and prosperity. That's why I have written this book.

In the final chapter, I discuss the importance of liquidity in times of financial uncertainty. It might surprise you that, among other strategies I will be outlining, I will show you how your ownership of real estate provides opportunities to profit from leverage while avoiding the risks associated with a collapsed U.S. dollar.

2009 UPDATE

The housing bubble burst as I predicted, but the rest, unfortunately, is not yet history.

Perhaps it's nature's way of protecting our sanity, but catastrophes never seem to be without light moments, and the real estate collapse brought us the witticism "jingle mail." On the small chance you haven't heard it, the term refers to envelopes containing house keys mailed to mortgage lenders by homeowners with the implicit message, "The place is all yours, pal. I'm better off without it." It has become commonplace for homeowners to simply walk away from upside-down mortgages, where price depreciation, equity extractions, or a combination of the two have caused the mortgage liability to exceed the home's value.

It accents a serious point I made early in this chapter, that since real estate is all about leverage, the consequences of the real estate bust were going to fall mainly on the lenders, our financial institutions, and the economy in general. With so many mortgage loans being made with little or no down payment money, lenders were taking an inordinate amount of the risk. Having little or no skin in the game, buyers had a strong incentive to use the lender's money for risky bets and to overpay for properties. When the bets turned south, there was no incentive for owners to stay in their houses and every incentive for them to walk away from their mortgages. As more people awaken to the fact that they are in the driver's seat, the jingle mail increases and prices drop further.

I'm not recommending that people walk away from their obligations, whatever the circumstances (though in many cases doing so is the most logical course of action), but I am saying this: In the current market, while borrowers clearly have the upper hand, borrowers and lenders both have strong incentives to cut a deal. I firmly believe that if there was ever a free market situation the government should stay out of completely, this housing crisis is it.

Yes, the free market would cause foreclosures that government intervention might defer, but the result would be that people with the means and desire to be in homes would stay in homes, while people without equity and lacking the means and motivation to maintain homes would rent. (Obviously, this discussion does not apply to people who become destitute as a result of job loss, illness, and other factors. Although sadly such cases become more commonplace in bad economies, they are a societal problem handled by special governmental and nonprofit sources of assistance.) There are plenty of rentals available at a wide range of favorable prices, and people who go that route not only get more house for their money, they live free of property taxes and other owner headaches and are usually happier as a result. I, for one, have been living happily as a renter for years.

A free and direct negotiation between owners and lenders allows for various compromises and promises the best outcome for both parties, for the economy, and for society. The government's involvement is not only unnecessary, but it also creates distortions, presents moral hazards, invites corruption, and works against the interests of everybody. I think it's significant that foreclosure should emit a vibe so ominous that avoiding it at any cost has become a top national priority. Foreclosure is unfortunate, sad, and costly, but in the vast majority of cases it needn't mean homelessness. It's a practical matter that has been made to seem like the unthinkable antithesis of the great American dream, itself part of a distorted perspective. Somewhere along the line, we let the real estate industry hijack the American dream and redefine it as home ownership. The American dream is that any Americans, no matter how humble their beginnings, can work hard, save their money, and rise as high in our society as their ambition will take them, even become president. But getting rich by owning a home is not the American dream. Your home is your shelter. It does not replace the need to save your money for retirement. That misconception of the dream and the importance given to home ownership was a force driving the housing bubble and now is a force misguiding the policies dealing with the bust. The American people should understand that misconception and let go of it.

The Bursting of the Bubble

The pin that burst the housing bubble came in the form of securities backed by subprime mortgages that Wall Street firms bought and repackaged in tranches (bonds) that earned them investment-grade credit ratings. The tranches were then sold as collateralized debt obligations (CDOs) to hedge funds, banks, and other institutional investors willing to trade off liquidity for higher yields.

People who bought homes with subprime mortgages, which would eventually mean most home buyers, were the first to feel the pinch when the Federal Reserve in mid-2006 began notching up interest rates to discourage inflation. They began defaulting, and by the first quarter of 2007 subprime foreclosures had reached alarming levels.

Suddenly under pressure to meet redemptions and other liquidation demands, the funds and banks holding CDOs tried to sell them, but found no takers. CDO valuations they had been reporting on balance sheets prepared for their investors were far higher than anything they could fetch in the real world. In the absence of a secondary market or any guiding precedent, they had been carrying these structured securities on their books at assumed market values derived using sophisticated mathematical modeling. Required by accounting rules then in effect to mark to market (rather than "mark to model," as their existing practice was facetiously called), they faced a reality check that would be their undoing.

A chain reaction ensued, just as I originally forecast in this chapter, in which firms too heavily exposed to subprime risk went bankrupt, others stopped taking subprime paper on, and finally subprime mortgage financing disappeared altogether for lack of originators. Deprived of their access to credit, subprime borrowers were completely shut out of the real estate market. Since it was the subprime home buyers who at the margin set real estate prices, prices started falling in their absence.

With prices dropping at a rate being accelerated by foreclosures, defaults spread quickly into prime mortgages, causing widespread losses at banks and other institutions holding mortgage-related paper. Those that weren't getting government bailouts were preparing to declare bankruptcy, or had begun hoarding the reserves they had. None of them were making loans, not even to other banks. With economic conditions worsening here and abroad and with foreign investors losing money on their large holdings of American mortgage-backed securities, international credit markets froze; and that condition prevails generally as this is written. Real estate prices continue to fall, but, with stricter terms and banks not lending, there are few buyers.

It is interesting to remember just how our leaders initially reacted to the subprime problem. Everyone, from President Bush to Treasury Secretary Paulson to Fed Chairman Bernanke, assured us that it was "contained." The point that everyone missed, and one I repeated often in my numerous television appearances and in articles posted on my web site, was that it was not a subprime problem but a mortgage problem. It was merely a matter of time before those problems surfaced in prime mortgages. The problems showed up in subprime first simply because those mortgages represented the weakest links. However, the entire chain was defective; it was just that the stronger links required a bit more pressure before giving way.

For those who still maintain that the problems in the mortgage and housing markets and the effect those problems would have on the overall economy were impossible to predict, this chapter proves otherwise. If anyone needs more evidence of just how predictable this entire crisis was, visit my web site at www.europac.net/video.asp and watch my November 2006 presentation before the Western Regional Mortgage Bankers Convention. Or if you prefer, simply go to YouTube and search "Peter Schiff Mortgage Bankers." There are eight clips in total. Watch them all and see if you think I left anything out.

Uncle Sam's Response

The government's answer to the larger economic crisis, as we know, has been an effort to restart the music that was playing before the party was so rudely interrupted. With specific reference to the housing crisis, remember my analogy in the original chapter comparing the real estate bubble to a beach ball suspended in the air by my outstretched hand? My hand, you'll recall, represented the easy money and lax lending practices making the ball appear to levitate. Damn if the government isn't trying to get its hand under the beach ball again. Applying the government's logic, the foreclosure problem and so-called toxic assets threatening lenders would be remedied by reversing the decline in real estate prices, which would also create home equity and encourage consumer spending.

As I feared, Uncle Sam is exploring all manner of gimmicks to prevent foreclosures, artificially prop real estate prices up, and eliminate toxic assets as a restraint on bank lending. To keep mortgage rates low, the Federal Reserve, having reduced the federal funds rate to near zero without measurable effect, has been buying long Treasury bonds which, with such heavy demand, were recently yielding around 3 percent, a ludicrously unrealistic return that will contribute to the bursting of a bond bubble, which I'll get into in the Chapter 7 update. Lowered mortgage rates encourage refinancing and, as I see it, only defer foreclosures to a later time. A $300 billion housing rescue bill passed in 2008 helps homeowners who are able to demonstrate severe financial duress avoid foreclosure. (If you're in the unbreakable habit of making timely payments, don't apply.) If you qualify for mortgage forbearance, foreclosure can be put off. Government-subsidized mortgage modification options, such as principal forgiveness, term extensions, or rate reductions, can keep people in their homes. But God forbid that we let the free market work to reprice houses and restore normalcy.

The Role of Fannie and Freddie

In this chapter, I wondered what the government would do when Fannie Mae and Freddie Mac, then government-sponsored entities, went bankrupt as I was predicting. Now, of course, we know. They made an implicit guarantee explicit and expanded operations, in effect socializing the mortgage industry. Now nearly all the mortgages in the country are being originated by or are owned by Freddie and Fannie. But some, a growing number, are guaranteed by the Federal Housing Administration (FHA), a near dormant agency whose 2006 market share was 2 percent.

When Wall Street had the good sense to exit the subprime market, the FHA saw an opportunity to fill the void. Guaranteeing mortgages that no private entity would touch, with 3.5 percent down payments (paid for with tax credits for anybody who hadn't purchased a home in three years) and refinancing at 125 percent loan to value, the FHA went into 2009 with 19 percent of a wide-open market. I'll wager we'll be looking at a bailout in the triple digit billions. How little we learn.

Actually there was a movement in Freddie and Fannie while they were still technically private entities to tighten their lending standards. But now that the government has taken them over, they've reversed that course and are trying to blow air back in the bubble by relaxing lending standards and increasing the size of the mortgages they'll buy.

The hard fact is that the economy and the American public would be better off without Fannie and Freddie as they now exist. Their original mission was to make housing affordable to more Americans, but that has been turned on its head. Now their apparent mission is to keep homes artificially expensive so that average Americans need subsidized mortgages to afford them. Without government involvement, home prices would fall to the point where average Americans could afford to buy without the subsidies. Why should the U.S. Treasury be co-signing every citizen's mortgage, which is what happens in effect when Fannie or Freddie buy or guarantee the obligation? It's nonsense and results in more mortgage credit being available at lower rates than would be the case in a free private market where higher lending standards would prevail because lenders would have to worry about default. The government's involvement distorts credit, causes higher prices, and undermines the economy.

If the government got out of the mortgage business, it would not mean fewer people would have the ability to buy homes. They would just have to pay less for them.

Since the house goes to the highest bidder, when all the bidders go to the bank and they all qualify for a $200,000 mortgage, that's what they borrow and the house sells for $200,000. In contrast, if the government wasn't in the way and stricter lending standards had to be met, everybody might get approved for $100,000 of mortgage credit. The house would still sell, but the price would be $100,000. Of course, lower home prices would result in fewer new homes being built, but given the current glut, that is exactly what we need. It would allow resources now wasted constructing houses to be used more effectively in other areas of the economy.

The best way to make homes affordable is not to find ways to borrow more money; it's to let prices drop. Anything the government does to interfere with the free market's attempt to bring prices down is counterproductive.

Why the Government's Intervention Is a Moral Hazard and Invites Corruption

Various government plans to help homeowners having difficulty making their mortgage payments are implicit moral hazards because the temptation to rearrange one's finances to qualify for government benefits is time honored.

President Obama's mortgage modification plan, which will subsidize mortgages where people can't pay, is fraud waiting to happen. Remember, many of the people in these houses lied about their incomes in the first place. There won't be any more checks and balances now than there were then, so absent virtue acquired in the interim, it seems unlikely they aren't going to tell the same lies in reverse this time around. In fact, the government is offering to pay mortgage brokers to recruit prospects for the new mortgage modification plan. Since they already have lists of folks they made liar's loans to, their job is a simple matter of picking up the phone and saying, "Remember me?" And to the extent there might be more checking, people who have been working overtime or whose spouses have been working can simply put those arrangements on hold until they get the mortgage modified, then resume them. Such huge national programs invite fraud that the free market wouldn't allow.

Since the whole goal is keeping prices from falling, a question arises as to how a present homeowner could ever sell an overpriced home in a market where buyers have to meet stricter lending requirements and make traditional down payments. Assuming prospective buyers would keep walking, owners, sooner or later, would stop making payments on a mortgage that is more than the house is worth. Prices artificially propped up are simply not sustainable.

Clearly, it makes much more sense to let home prices fall now until they find their natural level. When they do, people who can afford homes would buy them and have a vested interest in maintaining them. Of course, if home prices fell to true market levels, many of the lenders holding those mortgages would be insolvent, which is precisely what the government is trying to avoid. However, artificially propping up real estate prices simply to pretend that bankrupt lenders are still solvent merely compounds the problems that led to such dire circumstances in the first place. Real estate prices must be set

by market forces. Government attempts to keep them artificially high will only backfire, and end up doing more long-term
damage to our economy than the short-term effects of lender
bankruptcies.

Another political problem is that most homeowners are
unhappy about the prospect of lower home prices, as they were
counting on home equity as their primary asset. Homeowners
hardly see lower home prices as a solution, and are instead looking for a government "solution" that keeps prices propped up.
However, such "solutions" are impractical as they create even
bigger problems than the ones they purport to solve. When the
dot com bubble burst, no one asked the government to try to
prop up the prices of internet stocks. Investors who overpaid
accepted their losses and homeowners who made similiar mistakes need to accept theirs as well.

How the Free Market Approach Might Work
in a Direct Owner/Lender Negotiation

In a free market situation, a lender would contact the person with
the mortgage and try to determine if it's worth trying to keep that
person in the house. Let's say I'm a lender and I've lent somebody
$500,000 to buy a house that's now worth $300,000. The buyer
stops making mortgage payments, seeing no point in doing so.
I might say, "Okay, I know I lent you $500,000 and the house is
now worth only $300,000, so if I foreclose on the house, I'm going
to get only $300,000. How about I give you a new mortgage for
$250,000, provided you write a check to me for $50,000?" That's
the kind of deal a bank might offer. In exchange for a $50,000
check, the bank tears up a $500,000 mortgage and replaces it with
a $250,000 mortgage, a deal the buyer might well agree to do.

If, however, the person living in that house had no money—
couldn't write a check—it wouldn't make sense for the bank to
redo the mortgage for $300,000 because the owner would have no

equity. If the house continued to depreciate in value, the owner would only default again. In the meantime, with zero equity, the owner would be unable to fix a leak in the roof or finance any other upkeep, so the bank would be better off foreclosing. It could then sell the property to somebody who did have money and would therefore have a vested interest in maintaining the property. If the owner did not choose to reside there, he or she could rent it out, perhaps even to the person living there now, who obviously can't afford to own and maintain the home.

The lender wants an owner who has skin in the game, who is responsible enough to pay something down and have money aside in case something goes wrong. But all these factors and decisions are things a lender and an owner can discuss and negotiate directly. If foreclosure turns out to be the only solution, the person will rent something he or she can afford, often something nicer because rents will have come down. In most cases, foreclosure should not mean anybody is going to walk in shame into the cold.

Incidentally, if you renegotiate your mortgage and the lender forgives part of the debt, the law now exempts the forgiven portion from income taxes. That further strengthens the position of the borrower vis-à-vis the lender. Still, the real reason the government is propping up real estate prices is to help the lenders, not the little guy as they'd like you to believe. But the lenders knew what they were doing and they deserve to take their lumps. Ironically, though, in the end it's the lenders, despite the help the government is giving them, that are going to get hit the hardest, and that's because all the inflation being created is going to destroy the real value of the money they get paid back. The other real losers are the American economy and the American saver. They are seeing the value of their savings accounts, their investments, and their pensions decline because of all the inflation caused by the government's efforts to prop up real estate prices and finance bailouts.

The Mark-to-Market Issue

The lending industry and its political supporters won a victory in early April 2009 when the Financial Accounting Standards Board (FASB) ruled to suspend mark-to-market accounting rules. Lending interests had been arguing that the rules forced financial institutions to carry mortgages and mortgage-related investments at unfairly conservative current market values, thus impairing their capital. Market value is what the mortgages are really worth—what willing buyers and sellers are figuring the mortgage is worth based on the probability that it will at some point default. In effect, banks were blaming potentially toxic assets on mark-to-market accounting rules, which is like blaming your fever on the thermometer.

The banks held, for example, that if a 30-year mortgage is current, it is unfair to be forced to mark it down, since if timely payments are made over its term the lender hasn't lost anything. The reality, however, is the chances are considerably less than 100 percent that the loan will not default and the probability of default depends on various factors, such as whether and to what extent the mortgage exceeds the value of the property, whether it's a variable-rate mortgage with two years left on the teaser rate before it resets, or whether the borrower loses a job. So there are all kinds of factors to be considered in determining the market price of a mortgage. Wall Street and the banks prefer to ignore those factors and pretend that their assets are worth a lot more than what the current market price is.

The FASB ruling provides a quick and easy way to make balance sheets look better capitalized than they in fact are, giving people less reason to trust financial institutions. To the extent that banks ultimately fail, more money will be lost because of deposits made by people fooled by their accounting.

Mark-to-market accounting had been a factor in banks' reluctance to make loans because they feared that once they did, the mortgage would be marked to a lower market figure. That was an obvious signal that home prices are still too high and lending standards too lax, and that such loans should not be made in the first place. If home prices were allowed to fall to fair market levels, with buyers taking on mortgages they could actually afford to repay, marking to market would never have been an issue.

Commercial Real Estate: Another Shoe to Drop

The real estate story has so far been all about the collapse in residential housing, but an 800-pound gorilla has been waiting in the closet in the form of commercial real estate. As the phony consumer economy unravels, the real estate structure that supported it—the shopping malls, fitness centers, financial services offices, and the rest—has become increasingly redundant. So we have all these buildings that have been leveraged up that now represent potential loan defaults. Unlike residential real estate mortgages, commercial real estate loans are generally shorter-term, between three and seven years typically. This money was borrowed based on rosy rental forecasts, and as obligations become due, borrowers, faced with tight credit, higher borrowing costs, and reduced revenues, are going to be hard-pressed to roll them over. According to an Associated Press report, an estimated $36 billion of commercial real estate debt will expire in 2009 and about $55 billion of debt on average will roll over annually by 2012.

Now gone, but not forgotten, George W. Bush once explained the real estate debacle with the observation that "Wall Street got drunk." Well, so did Main Street, but let's not forget where the booze came from. It came from Uncle Sam, and how salutary it would be if somehow he could be kept out of the recovery process.

7

Come On In, the Water's Fine: Our Consumer Debt Problem

Not since Tom Sawyer cajoled all those neighborhood youths into paying him for the privilege of putting three coats of whitewash on his Aunt Polly's fence has there been a con job equal to one the United States has pulled on foreign economies. By convincing Asians that the toil of the harvest is a reward made possible by the Americans who enjoy its bounty, we might just have done young Tom one better.

As seen in Chapter 1, having become a nation of consumers instead of producers, the United States has been destroying wealth instead of creating it.

By borrowing to finance consumption, instead of saving to finance production, our country has dug itself into an economic hole far deeper than has any other nation in history (see Figure 7.1).

This chapter focuses on debt and how its misuse at both the national and personal levels is leading toward economic collapse and a realignment of global purchasing power.

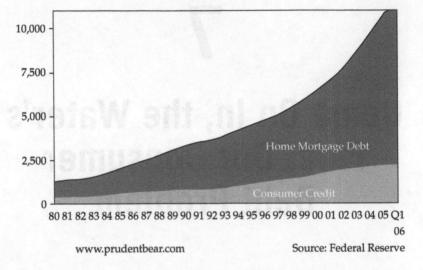

FIGURE 7.1 *Consumer debt outstanding, 1980–2006.* The explosion in consumer debt reveals the phony nature of the consumption-based U.S. economy. If, instead, consumer spending had been financed by legitimate increases in real incomes and production, our prosperity would have been genuine.

Source: Reprinted by permission from David L. Tice and Associates (www.prudentbear.com).

An economic dislocation of the magnitude expected will cause shockwaves worldwide, but will also present unique opportunities for Americans who have liquidity and an understanding of the events transpiring. The information in this chapter, together with practical suggestions I offer later in Chapter 10, will enable you to protect your personal assets and take advantage of those opportunities.

WHY AMERICA HAS GOT IT WRONG

A viable economy grows by savings and underconsumption. In the United States we have turned this basic economic concept on its head. Americans are encouraged to go deeper into debt to overconsume.

A sensible economy underconsumes so that it can generate the savings necessary to finance capital formation. An economy in which government policy is deliberately designed to discourage underconsumption is doomed to fail.

I find it ironic, to say the least, that our country is actually encouraging its trading partners to follow in its misguided footsteps. More often than not, at high-profile international economic summits, American delegates, representing the world's largest debtor nation, are found advising delegates from the world's largest creditor nations on ways to improve their economies.

That is analogous to an F student advising honor students on ways to improve their grades. His advice to party more, skip class, and smoke dope should be afforded as much respect as our advice to consume more and save less. For some reason, it doesn't seem to occur to the American delegates to wonder just who would do all the saving and producing if the rest of the world adopted our borrow and consume philosophy. Everybody can't ride in the wagon. Someone has to be outside doing the pushing!

HOW DID A NATION OF SAVERS BECOME A NATION OF BORROWERS?

Obviously it wasn't planned. At one point the U.S. economy was much freer, was much less regulated, and had much lower taxes. We thus had more money to save and became accustomed to a certain standard of living.

I think what happened was that government got more expensive as it started to expand and increased taxes to pay for that expansion. Americans resisted the reduction in their standard of living that the higher taxes required, so we used our savings and when the savings were gone we went to debt.

It was the resistance to giving things up that helped perpetuate the problem. We bought some time when women entered the labor force and added to the number of people working to help pay the higher taxes. But then came more regulation, more insurance, more necessities that cost more money, higher interest because of more borrowing, and more costs with the government involved more in health care and education. All those costs resulted in even higher taxes and made our standard of living harder to maintain.

So we started borrowing more and since there were no repercussions we kept doing it and things seemed to be going just fine.

Saving, by contrast, means sacrificing, seeing something you want and not having it. It's harder and requires discipline.

But consuming—buying what you want when you want it—is fun, childishly so, but still fun. And the world played right into this. They wanted dollars and were happy to supply us with all the stuff we wanted.

Of course, the Asians didn't realize that the dollars they wanted so badly no longer had gold backing and the fiat currency of a nation turning into a wasteland would soon become worthless. So they kept shipping, we kept borrowing, and here we are.

But it wouldn't be fair, either, simply to blame the decline in the savings rate on the American character. Our politically driven system of government has a built-in bias that encourages consumption at the expense of saving.

The most blatant example of this is the Social Security system, which, under the pretext of doing our saving for us, takes our money and promptly spends it. Social Security and other unfunded pensions, which people understandably think of as a form of savings, are in fact liabilities and a form of debt. Another example is the tax code, which allows deductions for interest expense related to home equity loans, for example, but fully taxes interest income. How's that for an incentive to borrow and a disincentive to save?

Figure 7.2 traces the rise in the financial obligation ratio— the ratio of household debt payments (including mortgages, consumer debt, auto lease payments, rental payments (tenant-occupied), homeowner's insurance, and property tax payments) to disposable personal income.

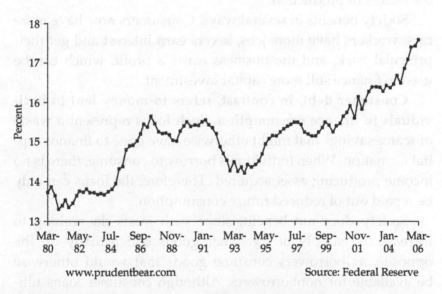

www.prudentbear.com   Source: Federal Reserve

FIGURE 7.2 *Debt service: the Fed's financial obligation ratio for homeowners, 1980–2006.* American homeowners continue to leverage their homes to finance excessive consumption or in many cases just basic necessities. In the future, they will have to pay for not only current consumption, but past consumption as well.

Source: Reprinted by permission from David L. Tice and Associates (www.prudentbear.com).

GOOD DEBT AND BAD DEBT

There is nothing inherently wrong with having debt. It all depends on the purpose for which it is incurred.

Capital debt, or investment debt, refers to loans made to businesses to finance capital formation, such as an automobile manufacturer building a new plant. Such loans benefit society and lead to higher living standards. The earnings the automobile company gets from its increased production enable it both to pay the interest on the debt and to repay the principal. Anything left over represents profit, which is the return on investment that a business deserves for taking risk and for successfully combining the factors of production.

Society benefits in several ways. Consumers now have more cars, workers have more jobs, savers earn interest and get their principal back, and the business earns a profit, which can be used to finance still more capital investment.

Consumer debt, in contrast, refers to money lent to individuals to finance consumption. Such loans represent a waste of scarce savings that might otherwise have gone to finance capital formation. When individuals borrow to consume, there is no income-producing asset acquired. Therefore, the loans can only be repaid out of reduced future consumption.

Society does not benefit, since such loans do nothing to increase the supply of consumer goods and actually do the opposite, as borrowers consume goods that would otherwise be available for nonborrowers. Although consumer loans ultimately enable savers to be rewarded with interest, assuming they are repaid, they are of no benefit to society as a whole. In fact, by redirecting savings away from capital investment, they actually undermine the higher living standards that might have been achieved in their absence.

It's often argued that consumer credit, by enabling consumers to make purchases they would otherwise have to defer, helps businesses earn profits and provide jobs.

That dog won't hunt. Demand exists with or without consumer credit. All goods will be sold. Prices that are too high will adjust. Consumer credit merely alters the composition of the buyers, enabling one person to consume more at another's expense. This contrasts with capital loans, which enable everyone to consume more.

WHATEVER HAPPENED TO SAVING UP?

Unless you were born late in Generation X, you'll probably remember how we used to save up so we could buy something we wanted. You don't hear that anymore. Now everything's bought with consumer credit.

Consumer credit is now so ingrained in the American culture that if you don't know your FICO score, you'd better respond to one of the myriad TV and Internet ads offering to show you how to get it. FICO, of course, is your personal credit history, reduced to a numerical score (using software developed by Fair Isaac and Company, hence FICO). A low FICO score doesn't necessarily mean you can't get credit, but it means you'll pay more for it. It's a comment on how credit has pervaded our economy that you see ads all the time that say, "Bad credit okay."

This is all fairly new. We used to be a nation of savers, where thrift was considered a virtue. Amazingly, we managed to become the wealthiest industrial nation in the history of the world without a single credit card or home equity loan. Rather than helping to build our economy, such innovation merely helped pave the road to financial ruin.

Younger readers might wonder how average Americans ever survived without consumer credit. Those longer in the tooth will remember such things as layaway plans and Christmas clubs, which at one time were quite common but no longer exist in modern America.

Layaway involved a consumer asking a merchant to set aside an item (put it on layaway) while the purchaser made payments to the merchant. Once the full amount of the purchase price had been paid, the merchant would release the item to the buyer. Christmas clubs were special bank accounts to which workers would designate small amounts of their paychecks. Come Christmas, they would have accumulated the money to pay for the gifts they wished to purchase.

By saving up instead of borrowing to consume, society benefits in two ways: It can finance more capital formation, leading to greater prosperity. And consumers are relieved of burdensome interest payments.

Saving also reduces the cost of buying. By saving to make large purchases, individuals accumulate interest, which reduces the cost of the purchase. Borrowing to make the same purchase increases the total cost by the amount of interest required to be paid.

Consumption financed by debt actually reduces future consumption, as borrowers make interest and principal repayments with money they would otherwise be free to spend. *Only by saving or underconsuming today can consumption be enhanced tomorrow, as savers have the added benefit of spending compound interest.*

HOME EQUITY AND STOCK MARKET APPRECIATION ARE NOT SAVINGS

I frequently hear the argument that the methodology used to calculate savings is flawed because it omits the accumulation of home equity or gains in the stock market. This naive attempt by Wall Street to wish away a chronic problem reveals a complete lack of understanding of the concept of savings and the important role that concept plays in a free market economy.

Savings represent consumption deferred to a future date. It amounts to a personal sacrifice, the deliberate postponement of immediate gratification. Savers make their savings available to finance capital investments that ultimately lead to increased productivity and rising standards of living. In fact, savings are the lifeblood of a market economy. Without savings, capital formation is impossible, and true economic growth cannot take place.

While it is true that home equity may be an asset to an individual homeowner, its existence in no way adds to society's stock of savings. Home equity does not require the homeowner to forgo anything or to free up any resources for use in capital formation. In fact, the only way a homeowner can tap his or her equity is by accessing someone else's savings. If the homeowner does it by selling the house, the buyer either uses savings or borrows someone else's. If the homeowner does it by refinancing, the money he or she gets from the bank represents money saved by others.

Therefore, not only does home equity not represent savings, it represents a potential claim on society's legitimate supply of savings. To the extent that it is used to finance consumption, it preempts savings that might otherwise have been used to finance capital formation (see Figure 7.3).

The main reason American homeowners can access their home equity is that foreigners, whose savings ultimately provide the capital invested by their governments in U.S. Treasury and mortgage-backed securities, are willing, in effect, to lend them the money. Once foreigners come to their senses, mortgage credit will evaporate, and home equity will vanish along with it. Unlike legitimate savings that are permanent, provide real

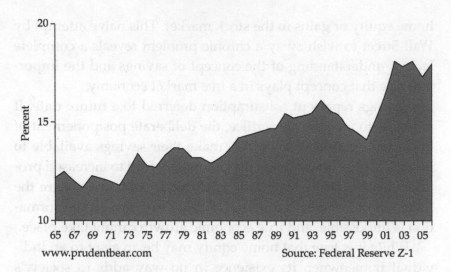

FIGURE 7.3 *Household debt as percent of assets, 1965–2006.* Even though the housing bubble inflated household assets, homeowners nevertheless managed to accumulate debt even faster. However, when the housing bubble deflates, the liabilities will not. Imagine what this chart will look like then.

Source: Reprinted by permission from David L. Tice and Associates (www.prudentbear.com).

security, earn interest, and represent future purchasing power, home equity will prove ephemeral, disappearing as quickly as it appeared.

From an individual perspective, counting home equity or stock market gains as savings is analogous to gamblers counting their chips while the card game is still in progress. Having a big stack in front of you means nothing if by the end of the game you're busted.

The same analogy applies to stock market gains. Rising stock values are not savings. Stock appreciation is clearly an asset from the perspective of the owner, but it in no way constitutes savings. Just like home equity, stock market appreciation can be accessed only if the owner borrows against it or sells shares. Again, either action would result in a drain of legitimate savings. In addition, while stock market wealth may be available to the individual shareholder in the case of financial hardship, those gains will certainly not be available to society as a whole. If a substantial percentage of the population fell on hard times, who would be there to buy all of the shares everyone was trying to unload, and at what prices would the shares ultimately sell? In such a situation, any paper gains would likely vanish at precisely the time when they were needed the most.

Legitimate savings, by contrast, can be accessed by individuals alone, or society as a whole, without anything needing to be sold. As such, they represent real security and can be relied upon to provide needed support during difficult financial times.

NOTHING SAVED FOR A RAINY DAY

Natural disasters provide a perfect example of why savings are so important. For example, take Hurricane Katrina, which struck the American economy at a particularly vulnerable time. By assuming that the sun would shine indefinitely and that economic levees (such as rising home values) would protect them from ruin, Americans literally had nothing saved for that rainy day. During the very month Katrina hit, personal income and spending data revealed a 1 percent surge in personal spending supported by a meager 0.3 percent rise in personal incomes. As a result the personal "savings" rate fell to what at the time was a new all-time record low of minus 0.6 percent.

Of course, as is always the case when disaster strikes, many naive economists looked for the silver lining in the hurricane's cloud, pointing to the spending necessary to replace what

Katrina destroyed as being an economic benefit. What such simplistic analysis overlooks is that resources devoted to replacing destroyed wealth are no longer available to create new wealth. Americans would have to either reduce spending in other areas or postpone such reductions through borrowing. Of course, in typical fashion, Americans opted for the latter.

Since the country lacked true domestic savings, the funds necessary to rebuild the infrastructure destroyed by Katrina had to be borrowed from abroad. As a result, our external debt grew by that much more, exacerbating our current account deficit and representing a drain on our future consumption for generations to come. However, once foreigners no longer make their savings available to Americans, the real burden of natural disasters will be more apparent. This harsh reality will expose the fallacy of our phony savings substitutes and provide a needed catalyst for the re-accumulation of legitimate savings.

Of course, such a process will require significant under consumption, and therefore could not take place without an accompanying recession. For most that would be the real disaster.

HOW WALL STREET FED THE CONSUMER CREDIT CRAZE

Wall Street accelerated the consumer credit revolution the same way it did the real estate bubble: It created a secondary market for credit card, auto loan, and retail paper by securitizing it— collecting it in pools and then reselling it as securities called by such names as plastic (credit card) bonds, certificates for automobile receivables (CARs), and other variations of the generic asset-backed securities (ABSs).

For an example of how it works, say I'm a merchant selling furniture. A customer buys a $5,000 furniture set with payments starting on some future date. I sell the paper to Wall Street, maybe to Merrill Lynch or another major firm, receiving $5,500, the difference representing interest and finance charges I would have earned had I held the paper myself instead of converting it to cash I could use to buy more furniture. Wall Street then pools the paper and issues securities that somebody in Japan, say, winds up owning at an effective cost of $6,000, that difference representing Wall Street's profit.

The point here is that the real price of the furniture set was $1,000 more than my customer paid, representing inflation that, having been created by easy credit, does not register as inflation. In effect, a lid has been kept on consumer prices because the merchant makes part of his profit on the interest.

What will ultimately happen, as the economy goes into recession and defaults begin to occur, is that the credit market will dry up. Then the Japanese either will not buy the paper at all or will demand much higher rates of interest for doing so. As a result, when the furniture dealer goes to Merrill Lynch with another $5,000 worth of furniture paper, he may find that they are no longer paying $5,500, but are offering only $4,500. That means the furniture dealer will have to raise his prices. That's when the inflation shows up.

So the Federal Reserve with its easy money policy was creating inflation that wasn't showing up as inflation because the cost of the credit was not in the price. As we saw in our discussion of the housing bubble, mortgage-backed securities were creating the same phenomenon.

Contrast the preceding example with a situation where the buyer saves instead of borrows. With interest compounded, the person with an eye on the $5,000 furniture set might have to put away only $4,750 to have the money needed for the $5,000 purchase.

CONSUMER BORROWING DEPRIVES SOCIETY

The economic point here is that by using credit, you are not only overpaying unnecessarily for what you buy, but you are also depriving society of scarce savings.

Anything that diminishes our savings diminishes our real economic growth and the real escalation of our standards of living. So consumer debt is a negative on many fronts, but we fail to recognize it as such because our measures of economic performance are focused on the gross domestic product (GDP). We're measuring economic growth by looking at how much we're spending, without any regard to how it is being financed and the negative long-term consequences consumer credit produces.

Another problem with consumer credit is that it raises interest rates. Borrowing to consume contributes to a process economists call "crowding out," meaning that there is additional competition for a limited pool of national savings better applied productively.

If we are going to keep on consuming, we're going to have to pay not only for our future indulgence, but also for the credit-related costs of all the consuming we have done in the past 10 years (see Figure 7.4). It's analogous to selling the cows to buy milk, or as the Austrian economist Ludwig von Mises put it, heating the house by burning the furniture.

But the people in the rest of the world, who have been forgoing consumption and building up income-producing assets, can look forward to a higher standard of living because they will get

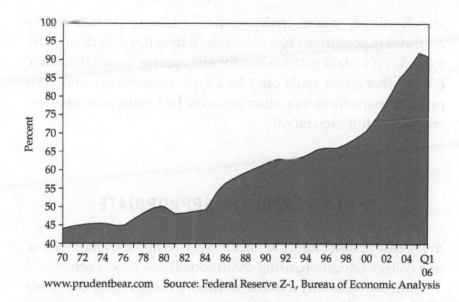

www.prudentbear.com   Source: Federal Reserve Z-1, Bureau of Economic Analysis

FIGURE 7.4 *Household debt as percent of gross domestic product,
1970–2006.* Note how debt in relation to GDP, which had risen
consistently since 1970, went ballistic in 2000. This coincided with
Alan Greenspan's "reflations" efforts following the bursting of the
tech bubble and the beginning of the housing bubble that followed.
Source: Reprinted by permission from David L. Tice and Associates
(www.prudentbear.com).

to spend not only their income but the interest on their savings
and investments, the principal of which they still have.

   Bright futures are not built on debt and consumption, but on savings and production.

COMMON MISUSES OF CREDIT

Some things clearly should not be bought on credit. These would
include items used in the routine of daily living such as groceries, gasoline, and clothing; purchases like household appliances

and furniture, where credit would add unnecessarily to the cost; and expenditures like vacations, where it is manifestly silly to trade off instant gratification for an ongoing financial burden. It's not that credit cards can't be a great convenience and even provide frequent-flier or other rewards. Just make sure balances are paid in full each month.

WHERE CREDIT IS APPROPRIATE

In the case of other big-ticket items, such as houses, automobiles, or a college education, using credit sometimes makes sense.

Borrowing to buy a house normally makes good economic sense, primarily because homeowners no longer have to pay rent. In effect, buying a house is like buying rental property where the buyer acts as his own tenant. Borrowing money to buy rental property is a perfectly legitimate use of credit, provided the rental income exceeds the cost of borrowing. The rent saved by a buyer who borrows is, in effect, phantom income that offsets mortgage payments. And owners who are their own tenants generally have few complaints about their landlords and vice versa.

Borrowing money to overpay for a house on the bet that a greater fool will be around to pay even more, which was common practice during the recent housing bubble, is speculation and obviously not recommended, as I discussed at length in Chapter 6 on the housing bubble.

Auto loans may or may not make sense, depending on the situation. To the extent public transportation is impractical and a car is needed to get to and from work, an auto loan can be viewed as a productive investment, since loan payments are covered by wages that could not be earned without it.

The same logic would not justify borrowing to purchase a luxury car, however, when an economy car can transport its owner to and from work just as effectively. Luxuries of any sort should always be paid for with cash.

Borrowing to finance a college education may make sense. There may be no alternative way to obtain a college degree, and the borrower's future income can be enhanced by an amount greater than the cost of the loan.

From a larger economic perspective, though, borrowing under government programs to finance education just because rates are low may be socially counterproductive for a couple of reasons.

One reason is that it uses scarce savings that would otherwise be available to finance capital investment that would provide multiple economic benefits, among them jobs for students once they graduate.

The other is that it causes tuitions to rise.

At one time very few Americans borrowed to go to college. My father, for example, worked his way though the University of Connecticut by waiting on tables each summer. Without help from his parents he graduated without a penny of debt. Today, UConn students can't work their way through because tuitions are sky-high.

However, high tuitions are no fluke. They exist as a direct result of government-guaranteed student loans. Without such loans, tuition could not rise beyond students' or their families' ability to pay. Because students have almost unlimited access to credit, universities are able to raise tuitions without the limits market discipline would otherwise enforce.

Any item for which consumers receive a subsidy to buy will naturally be more expensive with the subsidy than without it. It's ironic that as a direct result of government-subsidized student loans, students now need those loans to pay tuitions that, in the absence of such programs, they could have afforded to pay in cash. It is a good example of a government "solution" to a problem of its own creation.

And speaking of governments, let's look at the reckless consumer's national counterpart, Uncle Sam.

FLAWED HISTORICAL COMPARISONS

People who call me unduly pessimistic point to alleged parallels between today's current account deficits and those that existed during the nineteenth century. The difference is critical and goes to the same point I have been making about consumer credit: Nineteenth-century America borrowed to produce. Now we borrow to consume. Investment debt is self-liquidating, while consumer debt is self-debilitating.

This flawed comparison overlooks the fact that as a developing nation, the United States borrowed to invest, resulting in current account deficits that funded the construction of infrastructures and plants, which fueled American productivity.

When the country was still a colony, all the wealth was in England. The pilgrims had arrived at Plymouth Rock with nothing and the colonists were virtually without savings. So we borrowed money from the British and we used the money to build the infrastructure. What gave us an advantage compared to the British was that, as with its Hong Kong colony, there was less meddling than in the motherland, which gave us a significant entrepreneurial edge. We borrowed money from England, but with minimal government interference we used it to develop an economic infrastructure, first by building farms, then factories, railroads, and telegraphs, eventually becoming an industrial nation in much the same way the Chinese are now developing industrial sophistication.

So we borrowed to invest. Our investments enabled the production of vast quantities of consumer goods, which we sold back to our creditors to both pay interest and retire principal. In the end, our creditors got consumer goods and we were able to turn a huge current account deficit into a huge current account surplus. By 1980 we were the world's largest creditor and its wealthiest nation (see Figure 7.5).

The comparison between then and now is like night and day because back then we used the money wisely. In contrast,

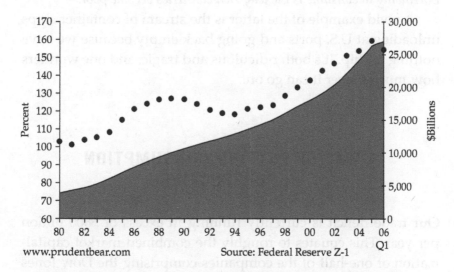

www.prudentbear.com   Source: Federal Reserve Z-1

FIGURE 7.5 *Total private nonfinancial debt outstanding and as percent of gross domestic product, 1980–2006.* Total private-sector nonfinancial debt has exploded from 75 percent of GDP in 1980 to 160 percent today. During that time period our GDP has been inflated by creative government accounting and is increasingly comprised of consumption, making the debt that much more dramatic when compared to the real wealth-producing components of GDP, such as manufacturing, mining, agriculture, and construction. Solid circles form a line plotting the annual growth in wealth-producing GDP. *Source:* Reprinted by permission from David L. Tice and Associates (www.prudentbear.com).

today's current account deficits mainly finance consumption. By squandering borrowed money on consumption, the United States has no way to repay the principal of its debts, let alone the interest. Borrowing to build factories is not the economic equivalent of borrowing to buy television sets, and it's amazing just how few modern economists can see the difference.

So when people point to that period of time to say that current account deficits don't matter, they miss the point that it all depends on whether a nation uses them productively or destructively. *Borrowing to produce is the way poor countries become rich. Borrowing to consume is the way rich countries become poor.*

A vivid example of the latter is the stream of container ships unloading at U.S. ports and going back empty because we have nothing to ship. It's both ridiculous and tragic, and one wonders how much longer it can go on.

A WAY OF PUTTING CONSUMPTION
IN PERSPECTIVE

Our trade deficit is currently running in excess of $800 billion per year. This equates to roughly the combined market capitalization of one-half of the companies comprising the Dow Jones Industrial Average, including Alcoa, American Express, Boeing, Caterpillar, Coca-Cola, Disney, DuPont, General Motors, Hewlett-Packard, Home Depot, Honeywell, McDonald's, Merck, 3M, and United Technologies.

That means that each year, Americans hock the equivalent of those 15 Dow Jones companies to foreigners in exchange for consumer goods. *We are literally transferring the wealth of our nation abroad purely to finance current consumption. Forget about merely selling the cows to buy milk, we are mortgaging the entire farm!*

"WE OWE IT TO OURSELVES, SO THE NATIONAL DEBT ISN'T A PROBLEM"

Back in the 1970s and 1980s when I was in school, economics professors claimed the national debt was really not a problem because it was largely "owed to ourselves." Although there was validity to that argument in the sense that the interest (the purchasing power) stayed in the United States, issues having to do with the distribution of income and wealth existed, since the debt holders represented a small minority of the population while the interest burden was shouldered by the people least able to afford it. Now, of course, the debt (what we owe) is largely held by foreigners.

The fact that the debt is now in large part held abroad poses a substantial problem in that interest payments made to foreign creditors now represent a net drain on national income and also shift purchasing power abroad.

As a result of persistent trade deficits, Americans accumulate liabilities, while foreigners accumulate assets. Servicing these debts will diminish future consumption in the United States while enhancing it abroad.

Economists, meanwhile, dismiss the massive buildup of debt, saying it comprises a traditionally acceptable percentage of our GDP. This naive rationalization ignores all the fluff in today's GDP figures, as well as the fact that over 70 percent of GDP represents consumption. Taken as a percentage of the wealth-producing components of GDP, such as manufacturing, mining, farming, and construction, the debt picture becomes a much more serious problem.

Also ignored is the short-term nature of the debt, most of which matures in two years or less, and the potential that rising interest rates will dramatically increase the burden of servicing it. So while doing so may be manageable now, given how low current interest rates happen to be, it will be far more difficult in the future when interest rates are substantially higher.

THE REAL NATIONAL DEBT

When we talk about the national debt, usually with astonishment at its size of $8.5 trillion, we should be clear that we are looking at the small part of the government's obligations that are funded. If we count the obligations representing contingent liabilities—promises and guarantees (explicit and implicit) for which no provision of any kind has been made—we are looking at an estimated $50 trillion plus, some six times the officially recognized federal debt.

Corporate accounting conventions vary, but contingent liabilities are required at minimum to be fully disclosed in the notes to financial statements, and when portions of such commitments are expected to become actual liabilities, actuarial estimates are required to be recognized. Not so with Uncle Sam.

Such unfunded liabilities include most notably obligations under Social Security and related Medicare and Medicaid programs, veterans benefits, congressional and other government employee pension benefits, U.S. Postal Service employee benefits, and a host of others, not to mention student loan guarantees, direct mortgage loan guarantees by Ginnie Mae, and other direct commitments or the implied Treasury backing of government agency obligations and those of government-sponsored entities such as Fannie Mae and Freddie Mac (to mention two whose vulnerability to mortgage defaults was covered the previous chapter, but are only two among many others).

The point here is that even when government backing is several steps removed, as for example an agency or service funded by congressional appropriation, you have to ask what the repercussions would be were the federal government not to rescue an entity having its implied backing. The loss of public faith in the responsibility of its federal government could have unthinkable consequences.

Yet even those unfunded obligations for which Treasury responsibility is officially acknowledged cannot conceivably be met with taxes, which is to say they can't conceivably be met—period.

THE GOVERNMENT TRUST FUNDS

Consider, for example, the government trust funds, the largest of which are the Social Security and Medicare programs. These trust funds are officially classified as "money that the government owes to itself." They are a mere illusion. There is nothing in them.

The way it works mechanically is that the government collects taxes. Revenues then go into these phony trust funds and the minute they get there, the government takes them right back out, puts some government bonds in the trust fund, then spends the money on current benefits or for general purposes such as the Iraq war, farm subsidies, or wherever it is immediately needed.

If you were to ask how much we have in the Social Security trust fund, the answer might be a trillion dollars, but all that would mean is that the fund has a government IOU for that amount. How is that any different than if you had nothing in the trust fund? It's no different, because if the obligation were to be met, the government would have to take the bonds in the fund and sell them to the public—in other words, borrow the money.

People perceive the bonds in the trust fund as an asset, which it would be if you or I held it. But in the government's case it's both an asset and a liability. It's like writing yourself a check and then claiming the amount of the check as an asset. That check is no more an asset when the government writes it in the form of a bond than it is when you or I do it.

In the words of a Congressional Budget Office report:

Federal trust funds are simply accounting devices. . . . What is in the trust funds is simply the government's promise to pay itself back at some time in the future. . . . When trust fund balances are drawn down, the government will not be using resources that have been saved for a rainy day. It will be using resources generated at that time—either by running a surplus in the rest of the budget or by borrowing from the public.

Of course the government does have other assets, but their values are highly questionable and are often based on inflated real estate or stock prices.

HOW SOCIAL SECURITY MADE A PIKER OUT OF PONZI

In December 1919, Charles Ponzi convinced a dozen Bostonians that he could return 50 percent on their money in 45 days by trading international postal coupons. Good as his word, 45 days later Ponzi paid $375 for each initial investment of $250. As he suspected they might, however, the investors gave it back to him to invest again and spread the word that he could make a person rich.

By the summer of 1920, Ponzi, now a wealthy man, was taking in $250,000 a day and was known coast to coast. When later that year a spiteful former friend brought Ponzi's prior criminal record to the attention of the Boston police, an estimated 40,000 people had entrusted some $15 million (about $140 million in today's dollars) to the Security Exchange Company, as his business was called.

What Ponzi had done was simple. He used money put in by new investors to pay off the old ones; and as long as more was coming in than going out, the scheme worked, although eventually, of course, like all pyramid schemes, it would have run out of people and begun unwinding.

But the Ponzi scheme lives in infamy as perhaps the greatest swindle of all time, with one notable exception: The Social Security system of the United States of America. As my father once wrote, the Social Security Administration should erect a giant statue of Ponzi to adorn its main lobby in Washington. In fact, the only real differences between the two are that Social Security is much bigger, involves an entire country, and was implemented without giving participants a choice. At least Ponzi didn't force anybody to buy in.

Social Security was established on the elitist premise that working-class people couldn't be trusted to save for their own retirements. Self-employed people were initially exempted, apparently on the theory that being self-employed meant that they were more likely to be responsible enough to save for themselves. But employees had to pay premiums (Social Security was initially sold to the public as being an insurance program and the taxes paid into it were referred to as premiums) into what was purported to be a massive trust fund.

To complete the illusion that such a fund was actually being accumulated, even though Social Security premiums were first collected in 1937 the first benefit check did not get paid until 1942. Of course, the insurance concept was just a con to get the public to support the program. The government spent every dime of the premiums the moment they were collected, using the very accounting gimmickry described in the previous section on government trust funds. Had the pay-as-you-go concept of today been proposed then, the system never would have seen the light of day.

Incidentally, the first beneficiary was Ida M. Fuller, who received check #00-000-001 in the amount of $22.45. She lived to be 100 years old, and although she had paid only $22.50 in Social Security taxes during those first five years, she collected over $20,000 in benefits. In Ponzi schemes it definitely pays to get in early. Unfortunately, the current generation of Americans will be left holding the bag, as their losses will ultimately pay for all the Ida Fullers who profited earlier.

The enormous significance of this is that the 6.2 percent (excluding Medicare) employers pay into the program is money they could otherwise be paying out as wages, some of which would presumably have been saved, as would presumably a portion of the 6.2 percent tax paid directly by the employee. Even worse, a self-employment tax of something around 12.4 percent was later introduced. That's a lot of money that self-employed people would, with even greater probability, have put in legitimate savings. Meanwhile, the Social Security trust fund saves absolutely nothing.

Bottom Line

By assuming responsibility for retirement savings and then spending every dime of it, Social Security has, in economic terms, done society a great disservice. It has actually helped destroy savings, thereby jeopardizing the retirements of several generations and depriving current and future generations of the benefits of lost capital investment. In the process, it has created a future liability that future generations will be unable to pay.

HOW MIGHT IT ALL RESOLVE?

All this borrowing to consume, both as individuals and as a nation, projects ultimately to bankruptcy at both levels, that or a reduction in the standard of living of a degree hard to imagine, although the recent economic collapse in Argentina and the hyperinflation and massive famine in the Weimar Republic following World War I provide some idea of what can happen as a result of unmanageable debt.

The immediate problem is the cost of servicing the $8.5 trillion of funded debt. As I mentioned earlier, our Treasury debt, over half of which is now foreign held and, thanks to the Rubinomics of the Clinton years, largely short-term, is steadily growing and, with interest rates rising, becoming more and more costly to service. In effect, the U.S. government has committed the American public to the mother of all adjustable-rate mortgages.

But there's no way we can keep issuing debt and still be the world's reserve currency. Of course, as more and more of our national debt shifts to foreign hands, foreign governments will naturally begin to worry about the political implications of what they see and will wonder why more Americans don't own their own country's debt. Adding even more liquidity is the time-honored expedient when debt reaches unmanageable levels, and, with a voting public in debt to its eyeballs, that would be a politically popular course of action, although not one calculated to please foreign central banks, since debt reduced by inflation is effectively repudiated.

At the same time, foreigners don't vote in the United States, so there isn't a lot they could do were our country to default on its foreign debt. For their part, American voters would typically be quick to blame the foreign governments for getting us into the problem in the first place.

Another thing we could do is extend the maturity of a foreign-held obligation from 2010, say, to 2040, making the creditor live with a 3 percent coupon for the next 30 years. Mandatory conversions are another alternative, whereby a 10 percent coupon would be simply replaced by a 3 percent coupon. Such measures have precedent in other countries similarly pinched.

Not that this sort of thing would be accepted cheerfully abroad. Foreign central banks would of course stop lending us money and foreign manufacturers would stop shipping us products on credit.

Nor would solving our debt problem with inflation leave us with acceptable domestic economic conditions.

With our manufacturing capacity largely dismantled, what would we have to consume if we had to consume out of our own production? And even where goods were produced domestically, only the richest Americans could afford to buy them. With the dollar collapsed, U.S. merchants would be able to get a lot more for their products abroad.

PROTECTING YOUR OWN MONEY

All the aforementioned exist as real possibilities, especially because as foreign investors finally begin to understand our economic problems, the measures they will take to protect themselves will only increase the pressures bearing on us.

Just like a family paying its Visa bill with a MasterCard, eventually our debt problem will catch up to us, necessitating a substantial reduction in our collective standards of living. However our debt problems are ultimately resolved, it is inevitable that there will be a realignment of global purchasing power that will be accomplished through a dramatic adjustment in exchange rates, with the dollar collapsing relative to the currencies of other countries. This will render Americans much poorer compared to the rest of the world, greatly reducing the ability of Americans to consume.

But not necessarily all Americans. Studying this problem from all angles has been my project at Euro Pacific Capital for a long time, and my recommendations for turning the situation to your personal advantage are in the chapters that follow.

2009 UPDATE

Bernard Madoff's scandalous undoing and our nation's tragic economic collapse have at least one thing in common: In both cases, motives notwithstanding, the underlying stratagems were doomed to fail. Pyramid (or Ponzi) schemes, which are what I'm talking about, are illegal for a good reason: They don't work. Any arrangement, public or private, that relies on a finite pool of new investors to repay earlier investors will eventually collapse.

Such scams, by definition, are deviously crafted, but the same dynamics can develop on their own, insidiously undermining well-intentioned objectives. There is no better example of a naturally occurring Ponzi dynamic, in my opinion, than the way consumer credit, the subject of this chapter, was misused by Americans. Debt was repaid by issuing new debt, with outstanding balances constantly increasing as the financial services establishment concocted one gimmick after another to keep the pyramid going. Now that credit has dried up, the phony economy it financed has predictably collapsed around us. Trade and budget deficits, excessive national and corporate debt, and bubbles in the markets for stocks, bonds, and real estate are essential parts of the story, but consumer credit was the fallacy at the root of the current economic collapse. Rather than trying to prop this phony economy back up by increasing debt, policy makers must let it collapse so that a legitimate economy can be built in its place.

At the heart of the financial crisis are the toxic assets that underlie bank balance sheets. However, the reason these assets are toxic in the first place is that they represent loans that American borrowers lack the means or desire to repay. Wall Street and the government claim the problem with these assets is a lack of liquidity. The real problem is lack of value. The assets are liquid, but the market prices are so low that current owners would be rendered insolvent if they actually sold at the bids.

The pyramid scheme analogy applies in other areas of the government where protecting the public's financial well-being is the name of the game. As I noted in the chapter, the Social Security Trust Fund is a pure case in point (see the subhead "How Social Security Made a Piker Out of Ponzi").

Another prominent example is the Federal Deposit Insurance Corporation (FDIC), which was reorganized in 2006 and recently given expanded powers. Its Deposit Insurance Fund is financed by insurance premiums collected from member depository institutions. That revenue represented 1.25 percent of the $4.29 trillion in deposits it insured at year-end 2008. Under Treasury Secretary Timothy Geithner's new plan to get toxic assets off the books of banks, the FDIC will guarantee loans to the high-risk public-private investment funds the Treasury will put together to buy them. I'll give you odds the FDIC will itself go bankrupt.

The primary reason our banks and other deposit-taking institutions are in so much trouble is that depositors generally don't care what risks these institutions take with their money. Why should they, when their deposits are insured by the FDIC? Thanks to FDIC insurance, institutions willing to take high risks continue to attract depositors with higher rates, while more conservative competitors lose customers. The FDIC thus creates a moral hazard because without the government backing banks would have to compete on safety as well as rates, and our financial system would be a lot healthier.

Ironically, the FDIC came into existence as a result of the Great Depression, where approximately 2 percent of deposits were lost to bank failures. As a result, while the FDIC now insures that no depositor will lose money, it guarantees that all deposits will lose value, as the government prints money to pay claims. My guess is that because of FDIC insurance, the purchasing power lost during the current depression will dwarf the amount of deposits lost during the 1930s.

As a country, the United States' history of never having defaulted has enabled it to borrow increasing amounts from its trading partners even though it has to borrow additional money to pay it back. As existing bonds mature, new bonds are issued to fund the redemptions. However, the stimulus programs have suddenly created new borrowing needs in unprecedented trillions of dollars. Foreign lenders, struggling themselves with recession, are increasingly worried about the United States' rapidly mounting debt levels and its continued ability to meet its obligations.

(An aside I can't resist: In one of Euro Pacific's weekly web site commentaries, I noted that with this growing anxiety on the part of foreign lenders, it would make sense if our government's primary emissary be someone exceptionally skilled at reassuring large groups of investors to stay invested in what amounts to a gigantic Ponzi scheme. I therefore fiendishly proposed that rather than putting Bernie Madoff in jail, President Obama should consider him for secretary of the Treasury.)

Gallows humor notwithstanding, it's a fact that we pay off our creditors in precisely the same manner Bernie Madoff paid back his early investors. Up until his scam went bust, no one had lost a dime investing with Madoff. Anyone who wanted his money back got it, as Bernie could always find a greater fool to supply the funds.

Ultimately our creditors will be faced with the same grim reality as Madoff's clients. When the supply of fools runs out, so too will our government's ability to "repay" its debts.

Personally, I don't see S&P and Moody's bringing themselves to downgrade the government's AAA rating, but it probably wouldn't matter much in any event. Both these rating agencies have been completely discredited, having kept AAA ratings on pools of subprime mortgages and other securities that ultimately became virtually worthless. My guess is their cozy relationships with our government will prevent them from ever issuing an official downgrade. However, unofficially the markets will impose the downgrade on their own, as our Treasury is issuing subprime, junk-quality paper any way you look at it. We have no choice but to go deeper and deeper into debt until our creditors blow the whistle, and when that happens our choices will be to default or to print money and create more inflation. Recent actions by the Federal Reserve have sent the world a clear signal that our choice would be to do the latter. More on that under the subhead "The Bond Bubble and the Final Collapse" at the end of this update.

How Consumer Credit Became the Monster That Brought Down Our Economy

It has become a mantra of the Obama administration, in its effort to get banks lending again, that "credit is the lifeblood of the economy" and that growth will not return until we restore the flow. As everybody who has read *Crash Proof 2.0* this far knows, however, the real lifeblood of a growing economy is savings, which is the well from which credit springs and becomes the source of capital investment and jobs, ultimately resulting in more savings and higher living standards. Credit that is used to buy consumer goods and services, by contrast, becomes a cancer. Rather than keeping our economy alive, it slowly kills it. Now that our economy lies near death, government policy threatens to smother what life remains.

How Securitization Made the Monster More Monstrous

When Wall Street, starting in the mid-1980s, began structuring asset-backed securities from pools of auto loan, credit card, and other consumer paper and marketing them to foreign banks flush with savings deposits, the wellspring of consumer credit became global. Once domestic savings were exhausted, we thus proceeded to borrow foreign savings. Instead of investing that money productively, however, we squandered it on consumption just as we had our own savings.

Out of this pseudo economy emerged the now-dominant service sector, which assumed all the borrowing and spending would continue indefinitely. The collapse of the credit bubble and the multiple malinvestments it generated has revealed that the service sector has expanded to the point that Americans don't have enough wealth to consume all the services. In the meantime, since we underinvested in manufacturing, we cannot export enough to repay out debts.

Now that the secondary market for consumer debt-backed paper has collapsed, only two buyers remain: the Federal Reserve and private investors that demand government guarantees regardless of how highly rated the paper may be.

Other Contributing Factors

So securitization, by making it possible to tap foreign savings, was a major factor in growing consumer debt to monster proportions, but not the only one. Pervading the credit system at large has been, I believe, a false sense of confidence stemming from several factors. One would be the myth that the distribution of risk through securitization somehow diminishes it. Another would be the ubiquity of real or implied government guarantees, including the "too big to fail" argument invoked, justifiably or not, to support government intervention where bankruptcy is imminent (of course it was the perception of being too big to fail that enabled such entities to grow so large in the first place). A third example would be the mistaken belief that technological and mathematical science, when put at the disposal of Wall Street's rocket scientists, makes it possible to hedge the risk out of anything, the example du jour being the credit default swap, whose insurance value has proven unreal.

It seems to me we're going to have to learn to live in a world where the majority of transactions are based on genuine creditworthiness confirmed by due diligence rather than risk management theory and insurance contracts of dubious value.

The American Public Wants to Help. Why Not Let It?

Generally speaking, American citizens, to their credit, realistically accept that they bought into a false paradigm of ever-rising asset prices and allowed the wealth effect to influence their decision making with respect to spending, saving, and preparing for retirement. In economic terms, we're watching free-market forces attempting to repair the damage and get us back on the right track.

The government, however, sees a danger in such realism and in free-market forces generally. It is saying that if American citizens won't take on any more debt, the government will do it for them. In a recent speech President Obama actually praised the hard choices to cut spending being made at family dinner tables around the country. However, his policies belie his words. Whatever progress families make paying off their own debts is offset by their share of the growing government debt. An economy correcting imbalances is going to feel some pain. Government efforts to avoid that pain through stimulus programs will only delay the reforms necessary to get the economy growing again and prevent even greater pain later.

At the risk of belaboring a point I've made many times before in different contexts, for savings and production to flourish, the government, which produces nothing, must stop borrowing, because that diverts funds from productive applications. It must also shrink in size, making it a lesser burden on the productive part of the economy and freeing human resources for productive work in the private sector.

We have to let people lose jobs in certain service sectors, such as financial services and retailing, and reemploy them making cars and other things that we can export to people who can afford to pay for them and who actually need them. Assuming we are not talking about a bridge about to collapse, spending taxpayer money now on infrastructure makes no more sense than a person who is broke borrowing to build a swimming pool in his backyard. I could go on, but everywhere we look there are opportunities to make sacrifices that are constructive and don't necessarily cause great pain. Where is it written that we need a new car every few years, or even every five years? In a proposed "cash for clunkers" bill, Congress is considering $4,500 per vehicle subsidies to encourage Americans to scrap fully paid for older cars in order to go into debt to buy brand-new ones! This makes about as much sense as an unemployed homeowner burning down his house so he can gain employment rebuilding it.

The Questionable Future of Foreign Borrowing

In the absence of domestic savings, we are forced to rely on our foreign creditors to finance the cost of our misguided economic stimulus plans. But with their own stimulus plans to finance, funding ours becomes a dubious prospect. Take China, which is our largest creditor. The argument that the Chinese own so much of our debt they have to put good money after bad to avoid collapsing Treasury bond prices weakens substantially when we ask them to back up the truck. China funds about 50 percent of our borrowing, and since we might need to borrow another $10 trillion over the next five years, they are effectively penciled in for $5 trillion more. I wouldn't be surprised if they decided to cut the cord and take their losses on the $1 trillion in debt they own now. Why should they incur even greater losses on what could be $6 trillion of exposure in a few years?

The Bond Bubble and the Final Collapse

In the final analysis, artificially low interest rates have created one final bubble that has yet to burst: bonds.

Rates on long-term Treasury bonds remained artificially low in the first months of 2009, meaning that bond prices (yields and prices being on opposite ends of a seesaw) remain artificially high. The benchmark federal funds rate, in a target range of zero to ¼ percent since December 2008, has failed to provide stimulus, and the Fed has been making massive purchases of Treasuries in an effort to keep rates down. The 30-year yields held in a range of 3 to 4 percent from November 2008 thru May 2009, representing record lows. In fact, in mid-December of 2008, the yield fell to an all-time record low of almost 2.5 percent.

Since no rational investor would buy 30-year bonds at such low rates with the intention of holding them to maturity, it is obvious that high bond prices are unsustainable. I believe leveraged hedge funds and other speculators are buying long-term Treasuries because they think their value will rise in the short term as the Fed proceeds with its announced programs to make purchases in the trillions of dollars. Foreign central banks are still buying, but are waking up to the fact that their risk is not default but reduced purchasing power.

When the dynamics reverse, these bond flippers, like the condo flippers in the real estate bubble, will go into sell mode. With a preponderance of sellers and few buyers, the bubble bursts. The greater problem comes as the Fed increases its purchases to pick up the slack. Since bonds merely represent future payments of dollars, as the Fed prints dollars to buy bonds it further lessens the value of those bonds left outstanding. This only chases more buyers away, necessitating even more Fed purchases and setting a vicious cycle into motion. Eventually the Fed remains the only buyer. However, given how fast the dollar loses purchasing power once this situation develops, the government must borrow even larger quantities to fund its rapidly rising expenditures. Once this dynamic sets in, hyperinflation is the result.

A prominent TV financial news anchor recently challenged me with the argument that if nations like China refuse to buy our debt, it's no problem since we can just print the money and buy the debt ourselves. What that otherwise knowledgeable person fails to understand is that when foreign governments bought our bonds, it was foreign money supplies that expanded, not ours. In effect we imported foreign goods and exported inflation. Now that the Fed is buying the bonds, it is our money supply that expands. The difference is that foreigners get to keep their goods and we get stuck with the inflation.

So as this final bubble bursts, we are faced with a self-perpetuating spiral. The more bonds the Fed buys, the more inflation it creates and the less the dollar is worth, making our bonds less attractive to outside buyers. That makes the bonds being currently issued a harder sell, never mind the multiple trillions of dollars that will have to be raised to finance President Obama's recovery program. Not only are foreign investors going to be inclined to pass on that debt, but I would also expect that with all the buying the Fed is doing, foreign investors would have second thoughts about continuing to hold the bonds they already own. That's why I say the real collapse is still coming. We've really seen nothing yet. The fact that foreign governments have been willing to lend us money this long has permitted the bailouts and postponed the pain.

When the bond bubble bursts, it's the U.S. government itself that will need bailing out. The question then becomes: Who, if anyone, is going to do the bailing?

8

How to Survive
and Thrive, Step 1:
Rethinking Your
Stock Portfolio

In my experience, nothing puts the Maalox mustache on a new investor faster than the mention of foreign stocks. Just the word *foreign* calls up a panoply of risks, real or not, that are unfamiliar and cause the jitters.

Foreign markets, to the contrary, are the most conservative place for your money right now. In this chapter, I explain why the risks people associate with foreign stocks and bonds are either outdated or unfounded. And I tell you exactly how to replace your endangered U.S. dollar holdings with a portfolio of foreign securities that offer less long-term risk, significantly higher current yields, and more upside potential.

I'm well aware that to exclude U.S. dollar investments from your portfolio flies in the face of conventional Wall Street wisdom, which holds conservative domestic investing to be conservative but regards foreign investing, by definition, as speculative.

That traditional focus on the risk factors contrasts sharply with my approach, which looks at foreign investing from a conservative perspective. I advise clients to invest abroad in pursuit of safety, wealth preservation, and purchasing power protection. My goal is to avoid the substantial risk I see in the U.S. market by seeking safe havens abroad.

The way I look at it, just as investors have choices when it comes to which stocks to buy, they also have choices as to which nations and, by extension, which currencies to invest in.

A responsible investor would obviously steer clear of stocks with excessive losses and high debt levels. By the same logic, why wouldn't the same investor avoid exposure in a nation that uses inflation as a means to repudiate its debts and deal with its economic problems, which is what the United States is doing? Nobody loves his country more than I do, but let's face it: The United States is unique among developed nations in its dire economic circumstances. It has gotten itself into a terrible economic mess, and is likely to try to inflate its way out of it. Conservative investors must seek safety elsewhere.

THE PROBLEM WITH TIPS

Wall Street's cookie-cutter solution for investors worried about inflation is to recommend investing in Treasury inflation protection securities, or TIPS for short. However, buying TIPS is a perfect example of trusting the fox to guard your henhouse. The basic problem with TIPS is that they are indexed to the consumer price index (CPI), which does not reflect actual

> inflation, but rather the government's highly understated version of it. Ultimately, the CPI can be manipulated to produce any result the government wants. As the supply of TIPS outstanding continues to increase, so too does the government's incentive to make them less costly by understating the CPI.

The operative part of the word conservative is conserve. What is it precisely that we are attempting to conserve? In the financial sense, most people would say they are trying to conserve dollars. When you really think about it, though, it isn't the dollars you are trying to conserve; it is the purchasing power that those dollars represent. What good is it to conserve quantities of dollars if those dollars buy little or nothing when you try to spend them?

As I have argued throughout this book, the dollar, on its present course, will salvage very little of its current purchasing power. Conservative investors really have no choice but to exclude U.S. dollar–denominated investments from their portfolios.

DEBUNKING THE MYTHS AND FEARS ABOUT FOREIGN INVESTING

Recent Historical Perspective

Remember when it seemed like just about everything worth buying was "made in America"? Sure, certain European imports were synonymous with high luxury, things like Hermès silks and Gucci leather goods. If something was made in Asia, though, the problem was getting it home before it fell apart. Generally speaking, American-made meant quality, while imported goods were suspect.

An interesting bit of trivia from the 1950s reveals what post-war Japan, in the early stages of its industrialization, was up against in its effort to compete with America's reputation for quality. Demonstrating inspiration and determination that we probably should have paid more attention to at the time, the Japanese actually gave one of their industrial cities the name Usa. Now they could honestly label products manufactured there "MADE IN USA." It's a flattering and amusing story, but it is also a serious comment on how hard Asian exporters had to work to make their products acceptable in American markets.

Not only did America have a reputation for quality, but it was known for low prices as well. European imports were perceived as high-priced. The word imported was almost a synonym for expensive. Being able to afford imported products was a sign of success, a status symbol. A shopper's observation that an item seemed expensive would be met with the explanation, "It's imported." Today, that would answer the question, "How come it's so cheap?"

So while at one time America flooded the world with low-cost, high-quality goods, today it is a high-cost producer with a reputation for poor quality. What's significant, though, is that when America was the low-cost producer, it also had the highest wage rates in the world.

It is a common misconception that low wages are the main factor influencing prices. The reality is that low capital costs, and the absence of taxation and regulation, are far more important. When Americans saved a lot and we had sound money, real interest rates were naturally very low. That meant lower capital costs, which allowed greater worker productivity. With very low taxes and minimal regulation, American manufacturers could pay the world's highest wages while they produced the world's lowest-priced goods.

Today, the high-quality, low-cost producers are all in Asia. Some countries like China have wage scales lower than those in the United States, while others, such as Japan, pay higher wages. However, the real difference is that costs of capital are lower because of higher savings rates, lower taxes, and fewer regulations. It sounds surprising, but in "communist China" entrepreneurs have more freedom than they do in America. It is far easier to go into business there than here.

Think about all the rules and regulations American businesses have to deal with. How can we compete with nations that don't impose those excessive burdens? Does anyone think that the United States could ever have become a great power with all the rules, regulations, and taxation that exist today? Could we really have actually settled the West if wagon trains had to meet onerous government safety standards and if employers had to deal with all the regulations that are in effect today, had to withhold taxes, and had to keep track of their expenses to pay their own income taxes as well?

China's Advantage Is That It Is *Not* a Democracy

Pundits will argue that China's economic viability is limited because it is not a democracy. I say the opposite is true, that it is precisely because it is not a democracy that China will likely be so successful.

What is of vital importance for economic success is economic freedom, meaning the protection of private property, the rule of law, and minimal regulation and taxation, not the right to vote. One could reasonably argue that with economic freedom, free elections are of secondary value, and without it, voting (suffrage) has no value. A choice between oppressors is tantamount to no choice at all. Remember, the old Soviet Union had elections and almost everybody voted, the alternative being frozen toes in Siberia.

The word *democracy* is used loosely these days, and it is useful to remember that one of the primary reasons for America's early economic success was that our founding fathers recognized a distinction between democracy, which they understood as populist government with counterproductive implications for capitalism, and republican government, which stressed checks and balances, such as the Electoral College and staggered senatorial terms, designed to keep the evil forces of democracy at bay. James Madison, the father of the Constitution, writing in the Federalist Papers, said, "Democracies . . . have ever been found incompatible with personal security or the rights of property; and have in general been as short in their lives as they have been violent in their death." After the Constitution was ratified, Benjamin Franklin was asked, "What form of government have you given us, Mr. Franklin?" His answer: "A republic if you can keep it." Perhaps if we could have kept it there would have been no need for me to write this book.

For those of you who incorrectly believe that the United States is supposed to be a democracy, just check the Constitution. The word *democracy* does not appear once. However, Article IV, Section IV, reads, "The United States shall guarantee to every State in this Union a Republican Form of Government." If you are still unclear, just recite the "Pledge of Allegiance" and listen carefully to the words.

The New Economic Alignment

The reality is that in the United States economic freedom, just like sound money, is a distant memory. So too are the low taxes, minimal regulations, and the high savings rates that went along with them. The comparative advantage we once had in limited government and freedom has been lost. Those advantages now prevail in Asia, and for that reason Asia is becoming the dominant factor in the global economy.

Just as the United States once replaced Great Britain as the world's leading economy, the economic baton will now be passed to the East. Japan and China will be the new leaders, with China possessing the potential to emerge as the world's single most dominant economy.

Go into any store, or look through your own home. Just about everything in it was made in China. And it's not all the result of cheap labor. There are plenty of areas in the world where labor is much cheaper than in China, but that export nothing. The real key to China's success is economic freedom.

China is communist in name only. People living under true communism are not productive. Did we import any manufactured goods from the former Soviet Union? Of course not.

China is set to overtake Japan as America's largest creditor. Did we borrow any money from the Soviet Union? No, in fact we lent it money every year. We had to give it credits just to buy our grain. China exports grain.

Once China allows the dollar to collapse, its domestic purchasing power will surge and its economy will quickly overtake the U.S. economy as the world's largest. Free from the burden of subsidizing America, the rest of Asia will boom as well.

As it now stands, the United States is the beneficiary of a reverse Marshall Plan, which costs Asian economies a fortune to fund. When they pull the plug, the U.S. economy will go down the drain, and Asian economies will see explosive growth and prosperity. Asia is where the real fortunes will be made. That is why I suggest growth-oriented investments be targeted to Asia. Investing there now is like investing in America in the late nineteenth century.

A free-floating yuan, especially if backed by gold, could well become the world's reserve currency. Though this may sound a bit far-fetched, I really think that it is a distinct possibility. A complete collapse of the dollar might make it hard for any other fiat currency to take its place. Gold backing could set the yuan apart from the rest, and China may just possess the ability to pull it off.

Europe certainly has its share of problems, but, unlike the United States, at least it lives within its diminished means. For all its socialism, at least the European Union enjoys a trade surplus and its people still manage to save. As a result the euro will likely be a principal beneficiary of the dollar's demise. That could give Europe a huge boost, helping to contain interest rates and consumer prices on the continent. As a result, the euro zone is definitely an area where we want to invest. Of course, we also want to invest money outside the euro zone, such as in Switzerland, the UK, and Scandinavia, which will also benefit from a strong Europe.

In the long run, the euro as a fiat currency may very well fail like the U.S. dollar. But being the largest nondollar currency issued by a major creditor, it appears certain to thrive in the short term.

Currency Exchange and Other Risks

Ironically, one of the risks most commonly associated with foreign investing, currency exchange risk, is the primary reason I'm recommending that you invest abroad in the first place (that, and my prediction back in Chapter 5 that the domestic stock market is substantially overvalued). The unfortunate reality is that the country with the greatest currency risk is our own. Here at home we call it inflation risk or purchasing power risk, and the way to avoid it is by investing in those foreign currencies that are expected to rise significantly as the dollar falls.

Other risks traditionally associated with foreign investing are not important as a practical matter when you deal with established companies in developed countries. Inadequate financial information used to be a problem, but foreign companies now provide abundant data, usually in English and accessible through web sites. Lack of accounting regulation was another risk, but these days the major U.S. auditing firms dominate abroad and standards of disclosure and transparency similar to those at home are more the rule than the exception. (Also, if my memory serves me, Enron, WorldCom, Tyco International, and the rest weren't headquartered in New Zealand.) Political risk, the risk that assets will be confiscated, is no greater a problem in the countries we'll be investing in than it is here in the United States.

Many investors also fear that somehow any foreign revenues or profits cannot easily be spent here. That's not true. You can readily repatriate what you hold and earn abroad. It doesn't matter that you live here and invest there. For example, let's say you have $1 million in foreign stocks that now produce the U.S. equivalent of $80,000 a year in dividends. When you get your dividends, say they're in Swiss francs, your American broker converts them into U.S. dollars, which you can then withdraw with a debit card or a check. If the dollar declined by 90 percent, that $1 million becomes $10 million and the $80,000 in income becomes $800,000. You're getting checks that are 10 times as big. So you can go to the grocery store and pay $1,000 at the checkout counter for what used to cost $100.

In short, foreign investing has become safe, economical, and very profitable. It's a matter of knowing how and where to invest. My purpose in this chapter is to explain how a conservative, income-producing domestic portfolio, exposed currently to a collapsing dollar, can be replicated in foreign currencies, while you live in the United States with no sacrifice of financial flexibility or convenience and with the added benefit of a higher yield.

MORE SMART MONEY HAS STARTED INVESTING OVERSEAS

Although foreign investing is my specialty as a broker, I'm in increasingly good company in seeking protection and opportunity abroad. The private client departments of the major Wall Street firms, which provide special services to wealthy clients,

have recently been recommending 40 percent to 50 percent portfolio allocations in foreign investments, where 5 percent to 10
percent allocations used to be more typical. Also, some of the
world's most legendary investors, such as Warren Buffett, Bill
Gross, Sir John Templeton, Jim Rogers, George Soros, Mark
Faber, and James Grant, are all advocating getting out of U.S.
dollars. Even former government officials such as Paul Volcker,
the former Federal Reserve chairman, and Robert Rubin, the former Secretary of the Treasury, have publicly addressed the risks
of a major dollar crisis and advocated foreign investments as a
hedge against it.

I like to remind people that the U.S. stock market is just one
stock market in one country in one very big world. Even absent
the dollar crisis, to my mind it doesn't make sense to limit your
investment universe to American companies traded on American exchanges, when there are exchanges all over the globe
trading stocks of companies that have no customers here, do no
business here, and pay dividends that you can often buy for less
than you'd pay here. In fact, the motto of my brokerage firm,
which specializes in foreign stocks, is "Because there's a bull
market somewhere."

Based on my outlook for the dollar, I'd have to be crazy not
to buy into an earnings stream based on euros, yen, Australian
dollars, or other currencies we'll discuss, especially if I can get
the same value for 8 times earnings that I'd have to pay 16 times
earnings for at home.

IF ONLY YOU HAD DONE THIS IN THE 1970s

If you're still not convinced that my strategy will work, consider
what happened in the 1970s.

Anybody smart enough to have invested abroad in the early 1970s would have made out like a bandit.

In 1972, after we broke from the gold standard and floated the dollar (which, of course, didn't float at all, but sank like a stone), you could buy 4.25 deutsche marks for a dollar, the Swiss franc was worth about 25 cents, and you'd get about 360 yen for the dollar. By 1980, the dollar had lost two-thirds of its value. The deutsche mark was at 1.5 instead of 4.25, the Swiss franc had tripled, and the yen was at 150 or 160.

So those with the foresight to have invested in portfolios of conservative foreign stocks in the early 1970s, although it was harder to do back then, would have tripled their money by 1980, not counting any appreciation in local currency or dividends earned, whereas those invested in similar portfolios of U.S. dollar–denominated stocks suffered through a brutal bear market.

The stock market between 1972 and 1980 went sideways, with repeated sharp drops, while bonds got clobbered and the CPI, a better inflation indicator then than now, more than doubled.

By the time the 1980s rolled around, those astute investors could have taken their highly appreciated foreign assets and bought the Dow Jones Industrial Average as low as 842 with a dividend yield of nearly 7 percent or bought the U.S. Treasury 30-year bond yielding more than 16 percent. Most Americans weren't in a position to make those investments because they got wiped out in the 1970s.

We're trying to anticipate a similar situation now, except this time the reasons for moving money abroad are far more compelling: Our economic problems are much worse and the United States is in a far more precarious position, meaning the dollar's decline and its impact on living standards could be that much more severe.

Assuming Americans learn from their experience, at some point we'll have reason to start reallocating our money back to U.S. markets, where there could well be a scenario similar to 1980: interest rates in the stratosphere, the economy and stocks in the tank, the dollar at rock bottom, and then, suddenly, light at the end of the tunnel. *To take advantage of potential bargains in the domestic market in the future, though, you first must take the necessary steps to protect your wealth today. That is what this chapter is about.*

WHAT IF I'M WRONG?

Like Damon Runyon's "longest floating crap game in New York," it is conceivable, if highly unlikely, that the U.S. government can keep the wool over the eyes of the public and the foreign central bankers for the foreseeable future and prove my forecast of the dollar's collapse premature.

Let's consider, then, from the investor's point of view, the possible scenarios, given that there are three variables affecting the profitability of a conservative foreign investment: (1) currency exchange, (2) dividend yield, and (3) local share price appreciation.

Scenario A: You take my advice and my forecast proves correct. You're obviously a very happy camper. I've saved you from poverty and despair, and you've not only preserved your wealth but also enhanced it considerably because you have dividend income, the stocks may have risen in value, and the foreign currency has appreciated against the dollar. Three for three. You are ideally positioned to buy back into the American market when its problems are behind it.

Scenario B: You take my advice and I'm wrong. Suppose you follow my advice and the U.S. economy doesn't collapse, there is no day of reckoning, and we just continue like we've been doing for the next 30 years.

Most authorities—legendary investors like Warren Buffett and Pimco's Bill Gross, even the big houses like Goldman Sachs and Morgan Stanley—are of the opinion that over the next 10 years the dollar is going to depreciate against other currencies, by what degree they're not sure. But it is widely believed that, despite occasional hiccups, the dollar will continue its 40-year decline. With our lack of savings and our current account deficits, it has to. If that doesn't produce a crisis, the one thing we know for sure is that it will produce a cheaper dollar relative to other currencies over time. That means if you're investing abroad you've got the wind at your back, not in your face, when it comes to foreign exchange.

So we're still going to make a profit on currency exchange.

Not only that, dividend yields are better abroad right now, a reflection of lower valuations there than in the United States. In other words, you can buy more earnings for less money in other countries than you can here. And you've got better growth potential because maturing global economies are growing rapidly, in contrast to the already mature U.S. market. So even if my doom-and-gloom scenario never materializes, you're still better off investing abroad than investing in the United States. Currency, dividends, and market value all have favorable indications abroad relative to U.S. markets.

Now, of the three sources of profit, dividends are most assured, assuming you selected stocks with sound fundamentals. If the stock goes down but the currency goes up, you've got the dividends so you're two out of three. Most of the time you're going to get at least two out of three. In the worst-case scenario, you're going to get two down and one up: currency down and stock down, but the dividend paid and offsetting the currency or the stock. It's hard to imagine a situation where you really get hurt.

Scenario C: You don't follow my advice and I'm wrong. Okay, so there was no disaster. You stayed in domestic investments.

Maybe you did better, but given the economic imbalances of the American economy and relative overvaluation of the U.S. market, you probably did worse anyway.

Scenario D: You don't follow my advice and I'm right. As Frank Sinatra once said, "Money isn't everything. You can't buy poverty."

Bottom Line

When you look at the various outcomes in terms of risk/reward ratios, it makes far more sense to follow my advice, right or wrong, than ignore it. You've got far more to lose if I'm right and you ignore me than if I'm wrong and you follow me.

It really goes without saying, but while I strongly recommend you put all your invested money in foreign currencies, you can always do it only to a degree. You might want to decide on a percentage you are comfortable with, and invest only that portion of your portfolio in foreign stocks.

GETTING DOWN TO BUSINESS: CREATING A FOREIGN PORTFOLIO

The foreign investment landscape is essentially the same as it is here at home. It offers the same basic asset classes, namely cash, stocks, and bonds, and the various alternatives within those classes.

Since my personal preference is for stocks, I will be talking mainly about the equity markets, although all investors should have an emergency fund in the form of cash equivalents and near-cash, such as money market funds or bank certificates of deposit (CDs), and very conservative investors may prefer bonds to stocks. Bonds can be bought and sold abroad essentially the same way as they are at home, but remember that fixed-income securities don't provide inflation protection.

My preference for equities is grounded in my belief that all governments that issue fiat currency will inflate, which will tend to reduce the purchasing power of those currencies over time. Although the nations in which we are investing are likely to inflate to a far lesser degree than will be the case in the United States, it still makes sense to hedge against those risks. By owning equities, whose income streams and value can rise to offset inflation, we get a hedge against foreign as well as domestic inflation. Also, current U.S. tax laws favoring dividend over interest income also apply to most foreign stocks (Hong Kong and Singapore ordinary shares, unfortunately, do not qualify). In addition, currency gains on foreign bonds or certificates of deposit are taxed as ordinary income at maturity. By investing in equities we can either put off taxes on foreign currency gains indefinitely or realize those gains but pay taxes at the lower capital gains rate.

Replicating a domestic portfolio assumes a portfolio currently exists and is structured in accordance with your investment objectives and your tolerance for risk. Whether that is true in your case or you are just starting a portfolio, one virtue of my plan is that it is structurally simple. One size really fits all.

Investment objectives are the first consideration in structuring a stock portfolio. Since I have made a specialty of conservative stocks that can be bought at an undervalued price and will provide generous and dependable dividend yield, three basic portfolio considerations—safety, growth, and income—are baked into the cake from the get-go. If your objective is income, cash your dividend checks. If your objective is growth, reinvest your dividends and watch the value compound. Safety, of course, is our first and foremost criterion.

As discussed in Chapter 5, since I buy when prices represent value, my portfolios have growth potential, but I view capital gains as a bonus. Dividends paid by a growing company will usually increase as profits grow, but dividend growth is also a bonus. *Current dividend income must justify the purchase. Longer-term investment goals are met as that dividend income is reinvested and compounded. So multiple objectives are achieved with the same stocks. It just depends on how long they are held and whether dividends are paid out or reinvested.*

Investors preferring the additional safety of bonds would schedule maturities to coincide with their objectives and use their interest for income or for reinvestment in other securities having appropriate risk and expiration features.

Risk tolerance, to use the term of art with investment advisers, is really irrelevant here. I assume everybody is risk averse. It's not that speculation is a bad thing, if you've got the stomach for it. There are speculative investments abroad that will provide exceptional returns if they pan out. But it's not what I'm recommending in this chapter.

Investment horizon, another term of art meaning how long you can wait for the payoff, is similarly irrelevant. When you hold a stock that pays off from the day you buy it, your investment horizon is the day you sell it or stop reinvesting dividends, so your horizon can be short or long.

Diversification is important but becomes less so to the extent the stocks in a portfolio are conservative. Ten to 20 stocks provide adequate diversification for us and will represent an assortment not just of companies, but also of sectors, markets, and currencies.

THE CASE AGAINST MUTUAL FUNDS, ADRs, AND PINK SHEETS

Because overseas investing has an intimidating reputation, advisers who do not succeed in discouraging people from foreign investing altogether will usually try to steer them into foreign mutual funds, into American depositary receipts (ADRs), or to domestic brokers that trade foreign stocks using the Pink Sheets.

I am against those alternatives. Here's why:

Mutual Funds

Foreign mutual funds are widely available and because they are diversified and professionally managed are tempting alternatives. If your choices are a dollar-denominated domestic fund or a foreign fund, I would certainly recommend the latter, provided it is not hedged and is truly foreign. (Funds called "international" are generally invested in securities outside the United States, while those called "global" are in both foreign and domestic companies.) But I avoid foreign mutual funds in general for the following eight reasons:

1. Mutual funds compete with each other on the basis of quarterly performance, which forces a short-term horizon and excludes some great opportunities.

2. The larger size of mutual fund portfolios precludes buying smaller companies, which often represent the greatest values.

3. Funds take greater company risk, which they then eliminate by unnecessary diversification. We buy safer stocks requiring less diversification and less expense.

4. Being forced to select from a universe of high-capitalization stocks, fund portfolios include mostly multinational companies with high U.S. dollar exposure and earnings heavily leveraged to the U.S. economy and American consumers.

5. Many funds then hedge the currency risk, unnecessarily increasing expenses and undermining our reasons for investing internationally in the first place.

6. Funds, to meet redemptions, are forced to trade, creating tax consequences.

7. Competition to show high short-term returns precludes buying solid value stocks that are out of favor and bargain-priced.

8. Fund management expenses reduce returns.

American Depositary Receipts (ADRs)

American depositary receipts were invented to make foreign investing in stocks easier for Americans and have succeeded in doing so. They are receipts for the shares of foreign-based corporations held in U.S. bank vaults, listed on U.S. stock exchanges, and entitling their owners to dividends and shareholder rights, such as voting rights and reports.

I do not advocate this way of investing for the simple reason that ADRs are issued only by the largest foreign companies. Nissan Motors and Sony are typical examples and don't represent the values and dividend yields you can find in a wider conservative universe. Also, banks incur costs in creating ADRs and sometimes keep part of the dividend to cover their services.

Another possible drawback is that the underlying companies that sponsor ADRs are subject to the sometimes excessive and stultifying regulation American companies must comply with, such as the laws passed in overreaction to Enron and other scandals. Many well-run foreign companies choose not to subject themselves to onerous and costly regulation when they can avoid it.

The best solution is to invest in ordinary shares traded on foreign markets. Those stocks offer the best values, and many earn their incomes from sources completely removed from the U.S. market. Not only will their earnings streams not suffer from a collapse in the United States, they will likely benefit as increased foreign purchasing power results in greater sales and a weaker dollar diminishes their raw material costs.

Pink Sheets

Many ordinary foreign shares, or ords, as they are commonly called, are also traded by market makers through the Pink Sheets (both terms are explained shortly), and unless you enjoy paying through the nose, I strongly advise you to stay away from them and the brokers that use them.

Pink Sheets LLC is a New Jersey company that provides daily bid and offer quotes from market makers. Market makers are broker-dealers acting in their capacity as dealers, that is, as principals trading for their own accounts, rather than as agents, which is the capacity in which brokers act when representing buyers and sellers. Quotes are printed on pink paper for foreign stocks and domestic over-the-counter stocks and on yellow paper for bonds.

The usual problem with market makers is that they work on the difference between a bid and an offer price, called the spread, and treat themselves generously. That problem is compounded with foreign stocks, many of which are priced under a dollar per share. Such pricing is very common as a matter of custom in the United Kingdom as well as most Asian markets, excluding Japan, and is not indicative of high risk as would be the case for penny stocks traded here in the United States. In addition, most Asian markets require shares to be traded in round lot minimums called "board lots"; the requirements range from as few as 100 shares to as many as 20,000 shares.

For example, suppose you wanted to buy a Hong Kong stock that last traded for the U.S. dollar equivalent of 20 cents per share. Also assume the board lot was 10,000 shares. Even though the share price was only 20 cents, the minimum dollar quantity of shares you would be allowed to trade would be $2,000 worth.

If you wanted to invest more, any additional investments would have to be made in increments of $2,000. That would hardly constitute a penny stock, but from the point of view of a market maker, that is exactly how the stock is treated. The Pink Sheets market maker might make a market of 15 cents bid, 25 cents offer. Therefore, in order to break even on the trade, if you buy on the offer and sell on the bid, the share price will have to appreciate by 50 percent. That's a tremendous amount of return to simply hand over to a faceless market maker merely for executing your trade. Trying to protect yourself by placing a price limit on your order won't work because the market maker simply will not fill your order until he can do so at what he considers to be a reasonable profit (and you or I would consider to be an obscene profit).

Adding insult to injury, on top of that spread, most discount brokers will also charge a hefty commission reserved for large quantity penny stock orders, which unfortunately is the category the stock in our example would likely, if unfairly, fall into.

So don't give your foreign stock order to any brokerage firm, discount or full-service, that will route it through a Pink Sheets market maker for execution. Not only will you get hosed on the price, but you'll potentially pay a fat commission on top of that. Stay away from the Pink Sheets, period.

Bottom Line

The key to my strategy for trading foreign stocks is to have your order executed directly on the foreign exchange that lists the stock you want to trade. That ensures you get the best price.

SELECTING THE RIGHT BROKER

To trade directly in foreign markets, you will need a broker that specializes in foreign stocks. Most brokerage firms do not even provide access to foreign stocks, while others restrict access to a few securities. Worse yet, access is typically limited to trading through domestic market makers on the Pink Sheets. As we have seen, not only is this an expensive way to do business, but you don't even know how expensive it is because firms are not required to disclose dealer spreads or markups. My own firm, Euro Pacific Capital, specializes in foreign investing and handles brokerage orders for direct execution on most of the world's exchanges.

As a personal note, you should know that I am not recommending the purchase of foreign stocks solely because that is what my firm specializes in. Rather, my firm specializes in foreign stocks because I genuinely believe it is a smart strategy to own foreign stock. Though the firm has been in business since 1980, I renamed it Euro Pacific Capital in 1996 to reflect its new focus on foreign securities, a direct result of the changing economic landscape that I envisioned.

Back then, I merely recommended adding foreign stocks as a means of portfolio diversification. However, as the stock market bubble inflated, and particularly as I watched the government and Federal Reserve take pains to postpone the eventual bursting, I became progressively bearish on U.S. assets, and began recommending that my client portfolios be more heavily weighted toward foreign securities.

A growing number of other firms have begun offering foreign stock services, though often with high minimum investments required, limited market and security access, and high commissions.

Another alternative you have, although usually not practical, is to open an account with a local broker in the country where the foreign stock exchange is located. The problems with this have to do with different time zones and odd hours, international telephone communications, foreign currency conversions, and in some cases a requirement that meetings with customers be face-to-face. On top of that is the need to open a different account in every country in which you might want to invest.

In general, the only possible financial advantages to speak of with this approach would be lower commissions. Most people prefer to have a knowledgeable, English-speaking broker in their own time zone, with all the protections, for what they are worth, afforded by a firm registered with the National Association of Securities Dealers.

Even the big full-service brokers, who have offices all over the world and would seem to be in the best position to trade directly on foreign exchanges, are not set up to handle foreign stock orders of small or even average size. They will handle a big order—something in six figures, say—but handling smaller foreign stock orders at competitive prices is not cost-effective for them. Securities and Exchange Commission (SEC) regulations regarding unregistered securities, related custody issues, and redundant stock symbols make foreign stock trading a cumbersome business for firms not specially set up to do it. Consequently, the big wire houses either won't take small orders or will take them and fill them as market makers at high markups that they are not required to disclose and at exchange rates that are exorbitant and also hidden.

Recently, online brokers have begun offering foreign stock trading services, but it is a very small part of the e-trade business, and added to the usual computer glitches are other problems. They usually trade through market makers, and when they don't they add custodial and settlement fees to the price you pay.

So the best solution is a broker specialized in foreign investing. I recommend Euro Pacific Capital (with a twinkle in my eye, although I do think we reach out to our customers to an extent unmatched), but if you go elsewhere always ask these five questions:

1. What exchange rate do I get? Currency conversion should cost you 10 to 15 basis points (a basis point is 0.01 percent)

but you're apt to be charged 1 percent to 3 percent. That's
a big difference and you'll never know you paid it.

2. Can I be certain my order will be executed directly on the
local foreign exchange, and not by a market maker in
the United States using the Pink Sheets?

3. Can I place limit orders (orders restricting execution to a
specified price or better) in foreign currencies?

4. Can I elect to receive dividends as well as proceeds from
sales directly in a foreign currency?

5. Are there minimum transaction amounts, special fees
for overseas orders, other hidden costs, or miscellaneous
fees? Please provide a list of all charges.

PUTTING THE FOREIGN STOCK PORTFOLIO TOGETHER: A TOP-DOWN APPROACH

Step 1: Creating a Cash Account

Setting some cash aside is always common sense, so why not
put the part you don't need for emergencies in foreign currency
where its value won't collapse?

Financial planners usually advise a cash fund equal to six
months of income, but this will vary depending on your circumstances. You should bear in mind that the invested part of your
portfolio will be liquid (convertible into cash in a matter of a
week or so, usually), but subject to the day-to-day vicissitudes
of market values.

You can purchase foreign currency CDs through domestic
banks, but your best bet would be to ask your broker to help
you buy a no-load mutual fund invested in foreign money market instruments, such as the Merk Hard Currency Fund. You

can also buy short-term government debt denominated in the foreign currency of your choice though brokers such as Euro Pacific. Then there is always the option of opening up a foreign bank account directly. This will involve some extra effort on your part, in some cases a personal trip to the foreign jurisdiction, but the added privacy and security benefits may be important enough to you to justify the hassle. Countries such as Switzerland, the Cayman Islands, Liechtenstein, Panama, Austria, and Luxembourg are the traditional favorites.

Step 2: Deciding What Markets to Invest In

The next question is: Which markets should we go for?

Since we're looking for conservative stocks, we don't want to jump from the frying pan into the fire. So we avoid emerging, developing markets and developed markets where there is any question of political risk.

As noted earlier, there are exciting speculative opportunities in markets where those risks exist and have been discounted, but my primary reason for recommending that we invest abroad in the first place is to protect ourselves from the risks inherent in the U.S. dollar. We want our money safe. So I am recommending that people structure a diversified portfolio of conservative stocks with high dividend yields in developed markets.

In North America, the action is in Canada, which, surprisingly, now has one of the best-positioned economies in the world. We'll be looking at industrial sectors as our next step, but Canada happens to be part of the natural resource block, which includes *Australia* and *New Zealand* and, to a lesser extent, *South Africa* and the Scandinavian countries, like *Norway*. I'll explain in a second why I think natural resources are a great sector to be in—as we say in the business, a great play.

Then there are the producing and saving Asian countries, which are the real growth engines. My two favorites there are *Hong Kong* and *Singapore*, followed by *Japan*. I would also put some money, but not as much, in *South Korea*, *Taiwan* (though government restrictions make this difficult), as well as *Thailand* and the *Philippines*, which are stable, developed countries, just a peg below the top tier.

The Asian economies, as discussed at length in the previous chapter, have all the ingredients of fertile investment soil: high growth rates, low taxes, a pro-business regulatory environment, a high savings rate, an educated populace, and a latent appetite for consumption easily equal to the task of supplanting the American market.

Certain of these economies will be more vulnerable than others to temporary internal dislocations as the purchasing power shifts from West to East, and such considerations will be factors in our investment timing and diversification decisions.

While the world in general will benefit greatly once it no longer has to bear the burden of supporting American consumers, there are those individuals and companies that benefit from the status quo at the expense of the broader global population. The political influence of these factions is in large part the reason the dollar has been supported to the extent that it has. The fortunes of such companies and the economies dominated by them will be negatively impacted in the short run. Those companies that can retool and refocus their efforts will thrive, while those that cannot will fail.

The companies that fail, however, will liberate resources, such as land, labor, and capital that will be combined in more effective ways by entrepreneurs that follow them and that will thrive in revitalized economies. After the initial hiccup, those economies most affected by the initial disruptions will boom, benefiting from the higher standard of living that will result from a more efficient allocation of resources and from enhanced domestic consumption.

Therefore, the initial impact of a dollar collapse will be most disruptive in Asia, while Europe will be affected to a much lesser extent. As a result, in the short run, non-Asian markets might do better, but in the long run Asia has the most to gain from the dollar's collapse. The Asian economies bear the bulk of the cost of subsidizing the U.S economy, and they have the most to gain when those subsidies stop.

Europe can basically be divided into two distinct markets. First there's the *Euro zone*, which consists of the 12 countries that share the euro, namely *Austria, Belgium, Finland, France, Germany, Greece, Ireland, Italy, Luxembourg, the Netherlands, Portugal,* and *Spain*. The second European market consists of select countries outside the Euro zone (or Euro block or Euro land as it is also called), which currently would include *Switzerland* and the *United Kingdom*, where you get the ever-sturdy Swiss franc and the pound sterling.

One of the biggest attractions of the euro is that it is seen as the most likely candidate to replace the dollar as the reserve currency. If that happens, the added demand for euros will help contain inflation and interest rates in Europe, providing a boost to its economies and asset markets.

Step 3: Attractive Industrial Sectors for Conservative Investors

Electric, oil, and gas utilities are attractive equity investments because they have a captive audience and enjoy constant high demand, their earnings are predictable because they can raise their rates, and they pay consistently high dividends. Because of their safety and consistency and the way they behave in the marketplace, utility stocks are sometimes called bond substitutes. But they pay better than bonds.

Utility investments are available everywhere as both stocks and bonds. Canada also has special business trusts, a form of income trust offering tax advantages along with high yields. However, due to recently proposed changes to Canadian tax law, those trusts could lose some of those advantages in the future.

Real estate, especially when it can be owned in the form of property trusts, as it can in most mature foreign markets, has both high yield and tax advantages. I prefer property trusts that are mostly commercial, such as those invested in industrial office buildings and shopping centers.

When you're buying property trusts, you're really not in the stock market; you're in the real estate market, and the rents are coming to you in the form of dividends. What's good about it is that you have diversification, immediate liquidity, lower transaction costs, and professional management, and you don't have to worry about collecting rents or getting insurance. It's a very convenient and easy way to buy real estate, particularly if it's halfway around the world.

Commodities and natural resources, which can be bought as stock or, in Canada, as tax-advantaged royalty trusts, in addition to offering attractive dividends are exciting economic plays.

I am particularly bullish on commodities. The supply and demand imbalances when it comes to natural resources are substantial, the result of years of underinvestment in capacity and exploration combined with overutilization, a natural by-product of their having such low prices.

For example, because oil was cheap for a long time the SUV came into being. It was only because everybody thought oil products would be cheap forever that nobody cared about gasoline prices. And that's what happens. When prices are low and people think they're going to stay low forever, the incentive to conserve is absent. For their part, producers, forecasting low prices as far out as they can see, have no incentive to invest in additional capacity. So low prices, if widely expected to persist, practically guarantee that high prices will eventually ensue.

We are currently in a major bull market in commodities. Commodity raw materials were in a bear market from 1980 to 2000, the exact opposite of the bull market in financial assets. As financial assets peaked, commodities troughed. So now people are moving out of claims to wealth into actual stuff—out of paper assets into physical materials, such as commodities.

But another reason I'm so bullish on raw materials is that I am looking at demand patterns and how they have changed over time. And right now, the biggest consumers in the world are Americans. Americans have a lot of things. For example, most Americans have a washing machine, a refrigerator, and at least one automobile. These things use a lot of steel, to be sure, and as they wear out they are replaced. But a replacement market is not an expanding market. Demands on our raw materials are not increasing the way they would be if we were an expanding market.

The other thing we do is consume a lot of gadgets, such as cell phones, digital cameras, and things of that sort. But gadgets like these are not resource-intensive.

So the United States may be the world's largest consumer, but the mix of products we consume is not making the same demands on our natural resources and raw materials as would be the case if we were a less mature society.

Now my thinking is that as the dollar collapses, the currencies that will rise the most will be Asian, particularly Chinese. When the focus of global consumption moves east and the world's producers strive to satisfy their own demand as opposed to ours, the type of products Asian consumers want will be far more natural resources–intensive than those currently in high demand here in the United States.

So I think we're going to see tremendous demand for the raw materials necessary to satisfy the demands of the far wealthier emerging Asian economies, once their full purchasing power is finally unleashed.

Commodities, natural resources, raw materials—all names for one sector—are therefore a great play in my judgment, and one of the beauties of this sector is that we kill two birds with one stone. Not only do we get the exposure to the sector, but we also get the exceptional dividends that the companies in this sector typically pay.

Normally, in foreign investing there is some trade-off between exposure and dividend yield. Here we can have our cake and eat it, too. Many Canadian oil and gas companies pay dividends of 12 percent to 15 percent. Coal producers pay dividends averaging something like 11 percent, and companies mining nickel, zinc, and lead are paying 7 percent to 10 percent.

Step 4: Selecting Particular Stocks

Having decided what sectors we want to be in, we can begin the process of individual stock selection. Our basic criteria, which are safety and yield, will narrow any field down considerably, and the rest of the process is applying valuation tools and doing, or obtaining, other fundamental research. This part of the process involves a bottom-up approach, a focus. Solid, well-managed, aggressive companies can do well even when the industries they are in are doing poorly.

In this connection, I want to mention an important category of stocks that falls between the categories of sector and company.

Special situations, although not a sector in the strict sense, always exist as opportunities to be stumbled upon. I'm talking here about stocks that have been around for a while and have good management, but, for whatever reason, are out of favor or simply being ignored. Interestingly, the number of companies that go off the radar screen like that but are basically sound and available at bargain prices has increased as the mutual funds and other managers competing on the basis of quarterly performance stop buying them and stop following them. You just have to find them, and they can be anywhere or in any kind of business.

What we won't be buying are companies that have significant exposure to the United States. Those companies will be good candidates to buy after the dollar collapses and their stock prices fall as a result of lost export sales. However, those countries most exposed are also the ones most likely to see the greatest gains in their currencies.

So the key here is to have exposure to the foreign currency through companies that generate their revenues in their own local markets (a Japanese retailer would be an example), not by exporting to the United States. This way, we earn currency profits while avoiding losses, and perhaps even seeing gains, in the underlying share prices. We can then use appreciated foreign currencies to buy the exporters' stock when the time is ripe, which would be after they take their lumps from the collapsed American market and their shares are cheap. Of course, the beaten-down exporters will be all upside potential when enriched Asian consumers emerge to replace impoverished Americans.

FINDING VALUE AND FINANCIAL VIABILITY IN COMPANIES

Securities analysis will never replace fly-fishing as a leisure-time activity, and if you already know the basics of it, you might want to skip this section.

Once we have identified buying opportunities abroad, which is what foreign securities brokers like Euro Pacific Capital specialize in doing, the problem becomes deciding which companies are the best values, have the strongest balance sheets, and are most likely to increase earnings and dividend payouts in the future.

My firm, of course, uses professional analysts, but it is important that investors understand basic analysis and valuation tools so they can understand the language of research reports, corporate financial information, and financial news.

Fundamental analysis is concerned with financial statistics. It gets into analysis of the balance sheets and income statements of companies in order to establish financial strength and forecast earnings. Fundamental analysts look at assets, earnings, sales, expenses, products, management, markets, and market-share statistics to predict future profitability and determine whether a stock is undervalued or overvalued at current prices and relative to industry norms.

Using a variety of tools and techniques as well as reading corporate reports and interviewing managers, fundamental analysts try to answer such questions as:

- Is management up to the challenges it faces? Are there any succession problems? Are there any imminent changes in senior management?

- Is the balance sheet strong enough, that is, liquid enough to pay current obligations, and not overloaded with debt?

- Are sales and revenues increasing and is the company gaining share in a viable market?

- Are expenses under control?

- Are any major capital expenditures being planned? If so, how are they going to be financed? (An issuance of additional stock might cause dilution, a given increment of earnings spread over more shares, resulting in lower earnings per share.)

- Did any special events affect last year's earnings?
- Are earnings per share increasing?
- Is the company's share price higher or lower than it should be relative to earnings per share?
- To what extent are the company's operations multinational? What is the exposure to foreign currency and political risks?

The annual reports of companies are good sources of information and are now available along with other stockholder information on the Internet. Just pull up the company.

You should be familiar with the following financial ratios:

Ratios That Measure Corporate Liquidity

Current ratio: This balance sheet ratio divides current assets by current liabilities. It measures the extent to which a company's short-term creditors are covered by assets expected to be converted into cash within a year or less. Generally speaking, a ratio of 2 would be conservative, although much depends on the kind of company and the composition of its current assets. The more liquid the asset mix, the better.

Quick ratio: This refines the current ratio by excluding inventory, the least readily salable current asset. The quick ratio, sometimes called the acid-test ratio, divides current liabilities into cash and equivalents plus accounts receivable. Ideally, this ratio would be 1.

Ratios That Measure Profitability

Operating profit margin: This is net operating profits divided by net sales. It is key to measuring a firm's operating efficiency because it reflects purchasing and pricing policies and control of costs and expenses directly associated with the running of the business and the creation of sales. It excludes other income and expenses, interest, taxes, and depreciation. This ratio is meaningful when compared to different periods or to industry norms.

Net profit margin: You get this by dividing net income by net sales, and it measures management's overall efficiency. In other words, it goes beyond operating efficiency and measures management's success in borrowing money at favorable rates, investing idle cash, and taking advantage of tax benefits. Businesses that work on volume (the quick nickel as opposed to the slow dollar) will have lower net profit margins.

Return on equity: Divide net income by stockholders' equity. It is the bottom line as a percentage of the money shareholders have invested. The higher the better, as long as it doesn't invite competition.

Ratios That Measure Leverage

Debt to total assets: Here total liabilities are divided by total assets to measure the proportion of assets financed with debt as opposed to equity. Owners usually like a high ratio because it means they are being financed with other people's money. Banks and other lenders like a low ratio because it is a cushion in the event of liquidation.

Long-term debt to total capitalization: This takes total long-term debt (bonds and term loans from other lenders) and divides it by total long-term debt plus stockholders' equity. It measures the portion of permanent financing that is debt as opposed to equity. Where the ratio is low, it might benefit the company's owners to issue bonds rather than stock or otherwise to increase its leverage.

Debt to equity (debt ratio): This most basic of ratios divides total liabilities by total stockholders' equity and measures the reliance on creditors, short- and long-term, to finance total assets. A high debt ratio makes borrowing difficult and a low ratio makes owners feel assured they will be protected in liquidation, since assets tend to shrink.

Fixed-charge coverage: Earnings before taxes and interest charges divided by interest charges plus lease payments results in a figure showing how many times fixed charges are covered by earnings. Put another way, it tells the extent to which earnings could shrink before the company is unable to meet its contractual interest and lease payments. Failure to meet interest payments is an event of default in most debt agreements. The ratio is sometimes calculated using interest charges only.

Ratios That Measure Stock Values

Price to earnings: Popularly called the P/E, this ratio is the market price of a share divided by the earnings per share, computed using the previous 12 months (trailing P/E) or, less commonly, estimated (projected) 12-month earnings (forward P/E). It reflects the value the market puts on a company's earnings and on the prospect of future earnings. The ratio is most meaningful when compared to those of other companies of the same type and size.

Price to book value: The market price of a share divided by the book value per share, excluding intangible assets, provides an indication of whether a company is over- or undervalued by the market relative to its net asset value. Since the basic rules of accounting require that inventories be carried on the books at the lower of cost or market value, and fixed assets, such as plant and equipment, are carried at their depreciated value, which may be more or less than their market value, the ratio is only the roughest measure of what shares would be worth in the event of liquidation. Having said that, though, there is no other ratio that relates share value to asset value, and a relatively (compared to similar companies) low price-to-book ratio might well be a sign of value and warrant closer analysis.

Price to sales: This ratio is market price per share divided by sales and revenues per share. It is preferred by some analysts to the P/E ratio because whereas earnings are subject to accounting methodology and are affected by a multitude of variables, sales and revenues tend to be less volatile and a more reliable indication of how successfully a company is competing in its marketplace.

Dividend payout: By dividing dividends per common share by earnings per common share, we learn what percentage of its earnings a company pays out in dividends. As a general rule, the more mature a company is, the higher its dividend payout ratio is, since rapidly growing companies tend to reinvest their earnings to finance growth. Utilities and property trusts usually have high dividend payout ratios.

Dividend yield: This is the company's annual dividend as a percentage of its market price. It is calculated by taking the company's most recently reported quarterly dividend and annualizing it, that is, multiplying it by four, then dividing by the market price per share. Dividend yield, as discussed previously, is the cash-on-the-barrelhead reward for owning a company's stock and is the basic feature of all the stocks I own.

WHAT I HOPE YOU HAVE LEARNED IN THIS CHAPTER

I hope I have convinced you that with relative simplicity and convenience, you can have a diversified portfolio of conservative foreign equities and earn an annual dividend yield of around 8 percent. Although the progress of all equity investments should be periodically confirmed as a matter of course, stocks of the caliber we've been talking about will probably never need to be sold and will provide a lifetime of increasing income. That income, particularly when augmented by rises in the value of the principal producing it, will likely offset declines in the purchasing power of the U.S. dollar and concomitant increases in the domestic cost of living.

Foreign equities also provide a hedge against foreign inflation, which, although much more moderate than domestic inflation, will still be a persistent force, robbing savers and investors of purchasing power over time.

I have stressed the importance of opening an account with a broker, like Euro Pacific Capital, that specializes in foreign markets and can help you structure a portfolio tailored to whatever might be unique about your objectives, risk tolerance, and financial situation.

Bear in mind, however, that the warnings and information contained in this book are wasted if you do not put my recommendations into action.

The U.S. economy has been pushing its luck, and short of winning some nonexistent cosmic lottery there is no conceivable way it can repay its debt and correct its trade imbalances without a collapse in its living standards followed by an agonizing period of sacrifice and rebuilding. I have shown you how you can protect your wealth, profit from the reconstruction, and in the event the U.S. economy does win that mythical lottery and avert disaster, still be better off than you would be had you stayed in dollar-denominated investments.

So don't wait! Don't wait another day.

2009 UPDATE

Think of Chapters 8 through 10 as a three-legged stool. Your stock portfolio, your holdings of gold and precious metals, and your liquidity are mutually dependent parts of my strategy for preserving and enhancing your wealth in the face of the economic collapse I predicted in *Crash Proof*. As I've been saying repeatedly, even with all that's happened, the real collapse remains ahead of us. This is still the overture; the opera itself hasn't even started. No fat lady is going to sing until the dollar hits its bottom. Since mid-2008 it's been rising more than falling, although I expect a clear bear market trend to resume shortly, probably before this revision is published.

Nothing has happened since I wrote Crash Proof *to change my outlook on the dollar or my recommendation that the average investor should have a portfolio of non-dollar-denominated dividend-paying stocks in fundamentally sound foreign economies that can be bought and held for the long term. In fact, everything that has happened between the time I wrote Chapter 8 in late 2006 and now has only reinforced my conviction. The fact that stocks have fallen in price while the dollar has gained value only means my advice to buy is even more timely now, despite the fact that many of my forecasts have already come true and that the collapse I envision is clearly well under way. It's like having the opportunity to buy fire insurance after the fire has already started, and at better rates then those who had the foresight to insure in advance!*

So what more needs to be said? Nothing, really, except that my critics continue to point to foreign market declines in 2008 as evidence that my recommendation to buy equities abroad was misguided, and my thesis that foreign economies can thrive even as the U.S. economy flounders, otherwise known as decoupling, is no longer valid.

Of course I totally disagree, but perhaps an explanation of why I do will be instructive. Their first mistake was to focus on one leg of the stool, this one, and ignore the others. But there are other problems.

The Background

Because my success in predicting the collapse caused a surge in publicity that raised my visibility and at times made it seem as though I fancied myself as some kind of clairvoyant, I became a sitting duck for media critics who, although totally off the mark with their own rosy forecasts, saw in me a poetic justice story with just one piece tantalizingly missing: "Doomsayer Peter Schiff, who saw the economic collapse coming when others didn't, may have been right about that, but he was dead wrong about. . . ." When foreign stocks tanked in 2008, they saw their chance to fill in the blank and seized on that as evidence that my investment recommendations were as wrong as my economic predictions had been right. Even the *Wall Street Journal* chimed in with a January 30th, 2009 article entitled "Right Forecast by Schiff, Wrong Plan?"

Of course, more disingenuous still was criticism from other investment professionals, whose long-term investment track records left much to be desired. Embarrassed by their own failure to see this crisis coming, they were quick to throw stones at one of the few who did, despite the fact that they did so from their own very fragile glass houses.

The Long and Short of It

The simple truth is that my critics and I are in totally different conversations and that should be the end of it. They are working within a short-term horizon whereas *Crash Proof* is emphatically based on a long-term, buy-and-hold strategy. For *Crash Proof* investors, an isolated bad year is an opportunity to add portfolio value. It is good news, not bad news. Using foreign stock performance in 2008 to make judgments about my investment strategy is like using a broom to brush your teeth. A broom is a form of brush and both are for cleaning, but it's a nonstarter.

People looking for short-term ways to capitalize on the crisis had plenty of options, although they had nothing to do with these chapters. They would include shorting stocks or buying puts on stocks of home builders, automakers, financial services companies, retailers, and other businesses likely to have tough sledding. People who shorted subprime mortgage paper in 2007, as some of our clients did based on my recommendation, or as others might have done based solely on what they learned about the coming real estate debacle by reading my book, obviously made out very well when the mortgage market imploded.

In fact, the only way to have made money in 2008 was short selling. But that's another book for another writer. *Crash Proof* is subtitled "How to Profit from the Coming Economic Collapse", not "How to Profit from the Coming Stock Market Collapse." The economic collapse is still in its early stages, its progress being delayed in ways that only ensures greater devastation when the process concludes. I'm, confident that by the time it does, the *Crash Proof* subtitle will live up to its billing.

As a broker, I generally referred short sellers to discount brokers, although some of my clients used their Euro Pacific accounts to short stocks, typically financials and home builders, as they were my favorite shorts. However, my main way of adding value is providing a mechanism by which people can get access to the types of stocks that I think in the long run will deliver the best performance and that will protect them from the collapse of the dollar. Very few of my clients bought on margin or were otherwise engaged in speculation. My advice in *Crash Proof* is for conservative ordinary investors positioning themselves ahead of the storm.

I did make one somewhat more aggressive recommendation in *Crash Proof*. I suggested that people who could not sell homes they owned outright or had substantial equity in, and who were willing to assume the risk, consider getting a mortgage that locked in a low fixed rate and using the proceeds to buy high-dividend-paying foreign stocks. Home loans are not subject to margin calls unless you stop making your payments. Obviously, if somebody locked in a good 30-year mortgage and bought foreign stocks, even though the stocks may be down now and some dividends may have been reduced, the dividends should still provide ample cash flow to meet mortgage payments.

2008 and *Crash Proof*

My comments updating Chapter 1 noted that 2008 was a year when, paradoxically and irrationally, the dollar reversed a steep decline and strongly rallied. Foreign stocks, reacting to growing financial turmoil in the United States, dropped sharply as I had predicted they initially would, but with the rising dollar turning currency gains into losses, portfolios had total returns that were, on paper, substantially negative.

Investors who had been following my advice in *Crash Proof*, however, not only were prepared to hold, but they also had liquidity in the form of cash on the sidelines. They could thus add to their positions at fire sale prices with the additional benefit of stronger dollars, thus twice enhancing their portfolios' value. In addition, those who did not need their dividends to meet current expenses could reinvest them at more favorable prices.

Sadly, others who might have bought earlier sold to preserve diminishing paper profits while still others who fully invested near the top might have sold to cut their losses. Whether they sold because they panicked or because they needed to raise cash, those investors could have reduced or avoided losses had they taken my advice to be less than fully invested and preserved some liquidity or remained focused on the long-term big picture, rather than be distracted by short-term volatility.

As you'll soon be reading, in 2006 under the Chapter 10 subhead, "How Much Liquidity Is Desirable?" I wrote, "The investment recommendations I made in Chapters 8 and 9 are investments you would continue to hold for income (excepting bullion) and would not want to cash in when their prices are temporarily off because markets are adjusting to economic shocks. . . . Depending on the outlook at the time you read this book, you might want to expand the liquid portion of your portfolio beyond what would cover personal emergencies . . . to take advantage of the opportunities likely to occur during the adjustment period."

That quote, by acknowledging the prospect of economic shocks and stressing the importance of holding, not selling, clearly confirms both my long-term investment focus and my realistic understanding that short-term challenges should be expected. Both themes are repeatedly expressed throughout *Crash Proof*, yet completely ignored by my critics. It is also interesting that those who were so quick to jump on the "criticize Peter Schiff's investment strategy" bandwagon were also among the most vocal critics of my dire economic forecasts prior to their coming true. In the end, these critics will look just as foolish dismissing my investment strategy as they now look having dismissed my economic forecasts.

I'll admit I was surprised by how sharply the dollar rallied as the crisis I warned about first began to play out. I was also surprised, although the two dynamics were related, that foreign stocks dropped as much as they did. Surprised, however, doesn't mean unprepared. I had established that the fundamentals of the developed, producing foreign economies I had been recommending were sound. I knew that decoupling would eventually take place, but that the transition would take time and initially cause problems for those foreign economies supplying us with credit and products. And I had prepared investors for surprises by stressing the importance of liquidity as an integral part of my survival strategy.

Other Issues I Have with My Critics

Having reduced my three-part survival strategy to foreign stocks investing, my critics proceeded to claim that foreign stocks took a worse hit than domestic stocks in 2008, categorically giving my investment judgment a thumbs-down.

Any way you look at it, foreign stocks saw a substantial sell-off in 2008. But comparing the relative performance of foreign and domestic stocks is a tricky business, getting into questions of the comparability of different indexes, the timing of comparisons, and what factors comprise returns.

On average, foreign stocks got hit harder than domestic stocks when you factor currency losses into the figures you're comparing, the more so as the dollar gained strength during the period. Depending on when somebody read *Crash Proof* and followed the advice, the foreign stock portfolio may have been down more in dollar terms than a diversified portfolio of U.S. stocks, a point of possible but slight relevance in cases where investors replaced diversified domestic portfolios with foreign stocks. That the dollar had fallen to new lows several months before publication of *Crash Proof* explains why the dollar bounced so high in the second half of 2008 and foreign stocks, which had risen on the weakness of the dollar, dropped so sharply.

Another notable factor was the incredible outperformance of foreign stocks over American stocks in the eight years prior to 2008. Given such a run, it's only natural that they would experience a greater fall. However, judging the effectiveness of my strategy of investing in foreign rather than domestic stocks (something I have done for the past 10 years) based solely on 2008 is absurd. Thus far, 2009 is shaping up to be another year of foreign stock outperformance, a trend that I expect to continue for another decade or longer.

Of course, no pains were taken by my critics to note such mitigating factors, but it hardly matters since they had little or no relevance to my investment recommendations in the first place. I recommended foreign stocks because they got investors out of what I forecast to be a collapsing dollar, bear market rallies notwithstanding; because they paid better dividends and would have the additional benefit of currency profits; and because they were based in fundamentally strong economies that would ultimately decouple and enjoy substantial growth. The fact that when stocks dropped, they got very cheap in Asia but never really got cheap in the United States (cheap referring to comparable valuations at bear market bottoms) confirms that *Crash Proof* investors are in the right place for finding value. Otherwise, the foregoing discussion of price comparisons has little application to what I'm doing. Prices matter only when you sell, but my strategy is about holding. What happened in 2008 was that prices went down while earnings and dividends dropped to a much lesser extent, so their multiples got compressed. Only a fool would sell in that market. But *Crash Proof* is about not having to sell and having the liquidity and dividend income to buy when such rare opportunities present themselves.

As you will read, I clearly noted in Chapter 10 that "those who followed my advice and put their dollars into high-yielding investments in foreign currencies may see temporary pullbacks, but will be well positioned for the longer run." My entire thesis is long-term-oriented, and since my critics still do not understand the long-term challenges facing our economy it is no wonder that they fail to appreciate my investment strategy.

So much for my critics.

The Outlook for Foreign Stocks

As I write this in early 2009, foreign stocks are still a bargain, although by the time this revision is published my guess is the bargains will no longer be as great. Depending on when you're reading this book, it is possible that 2008 losses will have been completely erased. If you're lucky, the dollar could still be high then, and if foreign stocks have still not recovered, it will be a great time to buy. In any event, I recommend buying foreign stocks, so long as valuations are attractive, even if less so than at current levels.

I don't think we're going to see a repeat of 2008, in which people mistakenly think decoupling is not going to happen, that the rest of the world is in worse shape financially and economically than the United States, and that the dollar is a safe haven. The world fell once already for the old head fake and everybody started running in the wrong direction, but it's highly unlikely they will make the same mistake twice. The world is rapidly waking up to reality.

But a global depression, which I just don't see happening, is still being factored into the economic analysis, and that means opportunity. We are already seeing signs of decoupling, and when it happens you're going to see real prosperity in the producing countries. I'm talking prosperity and growth unlike anything we could imagine when those nations had their wings freighted with the United States' excessive debt and trade imbalances. And if you think our debt was excessive then, just wait.

When foreign stocks dropped, one of the drivers was that everybody was running away from assets and from risk generally and getting into the perceived safety of cash and U.S. Treasuries, which they regarded as a default-free cash equivalent. They were paying off debt and were raising cash to fund redemptions and meet margin calls. They weren't concerned with yield as long as they didn't have to worry about asset prices falling. As I've discussed in other chapters, people were focused on numerical value, the amount of dollars or Treasuries they had, not what those dollars would ultimately be worth in purchasing power.

But, as noted elsewhere, that's about to go into reverse, with people stampeding *out* of depreciating currency and equivalents and back into dividend-yielding assets. Nobody's going to want to sell; everybody's going to want to buy, and prices of foreign stocks are going to go straight up.

You can't wait for that condition to happen, though. You have to act in advance. So that's one reason I didn't recommend staying in all cash. I said you have to have assets because the risk of holding all cash is too great. What if I had told people to stay in cash and the dollar had collapsed sooner rather than later? They would be broke and have no real wealth left to preserve. In hindsight it is very easy to know exactly what should have been done. However, without such knowledge, you have to prepare for the most probable outcome and safeguard against the most devastating consequences. So I recommended foreign stocks with enough liquidity retained for emergencies and bargain buying.

Readers of my other book, *The Little Book of Bull Moves in Bear Markets* (John Wiley & Sons, 2008), which was more prescriptive in its recommendations, can be assured that my enthusiasm for commodities stocks, such as copper, lead, nickel, agriculture, and energy, is stronger than ever with a resurgence in demand and limited capacity promising higher prices and huge gains. I am certain that the recent sharp decline in commodity prices will reverse, and that bull markets will return stronger then ever. As the world's producers begin making more for themselves and less for us, they will demand even more basic commodities, while recent capacity reductions will further limit supply. The fact that many commodity producers were badly burned during the recent downturn and credit crunch means they will be hesitant to add new capacity until they see much higher prices sustained for prolonged time periods. Once inflation is thrown into the mix, it will be the perfect storm.

One interesting bit of irony is that *The Little Book of Bull Moves in Bear Markets* received some criticism as I wrote it at the height of the recent rise in both commodities and foreign stocks and at the low point for the dollar. Critics tried to discredit the book based on how poorly my investment recommendations performed between the time I wrote the book and its publication in October of 2008. However, October 2008 marked the low point for both foreign stocks and commodities and the peak in the dollar, and judging an investment book based on how poorly its strategy performed before it was published makes no sense at all. Apart from the fact that my advice was long-term oriented, anyone who actually bought *The Little Book* and followed its advice is sitting on some fat short-term gains as this is being written. If these trends persist, *The Little Book* may well end up being the best-timed investment book ever written!

People new to *Crash Proof* and still in U.S. stocks have a great opportunity now to take tax losses on still overpriced domestic stocks and buy foreign stocks at bargain prices. As I observed earlier, the fact that U.S. stocks have performed so poorly over the past decade has led many to jump to the false conclusion that buy-and-hold investing does not work. Nothing could be further from the truth. It's overpaying for low-yielding stocks and holding and hoping for speculative gains that does not work. If you buy value and collect high dividends, you can hold quality stocks forever and make out like a bandit.

My greatest fear is that people who stayed in cash and think they did the right thing based on 2008 will stay in cash too long and watch their cash lose its purchasing power. For now those still holding cash feel like they dodged a bullet. However, what they fail to realize is that they are standing on a land mine!

9

How to Survive and Thrive, Step 2: Gold Rush—Be the First Person on Your Block to Stake a Claim

Buzzwords and catchphrases come and go, but one I especially liked was *Goldilocks economy*, a term the "new era" crowd coined in the 1990s to describe the utopian result of the Federal Reserve's mastery, at long last, of monetary fine-tuning.

Like the porridge sampled by the ironically named Goldilocks, the economy, as then perceived, was not too hot, not too cold, but just right.

Significantly, the porridge belonged to a family of bears, whose growls of displeasure when they got home sent Goldilocks running back into the forest. Had Alan Greenspan been similarly dispatched, I might not be writing this book.

In Chapter 3, I explained why gold- and silver-backed money substitutes, once replaced with nonredeemable fiat money ("IOU nothings"), removed the restraint preventing central banks from creating inflation and debasing currencies. As I have argued throughout this book, the most egregious case in point has been our own Federal Reserve, whose misguided monetary policy following abandonment of the international gold standard in 1971 has brought the dollar to the brink of collapse.

In this chapter, I discuss various ways of capitalizing on the bull market in gold, and also in silver, which has its own attractions, and suggest how these precious metals can add both safety and exciting growth potential to the conservative foreign stock portfolio covered in Chapter 8.

First, however, I want to explain why I think gold, which has already risen in price from a low of around $255 an ounce in January 2000 to a recent high of over $700 an ounce, is at the beginning of a bull market and is poised to rise substantially, perhaps spectacularly, higher. The reasons go well beyond gold's traditional attractiveness as a safe haven when the dollar and financial assets lose value. *There is a good possibility gold will be reinstated as official money by governments or, in a scenario made plausible by modern technology, by a private sector determined to have sound money even if politically driven governments resist it.*

WHY GOLD IS SUBSTANTIALLY UNDERVALUED AT PRESENT LEVELS

Even with its impressive recent gains as the dollar has fallen, gold remains extremely undervalued in my opinion. Here's why I think so.

Gold is not currently functioning as money. The significance of this is that whenever money has been based on gold, which it

was at least somewhere in the world continuously between 2500
B.C. and just 35 years ago, gold has enjoyed a monetary premium.

The monetary premium, the higher price it commands by
having a monetary function in addition to its commodity value,
shows up when there is an expectation that gold will be reinsti-
tuted as money. For example, when inflation was rampant and
openly acknowledged at the end of 1979 and gold was nearing
its all-time high of $877 per ounce, it had a ratio to copper that
if applied in mid-April 2006 would have given it a price of over
$1,500 an ounce instead of $625 an ounce.

As this is written in late August 2006, gold does not reflect
any monetary premium, an eloquent comment on the government's success in hiding real inflation and the public's misplaced
confidence in paper money.

What happened was that after Fed chairman Paul Volcker
declared war on inflation in the 1980s, the world began to forget why gold became money in the first place and became completely complacent and trusting of central bankers. It can almost
literally be said that the newfound skill and power of central
bankers, in the so-called new era unfolding, became "good as
gold" as the public misperceived it. Alan Greenspan, who succeeded Volcker in 1987, became a personage tantamount to a
deity, the personal embodiment of that misplaced trust. After
his retirement in 2006, no lesser an eminence than Queen Eliza-
beth II conferred on him an honorary position as adviser to the
Treasury in the United Kingdom. Not bad for a boy who started
out on clarinet and sax.

Between 1980 and 2000, in a process that fed on itself, investors began losing interest in gold, which paid no cash return, and
turned to paper assets like stocks and bonds that paid dividends
and interest. As gold prices fell and offered negative returns,
paper assets rose, and as the difference became more dramatic,
gold went increasingly out of favor. Central banks, which have

always held gold as part of their reserves, saw prices falling and began selling or leasing gold into the market, diminishing their gold reserves and making the demonetization of gold virtually complete.

As the 1990s wore on, gold and financial assets continued to move in opposite directions, with gold finally washing out and financial assets peaking at unrealistic levels.

But other dynamics had been at work while the bear market in gold progressed. There was very little money going into the gold market for exploration or anything else. Moreover, with prices falling, many of the producers were hedging, further depressing the price and making gold uneconomical to mine. Mining companies found difficulty borrowing money to operate. Before granting a loan, banks were requiring that they hedge even though the prices were low. The equity markets for financing were unavailable because nobody had any capital for the gold sector.

With so little going into exploration for a period of 10 years or so, no significant global supply was added. Mine production in South Africa, for one example, is now at an all-time record low. New production will take many years to come on stream, especially where the process has to start at the exploration phase. So there is a huge supply and demand imbalance in the gold market.

WHY DEMAND IS ABOUT TO EXPLODE

So the long bear market in gold ended in the early 2000s, concurrently with the end of the long bull market in stocks. As previously noted, gold bottomed out at around $255 an ounce and reached $725 in May of 2006, then had a technical pullback and has mostly traded over $600 since June. Here's why I think the bull market in gold is just beginning:

Our experiment in fiat currency and the complacency that went with it has run its course. Gold is now gaining value against all the world's currencies and the world's savers are waking up to the fact that the central bankers, including not just the Federal Reserve, but also the Bank of England, the Bank of Japan, the European Central Bank (ECB), and others, have been creating inflation and debasing currencies. As that sinks in, more people are going to be rediscovering gold as sound money, as a safe haven, as a store of value, and as a medium of exchange. Once that starts to happen, you'll begin to see the premium of money being built back into gold.

Sure, there will always be those who say gold is a "barbaric relic," that gold standards don't work, and that there's not enough gold to make a monetary system viable. That's all nonsense. Scarcity is what gives gold its value, and price structures will adjust to reflect the money supply. Governments themselves will naturally resist a return to the gold standard because it forces discipline they don't want. It forces them to make a choice: get more gold, reduce spending, or raise taxes.

The modern world has never been better positioned to use gold as a medium of exchange than it is right now.

Back in the early days, if you wanted to use gold you had to either carry it around or store it with a goldsmith and obtain a receipt; for smaller transactions, you had to use lesser metals, copper as in pennies, nickel as in nickels, and silver as in dimes, quarters, half-dollars, and, optionally, dollars. You couldn't break gold down beyond a certain point.

But today, with the Internet and with debit cards, it has never been easier for the world to transact in precious metals. If gold could have been money in years past when we didn't have the technology to make it convenient, imagine how well it would work today. This is the best of all worlds for the gold standard.

If governments don't want to reinstitute gold standards, private citizens will do it on their own. What I expect will happen ultimately is that financial institutions, such as a European bank, or other companies, such as Brink's, will emerge that are reliable depositories of gold and, in conjunction with Visa or MasterCard, will offer the opportunity to hold deposits in bullion.

Already, Americans who travel around Europe can walk into a restaurant and have a meal for 200 euros, then whip out a credit card and pay with it even though they don't have any euros in their bank account. The reason that's possible is that when the card company gets the bill, it does a currency conversion and takes enough dollars out of that account to settle the euro bill.

So it's just going a small step further to imagine how someone with 200 ounces of gold bullion on deposit with a company issuing a credit card could walk into a restaurant and have dinner and when the bill was presented, which could be in any currency, have their account debited the grams of gold equal to the exchange rate of the currency in which the bill was presented. Being a cyber transaction, there would not be a problem breaking down a bar of gold since the service company would simply charge your account and keep track of the amount of gold remaining.

As governments realize that citizens have the option of doing business privately in gold as an alternative to holding currency and watching it be debased, they will be under pressure to manage their economies more responsibly.

So I think individuals will start moving to these gold standards, and nations might follow. Officially or unofficially, the function of gold as money will be restored. The result will be an explosion of demand and, with supply as low as it is, gold prices will rise dramatically.

Other countries with troubled currencies may turn to gold rather than stronger fiat currencies. Once countries, such as Argentina, Venezuela, and Russia in the recent past, see the mighty dollar has gone the way of the Mexican peso, they will tend to avoid fiat currencies in general and move to gold.

The dollar's problems will expose all the fiat currencies as prone to monetary mismanagement and invite the observation that if the dollar can be debased, so can the euro or the yen. Countries like the aforementioned that have traditionally turned to the dollar during times of monetary crisis have failed to understand they were trading one worthless fiat currency for another. Just like Buster Douglas exposed the vulnerability of Mike Tyson, the collapse of the dollar will expose all fiat currencies for what they are and in so doing create greater demand for gold.

Central banks are becoming buyers instead of sellers. After years of selling, my guess is that the world's central banks will soon compete with one another in efforts to replenish their gold reserves.

When the dollar finally collapses, other national fiat currencies will also come into question. To reassure confidence, governments will need adequate gold backing for their currencies. After all, if the dollar is suspect, what good are dollar reserves? A currency backed by dollars may seem no better than a currency backed by nothing.

Gold will be required to restore credibility and preserve the public's faith in national currencies. This added demand will only fuel gold's ascent.

Mining companies will be unwinding hedge books. Now that gold is rising and real interest rates are low or negative, there is no longer any incentive for mining companies to hedge. In fact, there is now a powerful incentive to unwind those hedges that already exist.

Unwinding their hedge books is often the best way for gold companies to increase reserves. It's certainly a lot cheaper than prospecting and drilling for them. The absence of additional hedging and the buying that is required to close existing positions will be another powerful force driving gold prices higher.

In addition, as the gold bull market gains traction, gold mining companies will be able to attract equity financing without the need to hedge. Wall Street has been assigning premium valuations to unhedged versus hedged gold companies, providing even more incentive not to hedge.

Short covering will cause gold to rise. Perhaps one of the biggest sources of new demand will be the covering of short positions.

Borrowing and then selling non-interest-bearing gold, and then investing the proceeds into interest-bearing debt instruments, has been the world's ultimate carry trade for years. However, as gold prices continue their ascent, these carry trades will ultimately prove too heavy to support. Compounding the problem will be the fact that many of the debt instruments providing the carry may lose value or even go into default.

The rush to cover money-losing short positions (what traders call being in a short squeeze) will only intensify gold's price rise, forcing even more shorts to cover.

In fact, it is very likely that many of the gold shorts will go broke and will not be able to return the gold they borrowed to the rightful owners. This will mean that many investors, including central banks that have lent out significant percentages of their reserves, will not get their gold back. As a result they will have to reenter the market to buy back the very ounces they thought they already owned. Of course, with all that buying, they will be paying much higher prices.

Wall Street will rediscover gold. Traditionally Wall Street had always included gold and gold mining shares as an asset class in investment portfolios and included them in their allocation models. In addition, most equity mutual funds held gold shares, and the shares themselves were fairly represented in popular indexes, such as the Standard & Poor's 500.

However, during the 1990s this practice became passé. Gold and mining shares had performed so poorly for so long that holding them actually became an embarrassment. Today, Newmont Mining remains the sole gold stock in the S&P 500 index. The total market capitalization of all publicly traded gold stocks is actually less than the smallest (in market cap) of the 30 stocks in the Dow Jones Industrial Average.

Also, with the advent of derivatives, gold lost its appeal as a hedge against bear markets or other unforeseen economic shocks. The poor performance of gold and mining shares following the 1987 stock market crash helped to solidify the view that gold no longer served its purpose as a legitimate hedge.

I'm convinced, however, that this thinking is about to change, as gold, the "barbaric relic" and ultimate old economy asset, makes a comeback. Once holders of derivatives discover that the hedge value of derivatives is only as good as a counterparty's ability to pay, gold will reclaim its former role. Gold is not simultaneously someone else's liability; it has intrinsic value and therefore provides the ultimate insurance.

Also, when the market crashed in 1987, gold was seven years into its bear market, and the fundamentals were decisively different than they are today. Back then, many investors and mutual funds still held gold shares as insurance, and they tried to cash in on those positions after the crash. As a result of all that selling, gold and gold shares plunged as well. Expecting this phenomenon to repeat itself, many potential gold buyers are watching today's stock market from the sidelines, waiting to buy. When the stock market collapses this time, the gold price will be supported by fence-sitters looking to buy instead of a lot of owners trying to sell.

Gold is special for other reasons. The supply of gold can expand only to the extent it can be mined. And historically, the supply of gold has expanded only 2 percent a year. It will always be a scarce commodity.

The good thing about gold is that all the gold that was ever mined is still here. It doesn't tarnish or corrode. When sunken ships are salvaged, the gold is as good as new.

Gold represents real effort. An ounce of gold in coin form represents all the effort it took to discover it, mine it, refine it, and mint it—all that effort is embedded in that coin. The government can print a $1 bill at the same cost it can print a $1 million bill. But there's a big difference between a 1-ounce gold coin and a 100-ounce bar. A 100-ounce bar takes 100 times the effort. So once the distinction between paper money and sound money is clear to everybody, the choice becomes a no-brainer. Why put your faith in some government's promise to keep something scarce when you can put it in something that's already scarce and destined to stay scarce?

And there's an awful lot of money yet to be printed. When people become fully aware of all the demographic time bombs and all the promises that all the politicians in the United States and around the world have made to provide Social Security–type benefits where they haven't set aside any reserves and are counting on the productivity of future generations, the need for a gold standard to restrain central banks from creating inflation becomes obvious.

There's simply no way future promises can be met except with a printing press. Our country's funded debt, astronomical as it is, represents the tip of an iceberg. As indicated earlier, unfunded liabilities of the U.S. government are estimated to equal some $50 trillion, including not just the obvious Social Security, Medicare, and veterans' benefits, but all the government's loan guarantees as well. Despite knowing that a certain amount of the debt being guaranteed is going to default, the government doesn't take any kind of accounting charge for what the actuaries are saying is going to happen.

So that's an idea of the amount of money the government is committed to print in the future, because it sure isn't going to raise it with taxes.

Obviously something will have to be done about the nation's forward obligations. But whatever is done, massive obligations will remain and the temptation to print money will be there, big-time.

It's hardly surprising that such realities take time to sink in. People will believe some very foolish things for a short period of time. It wasn't that long ago that we were killing witches in Salem. Look at the NASDAQ bubble, and now the real estate bubble. So people have believed for a long time that fiat currency was as good as gold and that politicians would act responsibly and not deficit spend to get votes. But since the first Greek democracy they have never been able to resist that temptation.

The important point is that people are waking up to these facts and beginning to realize that the difference between real and paper money is like the difference between an original oil painting and a print being run off in the millions. The time is getting ripe for gold.

HOW HIGH COULD GOLD GO?

One way of getting an indication of how strong the bull market in gold could get is to look at a recent historical precedent.

In 1968, with the country still on the international gold standard, President Lyndon Johnson, who had financed his Great Society programs and the Vietnam war by printing money, tried unsuccessfully to prop up the dollar by keeping the price of gold at its artificially low official price of $35. It didn't work. Central banks continued to sell and find buyers as market forces dictated, setting the stage for two devaluations in the early Nixon years: one raising gold to $38, the other to $42. The gold standard was abandoned altogether in 1971.

Free to float, gold in that last bull market rose from $42 an ounce to its all-time high of $877 in 1980, a 20-fold increase. The current bull market in gold has not even seen a tripling yet. A similar move this time would give gold a price of $5,100.

GOLD AND THE DOW JONES INDUSTRIAL AVERAGE

While Wall Street pundits extol the virtues of the stock market and its promise of assured riches, they consistently denigrate gold and its value as an investment alternative. Gold, they chide, is as out of fashion as the leisure suits worn during the decade they naively perceive as the yellow metal's last hurrah.

At the peak of the bull market of the 1920s the Dow was worth over 20 ounces of gold. By the ensuing trough, the Dow was around 36 and, with gold officially $35 an ounce, the Dow-to-gold ratio was back to nearly 1 to 1.

By 1966 the Dow was again worth more than 20 ounces of gold, and by 1980, with the Dow at about 850 and gold at about $850, it was back to 1 to 1. So you had two occasions in the prior century when the Dow exceeded the value of gold by a ratio of 20 to 1 and then, within a short period of time after hitting 20 to 1, went back to 1 to 1 (see Figure 9.1).

The Dow's all-time record high relative to gold occurred in 2002, when it reached something like 44 to 1, an absurd level, more than double the previous peaks of 1966 and 1929. As this is written, we are at about 17 to 1. *Were we to repeat the history of the last century and go back to a 1-to-1 ratio, you'd be looking at a gold price of $12,000 an ounce, assuming the Dow stays about where it is. If the Dow goes to 5,000 it still puts gold at $5,000.*

Of course, the Dow could go to 36,000, as one best-selling book predicted not very long ago, but then a 1-to-1 ratio would

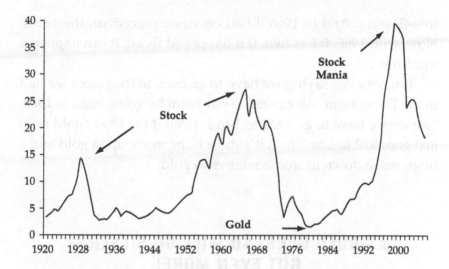

FIGURE 9.1   *Dow Jones Industrial Average divided by gold price,*
1920–2006. Since the Dow-to-gold price ratio returned to 1 to 1 after
both its 1929 and 1966 peaks, why should the current bear market
produce a different result? Even though the 1966 peak exceeded the
1929 peak by 67 percent, the ratio still returned to 1 to 1. Since the
2000 peak exceeded the 1966 peak by nearly the same percentage, why
should the reversion be any different this time around?
Source: Reprinted by permission from David L. Tice and Associates
(www.prudentbear.com).

put gold at $36,000. It doesn't matter where the two meet—just
that they get to 1 to 1.

   Imagine if I had said to somebody in the 1960s, "What if the
Dow goes to a 1-to-1 ratio relative to gold again like it did in
1932?" I suspect I would have gotten an answer like, "Are you
crazy? This is 1966. This the space age, the era of the Nifty Fifty,
the go-go 1960s, the electronic age. This is a new era. How can
you possibly think we'll go back to a Depression stock price?"
People would have thought it absurd in 1966 with the Dow at
1,000 and gold at 35. But to say gold could go 1 to 1 was actually
far more outrageous in 1966 than it is to say it now. Now gold is

free-floating. And in 1966 it had only one precedent, the 1920s. Now, with 1966, it has two. If it happened twice, it can happen a third time.

I'm not even saying we have to go back to the prices we had in the Depression. We can make our point by going back to 1980. Nor do we have to go back to 1 to 1. Even if the Dow/gold ratio just goes to 2 to 1 or 3 to 1, it's still a huge move up in gold and a huge move down in stocks relative to gold.

AS GOLD GOES, SO WILL GO SILVER— BUT EVEN MORE!

Silver historically has behaved similarly to gold in the marketplace and, since it is currently priced favorably relative to gold, it might be an even more profitable investment. I say that, though, with the caveat that silver therefore has a bigger downside should my predictions be wrong.

Investors in silver follow the gold/silver price ratio, which is currently 50 with gold at $600/oz. and silver at $12/oz. The ratio averaged 47 over the twentieth century. The higher the ratio, the cheaper silver is relative to gold. It hit its lowest point in 1980 at 17 when the Hunt brothers cornered the market in silver and the price spiked to $49.45/oz.

I would also have to caution that the arguments I have cited as favorable to an upward move in gold do not all apply with equal force to silver.

For example, the remonetization of gold that I believe is a highly likely development, whether it is done by the government or in the private sector, is not as likely for silver, even though silver was part of our country's bimetallic monetary system. The reason that silver was used as money in addition to gold had to do with its greater portability. Silver coins representing smaller amounts of money could be carried around on one's person, whereas an amount of gold equal to the value of a silver dime would be so small you couldn't see it. Modern technology in the form of digital money and debit cards renders carrying money unnecessary and makes spending 10 cents' worth of gold a simple matter of bookkeeping.

Silver is also in much greater supply than gold, but offsetting that is its wider industrial demand.

All that said, silver is a store of value second only to gold, has performed historically similarly to gold, is priced relatively cheaply in relation to gold, and could very well provide a better investment return in an environment highly favorable for commodities in general and precious metals with monetary attributes in particular. It is known for its volatility, and its variations in price reflect fluctuations in relative industrial and store-of-value demands. Between September 2005 and April 2006, silver doubled from $7 to $14 per troy ounce, evidently reflecting the declining dollar.

THE BOTTOM LINE: GET YOURS NOW

So people are slowly but surely rediscovering monetary sanity, but you still have time to get your gold (or silver with the caveats stated) before everybody else does. You want to get it while it's still cheap, before people catch on to the fact that gold, if not silver, is going be money again all over the world.

The fiats are all going to go back to gold, or if they don't, people are going to use it on their own. The value is going to increase. Just look at all the populations, such as in China and India, and imagine them all walking around with gold in their pockets (figuratively speaking). In reality what they'll have are gold debit cards representing gold on deposit in their names.

What I've described, I am convinced, is going to happen. Governments will try to resist it. They might even try to make gold money illegal and, in a worst-case scenario, cause a black market to be created. But it's going to happen and I believe it will drive gold and silver prices to sky-high price levels. Here's the advice I give clients on the best way to own gold and silver.

HOW TO OWN GOLD AND SILVER

Here are the different ways investors can position themselves in gold and silver.

Physical Ownership

The first and most obvious way to own gold or silver is in physical "bullion" form. Actual coins, such as the popular South African Krugerrand, the Canadian Maple Leaf, the Australian Kangaroo, and many others, can be simply bought from dealers and put in safe-deposit boxes.

My favorite way to buy silver is just to buy junk silver. A "bag" is a thousand dollars in face value of dimes, quarters, half-dollars, or silver dollars minted before 1965. They are 90 percent silver. The good thing about those is that they are legal tender and a little safer from confiscation than bullion that has no nominal currency value. Of course you wouldn't spend them for their nominal value because that would be less than their metallic value, which shows you the extent to which the money has been debased. (You won't find it in a bag of junk silver, but to dramatize the point, a $20 gold piece is worth $800 to $900 in metallic value.) These are regular, circulated, nonnumismatic (i.e., not for collectors) type coins.

Then there are other numismatic coins that are not necessarily bullion investments. They're collectibles. So people don't necessarily go and buy a MS 65 (MS refers to mint state and 65 refers to the grade) and pay 10 times the bullion content and think they're making a bullion investment. There may be a historical correlation between rare numismatic coins and bullion, but you're buying a collectible—a rare coin.

I am not recommending that people buy numismatics. I'm recommending they just buy bullion. These coins might do well in a bullion bull market, but there's a lot of risk there—a lot of big spreads—and I want to give conservative advice. So I mention numismatics but do not recommend this category unless your goal is speculating in rare items for their collectible value, not buying them because they happen to be made of gold or silver.

DEFINITIONS OF TERMS

Bullion refers to precious metals in their bulk form, cast as ingots (also called bars) in various sizes or minted into coins. Bullion coins issued by nations, such as the South African Krugerrand and the American Gold Eagle, are nominally legal tender with a face value, although their bullion value is much greater. Bullion value is determined by mass and purity.

Numismatics refers to uncirculated coins collected for their rarity value; they may have bullion value but their price is based on numismatic value. Numismatic value is determined by scarcity and condition, the latter indicated by a numerical grade ranging from 70 for a coin in perfect condition to 60 for a coin with scratches or a weak strike. The abbreviation preceding the numerical grade—MS—stands for mint state. A numismatic coin in perfect condition would thus have a rating of MS-70.

Perth Mint

The Perth Mint is a more than 100-year-old mint that is owned by the government of Western Australia and represented exclusively in 49 American states (Arizona is the exception) by my own firm, Euro Pacific Capital. Under the Perth Mint Certificate Program (PMCP), investors can purchase bullion gold, silver, and platinum at the Perth Mint spot (cash as opposed to future) market ask price with no markup. The only additional costs are a 2 percent service fee and a $50 administrative fee. For example, based on the program's minimum investment of $10,000, the total cost would be $10,250.

The PMCP offers free storage at the Perth Mint, eliminating a significant cost of physical ownership, particularly with bulky silver. Safety, which can be a concern with other certificate programs, is assured here because the metals remain on the premises and cannot be lent out. Another safety factor, the risk of confiscation, is also minimal. Unlike the U.S. government, which under the Gold Reserve Act of 1934 made it illegal for U.S. citizens to own gold, Australia has no such history. The mining industry is too vital an element of the Australian economy to disrupt in that manner. The Australian nation could ill afford to cause investors to lose faith in the scarcity of gold. Perth Mint accounts are fully guaranteed by the AAA-rated government of Western Australia and are further insured by Lloyd's of London, making the Perth Mint the only government-backed bullion storage facility in the world.

Although I recommend that investors keep some coins at home or in a safe-deposit box for emergencies, certificates are more convenient and it's also good to have something outside the country in case things get really bad here or the U.S. government makes it illegal to own gold. Should you be forced to flee the country because you're trying to be financially safe, it's good to have some money offshore waiting for you. The beauty of the Perth Mint is that it's not a bank account, meaning you don't have to disclose it. It's a government-owned vault and the storage is free.

Gold Exchange-Traded Funds

Gold exchange-traded funds (GETFs) are a specialized variety of exchange-traded fund (ETF), which is a security that trades like a stock but represents a mutual fund that typically holds an index or other specialized portfolio. GETFs track the price of gold and hold certificates for physical bullion that is on deposit and insured.

Although Spiders, the popular name for Standard & Poor's Depositary Receipts (SPDRs), a security representing the Standard & Poor's 500 index, have been exchange-traded since 1993, ETFs really started becoming popular in the past five years and GETFs are even newer. Two currently trading on the New York Stock Exchange are Streettracks Gold Shares (symbol: GLD) and iShares COMEX Gold Trust (symbol: IAU). Gold Bullion Securities (GBS) trades under the symbol GOLD on the Australian Stock Exchange; the Central Fund of Canada (symbol: CEF), which holds gold and silver, is traded on the Toronto Stock Exchange; and there are others in London and Switzerland. iShares Silver Trust (symbol: SLV) holds silver and is traded on the New York Stock Exchange.

The main risk I see with these investments is that it could turn out that the auditing has been false and that the metal they claim to have is not really there. I don't know this to be a problem, but anything can happen, and my feeling is why take the chance when you can own gold and silver directly?

Another drawback is that gold ETFs are legally a form of debenture (an unsecured bond), meaning that if there were trouble and the GETF provider went into liquidation, holders would be general creditors instead of outright owners as would be the case with a PMGC purchase.

Like physical gold generally, GETFs are subject to confiscation by governments, so you might feel safer with the Australian, Canadian, or British products.

Other considerations have to do with the liabilities and responsibilities of the market participants, such as custodians, and questions of valuations, fees, and expenses. Also, there is no self-regulatory organization in the mutual fund industry that would police fair market practices with respect to purity and other standard specifications.

On the plus side, ETFs, like stocks, can be traded using all forms of limit orders and stop orders and can be sold short.

Gold Money

There are also several places to buy gold on the Internet, and even several that offer storage programs. In general I would be very reluctant to trust most storage programs, but one exception is GoldMoney.com, founded by James Turk, a longtime gold advocate and widely respected figure.

Investors and shareholders of GoldMoney include two publicly traded gold mining companies, DRDGold Limited (South Africa) and IAMGOLD Corporation (Canada). GoldMoney's main office is located in Jersey, one of the British Channel Islands situated in the English Channel near the northwestern tip of France. Its web site and database servers, also located in Jersey, are housed in a secure, state-of-the-art data center.

GoldMoney is similar to online banking, but your account is denominated in goldgrams and mils, not dollars and cents. Each GoldMoney GoldGram you own is safely stored for you in allocated storage in a specialized bullion vault near London and is insured by Lloyd's of London.

When you buy goldgrams, you own pure gold in a secure vault.

GoldMoney also offers the added convenience of handling payments in gold between members in exchange for goods and services. Payments in GoldMoney are fast and convenient, and all transactions are processed instantly. The gold always remains safe and secure in the vault, but the ownership changes the instant a payment is made.

Commodity Futures

People can own gold and silver using futures contracts or options on futures contracts. I don't recommend options on futures contracts, which are for speculators willing to assume higher risk for greater leverage. But if you simply want 100 ounces of gold, for example, which costs about $60,000, you could fully fund your commodities account with the entire $60,000, buy one contract, and put the margin money in the bank or in Treasury bills. You could then use the interest earned to pay the difference between the cash (spot) price and the futures price (called contango) each time your contract was rolled over. The strategy would inherently be no riskier than owning the metal outright.

But to the extent you use leverage, say by buying $60,000 of gold for $2,000, then a small move could wipe you out. So the futures market is another way to be in gold that can be conservative if you do it right and very risky if you do it wrong.

One risk with futures contracts, however, is that if gold makes a big enough move up, the people who short that contract—for every long there's a short—could go bankrupt. They might not be able to pay, in which case the exchange, which could be the Chicago Mercantile Exchange (CME—the Merc), the Chicago Board of Trade (CBOT), the New York Commodities Exchange (COMEX), the New York Mercantile Exchange

(NYMEX), or any other exchange trading futures, could actually go bankrupt. That's called counterparty risk and it is the derivative industry's nightmare. People think they're hedged when they buy put options, but if the exchange goes under, they're out money. Derivatives markets operate on the assumption that what's happened in the past is going to happen in the future. But if some major blowup happens the model goes out the window. A suddenly collapsed dollar could be just such a blowup.

Mining Stocks

Another way to invest in gold and silver is by owning the stocks of the companies that mine it.

Stocks offer leverage. For example, a 10 percent increase in the price of gold could have the effect of a 50 percent increase in the bottom line of a mining company.

Of course, the price of gold has to increase faster than the cost of mining it. One of the recent problems of mining companies is that gold prices have been rising but they have been lagging the costs of production, particularly energy costs. It's ironic that mining companies have been the victims of inflation. Because governments have been so successful in convincing the people that there is no inflation, they haven't bought gold to the extent they should have, and so gold hasn't kept up with inflation.

Gold mining companies will offer great leverage to the rising price of gold and they will pay dividends. They haven't paid dividends recently because the cost of production is too high relative to the price of gold. But that will change. And one of the advantages is that stocks of gold mining companies generate capital gains at the favorable rate, whereas coins are considered collectibles and gains are taxed as ordinary income.

The Risk Pyramid of Mining Stocks   You have three basic categories in the mining sector, each with different risks for the investor.

At the bottom of the risk pyramid, you have the senior producers, companies like Barrick Gold Corporation, Newmont Mining Corporation, Gold Fields Ltd., AngloGold Ashanti Ltd., and Goldcorp Inc. Those are the biggest ones and should be a core part of your portfolio. They have tons of reserves, and even though some of those reserves are hedged, the majority are not. Barrick, one of the most notorious hedgers, has reduced its hedge book to about 2 million ounces, which is hard to believe since it was about 8 million ounces a few years ago. In addition, companies like Barrick still have exploration projects that would likely lead to more ounces being discovered than are currently hedged.

Then you've got the slightly less conservative but still very solid midtier group, consisting of companies like Newcrest Mining, Harmony Gold Mining, Agnico-Eagle Mines Limited, Meridian Gold, and Kincross Gold. Like the seniors, they should also be included in your core holdings.

Third, you have your juniors, which are smaller but have reserves and are in production. Companies in this category include Bema Gold, Northern Orion Resources, Golden Star Resources, Taseko Mines, and Northgate Minerals.

At the top of the risk pyramid, you have your exploration companies. They are the riskiest. They don't have any gold; they're just trying to find it. They may be doing joint ventures with other companies, or may have a claim, or are doing prospecting somewhere. These are the penny stocks of the gold mining sector, and while some of them will pay off big-time, I can only say watch out.

There's going to be a lot of fraud as the gold market gets hot. It'll be like the dot-coms, with scams and hoaxes. So you'll want to stay away from this part of the market unless you are personally involved or know the principals or know something about the company.

Ultimately I think there is going to be a bubble in mining stocks, a bull market that will end in a mania not unlike the NASDAQ bubble. I don't know how far that is in the future, possibly five or ten years from now.

STRUCTURING YOUR GOLD PORTFOLIO

My advice is for you to have a portfolio that includes at a minimum some physical gold in your possession; some physical bullion outside your possession and offshore, such as the Perth Mint; and a mixed portfolio of gold stocks, say 40 percent senior producers, 30 percent midlevel, 20 percent juniors, and then maybe the last 10 percent exploration companies and speculative stocks. That would be a solid portfolio of gold stocks, and if you like silver, you can blend that in proportionately.

I also prefer the foreign gold stocks. Generally, valuation is better abroad. In Australia there is more gold in the ground, and you can get more reserves for your money than you can in Canada, for example.

Then you have the political risk factor. Ounces in Zimbabwe are going to be worth less than ounces in Canada because there's a greater chance the government is going to take them. You always have the risk that a government is going to nationalize gold. So you're better off owning gold in a politically safe area, such as Canada or Australia, or even South Africa.

Is the United States politically safe? Right now there's no risk factor built into the U.S. mines, which I think is a mistake. I think that it is more likely that the U.S. government would nationalize gold mines than many other governments of countries in which gold is mined. The main difference is that for stocks in those other countries political risk is already discounted into the prices of the shares. However, in the United States no such political risk is priced in.

I think we're going to be in a real crisis and that the U.S. government could easily declare a national emergency and confiscate private holdings "for the good of the country and its population." I think gold investors worldwide are far too complacent on this issue.

Then there's the question of excess profits taxes. This is certainly less extreme than outright nationalization, but can be almost as damaging. The first thing that happens whenever the price of oil goes up is that somebody in this country says, "Let's have an excess profits tax." When gold goes to $5,000 an ounce, the same thing might happen. You want to have your mine in a jurisdiction that doesn't have a history of imposing excess profits taxes whenever somebody starts making money—particularly since gold miners are natural targets for vilification and apt to be seen as part of the problem.

The final point to consider would be how much of your gold portfolio to place in the physical metal itself and how much to invest in mining shares. I would suggest 20 percent to 50 percent in physical gold, with the balance in shares, depending on your risk tolerance. Obviously, the greater the percentage of mining shares, the more leveraged the portfolio is to the price of gold.

BLENDING YOUR GOLD AND FOREIGN STOCK PORTFOLIOS

What percentage of your overall portfolio should be in physical gold and mining shares? My recommendation would be 10 percent to 30 percent gold-related investments and 70 percent to 90 percent conservative foreign stocks. The more aggressive

investor would weight gold higher, while the more conservative investor, particularly if current income is required, would
weight it lower. So an aggressive investor could have a $1
million portfolio with $700,000 in conservative foreign stocks
and $300,000 in gold, apportioned as I suggested, while a more
conservative investor might have $900,000 in stocks and only
$100,000 in gold. The main reason for the relatively low weight-
ing in gold is so that if I am right a little gold exposure will go
a long way, and if I'm wrong you will not get hurt too badly.
Those who would want to overweight gold-related investments
could end up hitting the ball way out of the park but risk striking out entirely if my forecasts prove to be way off base.

Of course, depending on how much money you have, there
are plenty of mutual funds that invest in mining shares. Personally I would prefer to own the stocks themselves. I told you my
feelings about mutual funds in the previous chapter.

My reason for investing in foreign stocks is for safety and
income. My reason for investing in bullion is partially for safety,
talking here about nonleveraged physical bullion, which is very
safe but produces no income.

But part of my enthusiasm about gold, frankly, has to do
with growth and speculation. I think if you want to hit a home
run in real terms in any currency, the way to do it is with gold
mining stocks. You're going to get a lot of growth but not much
income. There's not a lot of dividend income now coming out
of mining shares and no dividends coming out of physical gold.
So it is speculation, by definition, because we're not getting paid
to own it. We're gambling on the future price, but I think it's a
gamble worth taking.

I'm not going to call it a once-in-a-lifetime opportunity,
because for people who were investing in the 1970s it's a chance
to make a killing again. But a lot of people missed that opportunity, and here's their second chance.

2009 UPDATE

The convulsive events of 2008 caused confusion in the gold and precious metals sectors the same way they did in foreign stocks, but I am more bullish now than I was when I first wrote Chapter 9—and that's bullish! Here's what's been going on.

The Gold Sell-Off

Gold initially rallied to a high of $1,012 an ounce in March 2008 from about $600 when I first wrote this chapter. Then, when Lehman Brothers went bankrupt and the deleveraging process started, gold went down in the general sell-off, along with foreign and domestic stocks, oil, other commodities, and just about everything else. Gold was a large and liquid holding of hedge funds and other leveraged players, and when they were forced to meet redemptions and margin calls they became big sellers. The gold price eventually bottomed out at $712 an ounce in November 2008.

Gold's 30 percent decline was significantly less than the 70 percent decline in crude oil, the 50 percent drop in the Standard & Poor's 500 index, a 40 percent drop in nonenergy commodities, and the general decline in asset values. Gold also recovered more quickly, selling at around $900 an ounce as this is written, a gain of almost 40 percent, while other assets, including those just mentioned, are still much closer to their November 2008 lows. More important, gold's rise put it within 10 percent of its record high, while other assets and commodities are nowhere near such levels. The bottom line is that gold bounced back because fundamental demand was so strong compared to demand for other assets.

The fact that during this period of deleveraging and flight to perceived safety the dollar strengthened while gold failed to eclipse its previous high reinforced traditional skeptics in their view that gold had seen its day. With the global economy in unprecedented shambles, the fact that gold was not selling at $2,000 per ounce or even challenging earlier records was enough evidence for them to conclude that gold bugs had it wrong and should go back into the woodwork.

Why the Gold Bugs Will Live Long and Prosper

The fact is, however, that gold did make new highs in the euro, the yen, the Swiss franc, the British pound, and every currency other than the U.S. dollar. It was especially strong in the currencies of countries where gold is mined, notably Australia, South Africa, Canada, and those in Latin America. It's clear to me that the short-term strength of the dollar is temporarily obscuring the underlying strength of gold.

But gold held its own, and the only reason we haven't seen the big move is that that foreigners are still propping us up—blowing enough air into our bubble economy to keep it from deflating completely. When our collapse finally comes, people holding gold will likely see even more spectacular gains than those living in Iceland and the United Kingdom. Those were two highly leveraged economies I avoided investing in as they were pushing the limits similarly to the United States only on much smaller scales. However, as their currencies lacked the reserve status, they did not get the benefit of an influx of foreign capital when their bubbles burst. Anyway, that gold stood its ground in a strong dollar environment means it should perform extraordinarily well in the weak dollar environment we are ultimately headed for.

Once the dollar loses its perceived status as a safe haven and starts to fall again, gold will start gaining strength.

Why Reserve Currency Status Is Bullish for Gold

As the dollar weakens, central banks will look to rebalance their reserves in favor of gold. Gold is an alternative to dollars, and as confidence in the dollar wanes, there is more incentive for central banks to hold gold. Lately China and Russia and other big dollar holders have been making noise about replacing the dollar as the reserve currency with another currency or with special drawing rights from the International Monetary Fund (IMF). While I don't think this is going to happen, I do think the dollar is going to lose its role as the reserve currency. I do not believe there will be an official decree to replace the dollar as the world's reserve. It will simply lose that status due to independent market forces. My guess is that central banks will began to hold more of their reserves in other currencies, such as the euro, yen, or Chinese renminbi, and significantly higher percentages in gold.

Remember that the only reason the dollar became the world's reserve currency was that it was not only backed by gold, it was redeemable in gold. The whole idea behind having reserves behind a currency is that currencies in and of themselves have no intrinsic value. Now that the dollar is backed by nothing, it makes no sense to hold dollar reserves, which is the same thing as having no reserves at all. So I think we are going to be moving in the direction of gold becoming a greater percentage of central bank reserves relative to dollars or other leading currencies. China recently announced it had quietly doubled its gold reserves from 2 percent to 4 percent of its total reserves and is now the world's leading gold producer. Also, Chinese sovereign wealth funds have been buying gold mining companies around the world. Those who maintain that the dollar will not lose its reserve status simply because no other currency presents a credible alternative miss a key point. Even though I disagree with the premise of no credible challenger for the dollar's title, the fact is that the world does not need a reserve currency. Rather than replacing the dollar with some other flawed fiat alternative, the world could simply return to the traditional gold standard that existed prior to Bretton Woods.

The Recent Rally in Mining Stocks and the Outlook

While gold bullion has held up very well in this environment as noted, gold mining stocks have not. Between mid-2008 and October 2008 the AMEX HUI Gold BUGS Index (Basket of Unhedged Gold Stocks), which tracks unhedged domestic mining stocks, declined by about 80 percent. Gold itself is highly liquid, while gold stocks are far more subject to volatility. So when a lot of people rushed to get out of their gold stocks, prices collapsed like a $30 suitcase for lack of buyers.

Since their October 2008 lows, however, gold mining stocks have considerably outperformed the Standard & Poor's 500 index and almost all stock sectors. Some stocks have quadrupled and quintupled from their lows, while most have doubled or tripled. They are still down from their highs, but not down anywhere near as much as they were. In fact, as I write, declines in gold stocks now seem on a par with the general market. So while gold is inherently safer to hold than gold mining stocks, I still believe mining stocks ultimately offer the most upside potential and that people should still buy them.

One indication that gold stocks hold significant value right now is that they are trading much lower in relation to today's gold price than they were when gold prices were at their highs a year and a half ago.

More important, gold mining has become a far more profitable business than it was because the cost of mining has fallen sharply. That's because energy costs as well as the cost of local labor and other local costs have come down. The cost of production has to be looked at in terms of the local currencies. For example, as the Australian dollar and the South African rand have dropped, the Australian dollar and rand prices of gold have skyrocketed.

Another factor contributing to higher stock and bullion prices has been the reduction of capacity due to bankruptcies in the past six or seven months of gold and silver miners that were highly leveraged and unable to get financing. In addition, many exploration projects have been put on hold and new mining production has not been brought on stream.

Government's Efforts at Economic Stimulation Will Benefit Gold

The big increase in the price of gold relative to the cost of mining it makes the surviving mining companies more profitable and their stocks more attractive. But on top of that, the prospects of commodity gold prices moving substantially higher are phenomenal.

Not only has the U.S. government exceeded my worst expectations in terms of how irresponsibly it would react to our collapsing economy, but I'm also surprised at the extent to which the European Central Bank (ECB) and other foreign central banks have adopted inflationary policies. All the major central banks have interest rates close to zero: The euro zone is 1 percent, the United Kingdom and Canada are 0.5 percent, Japan is 0.25 percent, Switzerland and the U.S. are zero. And everybody is printing money. This is the most bullish environment I have ever seen for gold.

And I think as central banks keep interest rates very low to stimulate phony economic growth and inflation starts to pick up, more and more people are going to reject national currencies and go for real money. The demand for gold will thus increase spectacularly around the world as people shun currencies and hold gold as a store of value and use it as a medium of exchange.

What that means is that all the world's currencies are going to lose value against gold. The dollar, however, will end up losing a lot more than the others. At some point, foreign central banks will raise rates once inflation more adversely affects their consumer price indexes. The United States will be more restrained in its ability to raise rates because of our status as the world's largest debtor. Where creditor nations are much freer to raise their rates, our heavily leveraged economy means we will leave our rates lower and keep them there longer, meaning our currency will weaken more. Comments by Fed Chairman Ben Bernanke that he stands ready to remove the excess liquidity—that is, to contract the money supply by rate hikes or other open market actions—at the first signs of inflation or when growth returns is mere talk. Putting the inflation genie back into the bottle will be impossible, especially since current policy makes our economy even more addicted to lower rates than ever before. If we cannot swallow the medicine now, what chance is there that Bernanke will force-feed it to us when it tastes even worse? So the environment for gold is even better now than it was when I first wrote the book.

The Dow/Gold Ratio

The Dow/gold ratio tells us how many ounces of gold we need in order to buy one share of the Dow Jones Industrial Average. The lower the ratio, the more investors are willing to pay for gold (hard assets) and the less they are willing to pay for stocks (paper assets).

A declining Dow/gold ratio is a bear market indicator.

When I first wrote this chapter, the Dow/gold ratio was about 16 to 1 and I discussed the possibility of a 1 to 1 ratio, as happened in the years following the market peaks of 1928 and 1966. The Dow actually got as low as 7.7 ounces of gold in early 2008 (though it could be lower by the time you read this), a rather spectacular 50 percent decline in the gold price of the Dow since I wrote the book. The total decline now in the value of the Dow since its peak price in January 2000 is around 75 percent.

A decline of that magnitude over nine years is already a huge bear market. But I think my projection for the Dow being close to 1 to 1 is on target, although it might take another 5 to 10 years to get there.

Buy Gold

Even though the price of gold has risen, it has plenty of upside and I strongly recommend buying it. And gold mining stocks are just that much cheaper and offer even more spectacular gains if I am right. I continue to feel strongly that it is wise to have some gold and silver offshore and recommend the Perth Mint for the reasons I gave in the chapter.

With my increasing worry about really high inflation along with black markets, price controls, and shortages, I feel more strongly than ever that people should also have gold or silver coins in their possession for use in their transactions. An important caveat, however: The high level of anxiety being generated by the current economic environment has caused the demand for gold and silver coins from individual buyers to be extremely high. The result has not only been shortages but dealers in all too many cases have been charging premiums over the spot (cash) price of bullion that are outrageously high—50 percent in some cases. It is normal for coins to sell at premiums over the bullion price because different coins have different supply and demand dynamics and there are cost factors involved with the production of coins that don't exist with bullion. But premiums on one ounce gold coins should generally be no more than about 8 percent above the spot price, including dollar markups. It is important therefore to check out the integrity of dealers and to compare prices. (By the time this book is out, in fact, I will be selling physical precious metals myself, either through my current brokerage firm, Euro-Pacific Capital or through my own newly created precious metals company. Readers interested in having metals in their physical possession might want to watch for these developments on my website, www.europac.net, or check with your Euro-Pacific account representative. You can also call 800-377-EPAC (3722) which will be the direct line for physical metals.)

How high can gold go? There's really no limit to the upside, because there's almost no limit to how low the dollar can go. The hyperinflation à la the Weimar Republic and Zimbabwe that I believed was a worst-case scenario when I wrote *Crash Proof* still seems unlikely to occur, but given current government policy, the possibility is now far less remote. In fact, if we continue current policy, hyperinflation is precisely where we will end up. It is still my belief that while we are headed in that direction now, we will change course before it is too late. But the longer we wait to do so, the harder it becomes, and the more likely we will arrive at that dreaded destination.

10

How to Survive and Thrive, Step 3: Stay Liquid

In bad times, cash is king, goes an old saying, with which I would agree as long as the cash is in a viable currency.

The monetary and economic implosion I have been predicting throughout these pages could happen tomorrow or could take a few years. It could be cataclysmic, as would be the case if the United States suddenly lost reserve currency status or there were a run on the dollar, or it could be gradual and so well disguised that the purchasing power of the dollar would simply be gone before we knew it and had time to protect ourselves.

But it's coming, and although the broad outlines of the global economy that will emerge are clear enough—a realignment of purchasing power to the producing nations, stagflation and possibly hyperinflation at home with an aftermath of sacrifice and painful economic rehabilitation—the immediate effect will be global disruption, confusion, and possibly panic.

That period of adjustment and uncertainty will cause a lot of people to lose money, but for those who understand the larger picture unfolding, it will hold opportunities for profit.

Americans who follow my advice in Chapters 8 and 9 and put dollars into high-yielding investments in foreign currencies or invest in gold may see temporary pullbacks, but will be well positioned for the longer run.

This chapter thus focuses on liquidity, not the kind created by the Federal Reserve that got us into all this trouble, but personal liquidity—having enough walking-around money to handle living expenses and also having a reserve of uncommitted cash to take advantage of opportunities to acquire assets at bargain prices. Such opportunities may result from panic selling here or abroad, or be in non-dollar investments, including such as multinationals and exporters, that become cheap before people realize a new consumer class was being born as the American consumer died.

Being liquid also means doing something about assets that are owned and losing value, such as a house you should sell but cannot. Staying liquid means converting existing adjustable-rate debt to fixed-rate debt, so that you don't lose the asset because of an inability to service the debt. There are strategies for turning fixed-rate debt into income that I will discuss.

Finally, staying liquid means managing your money intelligently. You should have a grasp of where your finances stand, how your living expenses break down between those that are fixed and those that are discretionary, and how much liquidity you need. In other words, you need to examine what the subjective elements are that determine the degree of flexibility and safety your particular situation requires.

HOW MUCH LIQUIDITY IS DESIRABLE?

In Chapter 8 I touched briefly on the wisdom of keeping a portion of one's investment portfolio in cash or near cash to cover living expenses when money is immediately needed and financial assets may be temporarily affected by unfavorable market conditions.

The liquid assets I referred to then are the same ones I would recommend here, but my focus in this chapter is on maintaining liquidity during a period of months or even a year or two, when global markets are unsettled as a result of the U.S. dollar's collapse. In other words, the investment recommendations I made in Chapters 8 and 9 are investments you would continue to hold for income (excepting bullion) and would not want to cash in when their prices are temporarily off because markets are adjusting to economic shocks.

Depending on the outlook at the time you read this book, you might want to expand the liquid portion of your portfolio beyond what would cover personal emergencies so that you would both have enough to cover the extraordinary expenses that might occur in a longer time frame and also have the available funds to take advantage of the opportunities likely to occur during the adjustment period.

Despite the grim outlook for the U.S. dollar, simply as a practical matter of being a resident of the United States you should keep a certain amount of cash available in domestic currency. The guide here is to keep no more than is necessary to cover expenses you would likely have during a three-to-six-month period and to make sure that any holdings you have in dollar debt instruments, such as certificates of deposit, have short maturities. Anything earmarked for future consumption should be in foreign currency.

INVESTMENTS PROVIDING LIQUIDITY

As covered in Chapter 8, it is possible to purchase foreign currency certificates of deposit through domestic banks, and there is always the option of opening a foreign bank account. Both alternatives involve complications that can be avoided by working through the specialized broker you will be using anyway to handle your other foreign currency investments.

Available through Euro Pacific Capital and other brokers, the Merk Hard Currency Fund is a no-load mutual fund that invests in a basket of hard currencies from countries with strong monetary policies chosen for their value as protection against the depreciation of the U.S. dollar relative to other currencies.

Although I normally recommend against stock mutual funds as an alternative to carefully selected and diversified personal portfolios because of their short-term focus and management fees, I strongly recommend this alternative to choosing specific foreign currencies or investing in currency derivatives. The Merk Hard Currency Fund is very well managed and very liquid. Unlike a conventional money market fund, however, which has a constant net asset value (NAV) and a fluctuating rate of interest, Merk's NAV fluctuates on a daily basis depending on the dollar's exchange rate versus the currencies in the fund.

Another alternative is to buy short-term government debt denominated in foreign currency through Euro Pacific Capital or other specialized brokers.

If, to be ultrasafe, you want to buy government bonds with the full faith and credit of a sovereign government backing them, they are available in Germany, Australia, Canada, and other countries. Shorter terms mean lower yields, but longer-term bonds with higher yields are available and are liquid, and one can have reasonable assurance that most of their principal will be recovered if they are sold prior to maturity.

If you want debt that's linked to inflation, most of these countries have those types of bonds as well.

When you're lending money to a foreign government, you obviously want to avoid going from the frying pan into the fire. The way to determine that a government has a solid currency is to look at its balance of payments, available on the International Monetary Fund (IMF) web site, among other places, and see if it is running trade or budget deficits. Countries that are running deficits in their merchandise trading are likely to incur inflation and you are less likely to be repaid in currency of value. Even when currencies are demonstrably stable, it is smart to diversify.

LONGER-TERM INVESTMENTS PROVIDING LIQUIDITY

Of course, for longer-term investments, I personally prefer equities to debt securities, for reasons already explained in Chapter 8. In general, the dividends paid on foreign stocks typically exceed the interest paid on foreign bonds, and the former usually qualify for favorable tax treatment, Hong Kong and Singapore being notable exceptions.

Otherwise, the only time you sacrifice favorable tax treatment is when the foreign company is classified as being a passive foreign investment trust (PFIT), meaning the asset is actually a holding company managed by a third party on a fee basis. But that's a question for your broker, who can tell you in advance if an investment pays a qualifying dividend. Of course, there's no telling how long that differential treatment is going to be in effect. But you get it now when you own stock, whereas bond interest is fully taxable.

In addition, stocks allow currency gains to be taxed as capital gains as they are incorporated into the price of the underlying stock. However, for bonds or foreign currency CDs, currency gains are taxed as ordinary income at either sale or maturity. For short-term holdings, the tax advantage of equities is lost.

Foreign equities are highly liquid, although there is always market risk. But the way I look at it, if we knew the collapse was going to happen tomorrow, we would put everything in cash or near cash and wouldn't buy the stocks. However, if the reckoning holds off for three or four years, we're giving up a lot of income. And if there is a decline, will it be enough of a decline to make up for all those years of lost income?

Let's say you buy one of these equities, and in the next few years it goes up from $1 a share to $1.40 a share. Then there's a major collapse, but the stock only goes down to $1.10. It's a big drop but the price is still higher than what you originally paid for it. So you're better off than if you'd been in cash all that time, and you've been getting a better return.

Of course, nobody knows what the timing is going to be. So you have to strike a balance. You keep some liquidity so you can take advantage of declines when they come, but you also keep some money invested in higher-yielding investments with the potential to appreciate.

So when we think of liquidity we think of cash, cash equivalents, short-term debt instruments, and money market instruments, alternatives all available in foreign currencies, on one end of a liquidity continuum. On the other, longer-term bonds and equities offer liquidity and income but some market risk. The sooner you think you'll need the money, the greater the liquidity should be.

Of course, it is important to point out that even if the foreign currency prices of many stocks fall in response to a major U.S. market decline or dollar crisis, the dollar prices of such stocks might not fall at all. In fact, from a U.S. dollar–based investor's perspective, foreign stock holdings should considerably outperform U.S. money markets, even if foreign markets fall sharply in sympathy with declines in the United States.

The way I see it, even if foreign share prices fall in terms of their local currencies, the dollar will lose even more value, meaning that the dollar prices of those stocks will rise even if their local currency price falls. Of course, the conservative, high-yielding stocks advocated in Chapter 8 should be far less vulnerable to sharp declines than more aggressive, export-oriented, lower-yielding, large-cap multinationals, which is one reason I prefer them in the first place.

Before we leave the subject, I should say that I regard bullion gold and gold coins, but not mining shares, as liquidity. You can barter them. You can easily cash them in for other currencies. Particularly since I expect the bull market in gold to continue, it may be the ultimate liquidity.

DEBT AND LIQUIDITY

To the extent you have income, there's nothing wrong with having debt. What you do not want is adjustable-rate debt, because as the economy turns down and inflation is making the debt less burdensome, you're stuck with rising debt service costs. And if you can't service the debt, you can lose the assets collateralizing it, if any. Your standard of living would be plunging and you'd be struggling to service debt.

The first order of business, then, is to convert adjustable-rate debt to fixed-rate debt with the longest possible maturity. This is nearly always possible with home mortgages. Various companies exist that will consolidate student loans at a locked-in rate that is reasonable since rate levels are low anyway for these loans, some of which are government sponsored and others private. Credit card revolving credit is adjustable and generally nonnegotiable, although borrowers able to prove hardship and willing to risk having their credit histories qualified can contract with credit counseling services that will negotiate lower fixed-rate arrangements with banks. If possible, though, pay credit card debt off, the highest rates first.

HOMEOWNER OPTIONS

What if you own a house? Should you borrow more money against it? I say yes, provided you can reinvest the proceeds at a rate that exceeds the cost of the debt.

If you can borrow at 6½ percent on a fixed-rate mortgage and invest in conservative, dividend-paying foreign stocks with a target dividend return of 8 percent, then for every $100,000 you borrow you have $1,500 a year in cash to spend. That makes sense under my declining dollar scenario because if the dollar were to lose half its value, that $1,500 becomes $3,000.

If the dollar really got clobbered, say by 90 percent, you would be earning $15,000 a year. In six years you'll be able to pay off the entire $100,000 loan. You would own the investment portfolio for nothing, enjoy all the cash flow without any debt to service, and be able to pay off your dollar debt with your appreciated foreign assets.

If you get a decent positive carry, as the differential is called, you'll still make something even if the dollar goes up.

So it makes sense to leverage your overvalued real estate and use the money to accumulate assets abroad.

Of course, by the time you read this, it may be too late to sell your house, but let's say you're lucky and have a $500,000 house with a $200,000 mortgage and you are able to sell it at full price. You would now have $300,000 to put in a portfolio of foreign dividend-paying stocks. With a yield of 8 percent, your income would be $25,000 a year.

If you can rent a house for $25,000 a year comparable to the one you sold, you are now living rent, insurance, and property tax free. You have taken the equity you had tied up in a house and used it to accumulate an asset that will pay your rent.

That asset is going to be there, and will appreciate in value. Meanwhile you take all that money you save and add it to your growing investment account.

People say you're throwing money away when you rent, but that isn't true if you're going to be saving money by renting. Plus what would you call interest-only mortgages, or worse yet, negative amortization mortgages? Since not a penny of the mortgage payments goes toward paying down principal, all the money is "thrown away." Trading expenses for rent is not throwing money away.

Compare this to buying a house with a 30-year mortgage. Here you wind up with an investment account worth three times the value of the house. So it's all about what you do with the money you don't pay in taxes, insurance, and mortgage payments. You're not building equity in a home but you are building equity, and because the equity you're building is throwing off investment income, it will grow by compounding, enjoy currency profits, and probably appreciate in value as well.

Obviously there are places where the rent versus own relationship is such that this wouldn't work out. Nor is it for everybody. You should seek professional advice before going this route from people like Euro Pacific Capital.

But in markets where you can't sell your house because the real value has collapsed, but the appraisers are still stupid enough to base appraisals on cost or on comparable sales from six months to a year ago when sellers were scarce and speculators were flush, borrowing the equity out is the next best thing to selling. By borrowing in a currency that's going to depreciate and investing in currencies that are going to appreciate, you're creating your own little hedge fund. You've got a positive carry trade, as they say in high finance. It sure beats investing in Yahoo! and hoping it will go up. That's just gambling.

Another idea: Let's say you want to stick with real estate and you own one house in the United States. You can borrow against the equity, give it to us at Euro Pacific Capital, and we'll invest it in global commercial real estate trusts in Singapore, Australia, New Zealand, Switzerland, France, the Netherlands, or other good markets. Now you're trading overpriced, residential real estate in the United States for fairly valued, commercial real estate abroad.

What would you rather have, residential real estate in the crashing U.S. housing market or income-producing commercial real estate around the world? When the dollar collapses, would you rather try to collect depreciating U.S. dollar–denominated rents from unemployed American tenants or receive appreciating foreign currency–denominated rents from the most credit-worthy commercial tenants in the world? Your call!

What you are doing here is making smart use of the fact that interest rates on dollars are still too low. Current U.S. interest rates do not accurately reflect all the inflation that exists. The bond market's got it all wrong. Because of all the foreign intervention and all the foreign central banks buying our debt, rates are being effectively subsidized.

So it certainly makes sense to borrow money under these circumstances. However, it never makes sense to borrow to consume.

THE ARGUMENT FOR SAVING

It is much smarter to save for what you want to buy than to borrow, because you'll ultimately have to work a lot less. As we discussed at some length in Chapter 7 on consumer debt, saving at a compound rate of interest not only makes the purchase effectively cheaper, it leaves you free of a debt burden. This becomes even truer if you can do your saving abroad, where you stand to gain the additional benefit of currency appreciation.

For example, instead of financing or leasing a new car, given the current outlook, drive something you can pay for that gets you by and enables you to save and buy a much nicer car at a later date. The same would go for any big-ticket purchase.

If instead of buying a house now, you rent and invest the down payment money outside the United States, you'll be able to afford a much bigger down payment in a few years and perhaps even own the house without any mortgage at all.

If housing prices decline 50 to 60 percent and the dollar declines 70 percent, a $500,000 house would become a $200,000 house that you could afford to buy free and clear if instead you invested the $50,000 down payment money in conservative foreign stocks. If the rent you paid was less than your mortgage payments would have been, the difference, saved and compounded, would have resulted in even more money.

Secondhand consumer goods, such as big-screen television sets, home furniture, boats, and used cars will become very inexpensive in a major economic downturn. Many people will be forced to sell such goods if they lose their jobs and have to struggle to make sharply higher adjustable-rate mortgage payments or merely pay for basic necessities, such as food or home heating oil.

Of course, prices for new goods will surge, as the collapsing dollar makes the cost of importing them that much higher.

But the used stuff that is already here (and hasn't been shipped abroad to wealthier foreign consumers able to outbid poorer Americans) should initially be available at rock-bottom prices. So why stretch to buy such items now, when you can wait and get them for next to nothing using your appreciated foreign savings?

IDEAS FOR PENNY SAVERS AND OTHERS

If you have enough time and wheelbarrows, here's a way to boost your wealth: Collect pennies minted before 1982, many of which are still in circulation, and nickels. The copper in pre-1982 pennies—the "melt value"—is worth 2.13 cents at today's commodity prices, which could go far higher. Nickels, with 25 percent nickel and 75 percent copper, have a melt value of 6.99 cents. Even pennies minted after 1982 represent a store of value. The zinc they contain has a melt value about equal to a penny.

Just don't get caught melting pennies and nickels or shipping them abroad in bulk. A U.S. mint rule effective in 2006 makes that illegal. It's another example of the government hiding the effects of the inflation it creates. Expect more capital controls as inflation worsens.

It has become difficult to find quarters and dimes minted before 1968, but they were made of silver, so if you have them, hang on to them.

Another smart thing to do is to stock up on things you use as part of your daily life, which are being subsidized, in effect, by the low dollar and will become substantially more expensive after the dollar collapses. Buying such items now and storing them for the future could be an investment providing high triple-digit returns.

The best examples would be items that require minimal storage space and are not perishable—things like batteries, razor blades, certain foods, and a million other things you'll think of if you put your mind to it. Replacement parts for things you use regularly are another example.

I was in Target the other day and bought my four-year-old son a pair of sneakers for about $6. The thought crossed my mind that in a matter of months or a few years, those same sneakers could cost $50. I was tempted to buy several pairs in escalating sizes and put them away. It's a small thing, but the idea could mean serious savings, especially for those living paycheck to paycheck.

Anything imported will get especially expensive. Imported wines, for example, whether you drink wine or not, could be an excellent investment. It will always be in demand and can be used as barter in exchange for other goods and services.

OTHER CONSEQUENCES OF ECONOMIC COLLAPSE

The social and political consequences of an abrupt and severe reduction in living standards have to be considered and should be factored into our planning.

Social unrest caused by deprivation on a massive scale can produce violence and anarchy. It is beyond the scope of this book to examine all the possible manifestations of social ferment compounded by a curtailment of municipal services and programs, but one can imagine how explosive things could become, and perhaps we want to give some thought to how and where we'd want ourselves and our families to be situated.

What extreme measures the federal government might take in the name of national economic necessity is also anybody's guess, but capital controls and confiscation of assets combined with legal authority certainly have precedent in other democracies under comparable pressure. Since the U.S. government seems to have no qualms about violating our individual liberties during times of apparent economic prosperity, the U.S. Patriot Act being only one example, imagine how much more draconian will be the measures during the economic collapse that awaits. Having your assets out of the country or in any of the popular offshore havens would be a wise move should foreign currency–denominated assets or precious metals be confiscated.

It would be a shame to have successfully avoided bankruptcy or to have made a considerable profit following the investment advice in this book, only to have the U.S. government confiscate it from you "for the good of the people" under the pretense of a "national emergency."

To add insult to financial injury, politicians would probably even seek to scapegoat those of us who had the foresight to invest in such assets in the first place as being to blame for the catastrophe! So-called speculators who profit from their forethought while most others are blindsided are often vilified by politicians looking to deflect public outrage. This has always been a popular tactic, as it appeals to the lowest common denominator, envy. The common thought: "Everyone is suffering. Why should the greedy speculators profit at our expense? Let's take away their ill-gotten gains and divide them among the rest of us."

Of course, failure to turn over such assets, should their ownership be made illegal, would make one a criminal, but that is a decision each of us will have to make when and if that time comes. My personal feeling is that under such circumstances it would be the government itself that would be acting criminally and any actions taken to protect one's wealth from a "criminal government" would be morally and constitutionally justified. Remember, as Americans, we do not swear oaths to protect the government or even the nation, but rather to protect the Constitution from all enemies both foreign and domestic. Clearly a federal government confiscating private property under the pretense of national security would be acting unconstitutionally, and resisting such actions would certainly have been considered patriotic by our founding fathers.

In an extreme example, was Miep Gies a criminal for not telling the Nazis that Anne Frank and her family were hiding in the attic? Closer to home, were those who harbored runaway slaves or who ran the Underground Railroad criminals?

Also, in the event things really get bad and you decide to physically leave the country, there would be an obvious advantage to having your money there to meet you. I doubt that under such extreme circumstances our government would let you leave with anything other than the shirt on your back.

We hope and pray it never comes to that, but it conceivably could. It's food for thought.

PUTTING THE PLAN INTO ACTION

In these final three chapters I have discussed various investment options that readers can follow to help preserve their wealth and protect the purchasing power of the savings they have worked a lifetime to accumulate. Investing using conventional wisdom will not work, as the conventional wisdom is rooted in the fundamental premise that the dollar is sound. By now you should be convinced that this premise is false. Therefore the conventional wisdom that follows must go out the window as well.

Never forget that maximizing the dollar value of your assets accomplishes nothing if the value of the dollar plunges. Again, what good is it to preserve your dollars if those dollars do not preserve their purchasing power? Since it is purchasing power that investors really want to preserve, my strategy is the best way of doing so.

Do not allow your current financial adviser or stockbroker to convince you otherwise. These individuals have likely been giving you bad advice for years, either out of pure ignorance or due to conflicts of interest. You need to fire those shills and take charge of your own financial destiny before it is too late.

But you do not have to go it alone. I have assembled an excellent team of investment consultants who not only specialize in

GET READY TO LIVE LIKE A WEALTHY TOURIST
IN A POOR COUNTRY

Say it's a year or so down the road and the dollar has collapsed against foreign currencies. But you were smart and invested abroad. Your wallet bulges with dollars representing freshly converted currency profits. How has the American marketplace changed for you?

Goods that were imported have risen significantly in price, but that doesn't bother you. You've got the extra dollars to pay for them. You haven't lost any purchasing power.

Some American-made goods, though, have increased in price more than others. A shopkeeper explains that those items, with the dollar so cheap, have become popular exports. "There's a lot of demand abroad and we get much better prices there," you're told. "The prices you're looking at here are globally competitive."

Services provided domestically, in contrast to goods, will be terrific bargains for you. Things like haircuts, manicures, massages, and meals in restaurants, as well as services of maids, fitness trainers, and nannies, will cost sharply less in foreign currencies because such services are not easily exported and American buyers are not in competition with wealthier foreign consumers.

You probably had the same experience when you took a trip to a poorer country, such as those in Eastern Europe. Sony television sets, for example, were selling at about the same prices they were in the United States. They might have been somewhat cheaper, reflecting lower rents or local salaries, but in general the global market for Sony products kept prices high and consumers in poor countries had to compete with those in wealthier countries for the same products. If you dined in a restaurant, however, you probably ate like a king for next to nothing. That is because most of the costs reflected the labor involved in preparing and serving the meal, local rents, and locally grown food. Except for the occasional tourist, a restaurant sells its services locally, not to wealthy customers from rich countries. Prices thus reflect local incomes and living standards.

Foreign tourists traveling in America will enjoy the same bargains Americans once enjoyed when traveling abroad. In 1957, Arthur Frommer's original book, *Europe on Five Dollars a Day*, was a national best seller. (The current version prices the trip at $85 a day, and doesn't appear on best-seller lists.) Europe was inundated with middle-class American tourists who, feeling rich when exposed to low European prices, acted priggishly and earned the epithet "Ugly American."

If the scenario I predict pans out, euro and yen versions of Frommer's travel book will be hot sellers abroad. Of course, you don't have to be a tourist to enjoy the benefits of an "America on sale." All you need is the tourist's currency. By denominating your savings and investments in currencies against which the dollar will decline, you'll enjoy all the bargains and save the airfare and hotel bills.

From a national standpoint, America's lower living standard—meaning lower real estate prices, rents, and wages—also means lower costs of production. That, if combined with reduced taxes and regulation, would be an economic trifecta. We'll be a poorer nation but once again a viable economy. With hard work and sacrifice, our grandchildren and great grandchildren could live in the hopeful America our parents and grandparents were born into.

this approach, but do so under my strict supervision. No matter which consultant you work with, you will always have the benefit of my guidance and expertise.

The information contained in this book is only the first step in your reeducation process. I suggest that you continue the journey by regularly visiting my web site at www.europac.net. While there you can read hundreds of my economic commentaries; listen to my live weekly radio program, "Wall Street Unspun" (plus

> To open a brokerage account with Euro-Pacific, either go to my web site at https://www.europac.net/account.asp or call us at 800-727-7922. Should you wish to transfer an existing account to Euro Pacific from another brokerage firm, the forms necessary to do so can be downloaded directly from my web site at www. europac.net/forms.asp. In addition, once your account has been opened, you will have free access to it on my web site as well.

download all previous episodes from the archives); sign up for my free online newsletter, The Global Investor; download any one of a number of comprehensive special reports; watch numerous video interviews and debates; and monitor my scheduled media and personal speaking appearances. In addition, I update the site daily with the latest relevant financial and economic news stories.

If this book has helped to open your eyes, then as its writer I have personally accomplished something. However, if you do not actually do anything as a result of having read it, as its reader you have accomplished nothing. Start putting this personal financial survival plan into action today.

2009 UPDATE

In these updates to the original *Crash Proof*, I've been discussing collapses in two tenses, present and future. The first, the credit crunch and recession we're currently experiencing as a direct consequence of the bursting of the real estate bubble, presents one set of challenges, while the far greater bubble yet to burst that defines the entire U.S. economy will present a second. The two are also interrelated, as the inflation being created to deal with the bursting of the smaller bubble will only make matters far worse once the larger bubble pops as well. Liquidity, the subject of this chapter, is a good example of how the two collapses require somewhat different approaches.

Has My Thinking about Liquidity Changed?

Underlining what I said in the Chapter 8 update, I do not see a foreign stock sell-off combined with a bear market rally in the dollar happening a second time. In other words, I think it is unlikely we'll see foreign stocks selling at such low valuations again, and think that holding cash will get increasingly risky as purchasing power declines, which it surely will. I see gold headed much higher, as discussed in the previous update.

Bottom line? In my view, the big asset sell-off has come and gone, so I don't see the same buying opportunities looking forward that argued for liquidity when I wrote the book, and I see more danger in holding cash. You may have your own reasons for wanting to have liquidity—that boat you've always dreamed of owning may come on the market cheap or even that house that used to be out of the question may become available on favorable terms—but that's your personal business. Gold or foreign stocks are better bets than liquidity from an investment standpoint. For emergencies, cash or liquidity in some form is always necessary, although you should consider alternatives to holding cash in dollars, such as junk silver coins.

Ways of Maintaining Liquidity

Basically the government, by creating potentially massive inflation, is declaring war on liquidity. Money saved (liquidity) is money not spent, and the government's short-term way of promoting economic activity is to discourage saving and stimulate spending, which is the opposite of what would be conducive to real recovery. For the moment, savings are being discouraged by low rates and potentially high inflation, which makes a strong case for investing abroad.

Yes, the personal savings rate has improved in recent months, but part of that is canceled out by the fact that the money is coming from mortgage payments, automobile loan payments, and other consumer debt payments people are no longer making. The rest is borrowed by the government, so net national savings are still falling at a time when they should be rising to make legitimate credit available for productive purposes. By penalizing people for saving and driving people out of the dollar, the government is making it impossible for the economy to recover. The government looks at people holding too much liquidity as part of the problem and is determined to force us to spend, no matter how deeply into debt they drive us in the process.

But the government has other arrows in its quiver. If the government imposes exchange controls, which I think is increasingly likely, foreign investing could become subject to transaction tax penalties or be made illegal. Such legal barriers would negate the value of having liquidity to scoop up foreign stocks that may be selling at bargains. To make sure that you avoid this trap, as well as escape possible future restrictions on ownership of precious metals, which is also likely, it would be smart to invest your money abroad now, while doing so is still legal or free from onerous transactions taxes.

Liquidity is a relative term in the sense that it can exist to varying degrees and still be ready money. Foreign stocks are liquid to the extent they have an active market, although you run the risk of selling at a time when your stocks are down, as was certainly the case in 2008. But they are nonetheless liquid; your choice isn't necessarily cash or illiquidity. There are foreign money market funds and other near-cash foreign investments, as discussed in this chapter. Another idea you might consider is structuring your liquidity so you have different pools to choose from depending on what's up and what's down. You might have some money in dollars, some in gold coins, and some in a selection of different foreign currencies. If an emergency comes up, dip into the pool with the highest water level.

Liquidity and the Final Collapse

Inflation is about as sure a thing as anything these days. Since it clearly benefits debtors at the expense of creditors, since debt becomes repayable in cheaper dollars, the smart money would logically run up as much debt as possible, provided there was reason to believe the effects of inflation were going to kick in immediately. Of course, we don't know when those effects will kick in. If the debt becomes due before the dollars become cheap, you are out of luck. So playing future inflation by taking on current debt is a risky game to play. There might be exceptions, however.

With mortgage rates below 5 percent, for example, it might make sense to buy a house that has dropped in price 40 or 50 percent, not because I think real estate has bottomed, but because if you can get a 30-year Freddie or Fannie mortgage, you can make money as a debtor. Even though real estate is going to lose value, the dollar will lose even more value, giving you a profit. Of course, if you have to make too big a down payment, you might be better off investing that money in foreign stocks if the dollar declines that much. Still, depending on the rental situation, it might pay to buy a house if you can get enough leverage at an ultralow rate.

As I said earlier, anybody owning a home that is unencumbered or has substantial equity should take out the biggest mortgage available while rates are below 5 percent. I have no idea where the rates might be when people are reading the book, but if you can borrow any where close to 5 percent it would make no sense not to do it. Just make sure you don't spend the money. Invest it in foreign dividend-paying stocks or, if you want to stay in real estate, you can buy commercial real estate trusts in Asia that yield much more than the cost of borrowing the money. Of course such a strategy is not for everyone and careful consideration of the risks involved is a must.

Of course it's not only personal liquidity that is important, but the liquidity of the companies we invest in. During the 2008 global stock market sell-off, highly leveraged stocks got clobbered, particularly those in the natural resource sector. While such stocks were certainly well positioned for the inflation scenario, they were ill prepared for the deflation scare that played out first. Those that leveraged up too much may not survive the battle, while those that had more conservative balance sheets are now positioned to win the war. My guess is that the experience of 2008 has caused investors to look at debt as a four-letter word when it comes to stock selection. As such, there are some real bargains among those companies perceived to have too much debt. However, having the right amount of debt is certainly preferable to having no debt at all; it's simply a matter of striking the right balance. In the end I expect inflation to render those companies with manageable debt levels substantially debt-free, implying huge transfers of wealth from bond to equity holders.

Other Consequences of Economic Collapse

Shortages, price controls, black markets, cuts in state and municipal vital services, along with increased crime, poverty, hardship, and civil unrest—these and all the other things I wrote about under the above Chapter 10 subhead are still in the cards. I am even more convinced of that now than I was then because it's now clear what road the government is going down. The worse things get, the more the free market will be blamed and the more government will expand. I expect the economy and the American lifestyle to get substantially worse before things turn around. Yet I'm also still convinced that there will eventually be a turnaround. We may travel far before that happens and be batdly bruised and battered from the trip, but I still believe the American spirit will survive the journey.

Epilogue

I hope that by now I've convinced you that the U.S. economy is a house of cards. It has an impressive facade, but its interior structure has deteriorated beyond the point of no return. One strong wind will topple it. How much longer do we have? That's impossible to say, although as an investor you have nothing to lose and much to gain by assuming the fateful moment will come sooner rather than later.

If you think of it as a bubble in search of a pin, it is simply a question of which pin it finds first.

The one thing I am sure of is that bubbles in search of pins ultimately find them, and the longer this bubble inflates, the more devastating will be the financial consequences.

Here are some of the scenarios, any one of which could be the tipping point, the event that starts the self-feeding cycle of high interest rates, dollar selling, inflation, recession, and eventually a choice between default and hyperinflation.

- The real estate bubble, already losing air, could pop first, sending the economy quickly into recession, which could cause a run on the dollar, force up long-term interest rates, create hyperinflation, and force defaults, refinancing, or other settlements with respect to personal and national debt.
- It could begin with a run on the dollar that forces up interest rates, that pricks the housing bubble and sets the series of events in motion.

- An expanded war or a confluence of natural disasters could overwhelm the federal budget, starting the process of financial cataclysm.

- Overleveraged consumers might finally run out of credit, stop spending, and, heaven forbid, start saving. That would push the economy into recession, triggering a run on the dollar and pushing interest rates even higher, thus pricking the housing bubble and leading to unthinkable stagflation.

- Some derivative-led chain of defaults or a major blowup among hedge funds may be the catalyst.

- Foreign central banks could start selling dollars.

- One of the series of record-high current account deficits could cause panic, causing foreign investors to stop buying U.S. Treasury and mortgage-backed securities.

- China might finally pull the plug on its currency peg, allowing the dollar to go down the drain.

- Inflation could get so out of control that it forces the Fed to raise rates high enough to cause a recession and prick the housing bubble.

- A surge in the price of gold could lead to a run on the dollar.

- An oil shock could overwhelm the economy's ability to pay.

- Insolvency at Fannie Mae, Freddie Mac, or the Pension Benefit Guaranty Corporation could create an international crisis of confidence in the country's ability to make good on its financial promises.

- A high enough rise in short-term interest rates could cause some form of default by the U.S. government, raising questions about full faith and credit.

I could fill pages with a continued list of potential catalysts. My point is that when a bubble is this big, there are just so many potential pins that it is impossible to guess which one it will find first. Of course it really doesn't matter which pin starts the process, only that the process gets started. Remember Murphy's Law? With so many things that could go wrong, there's a pretty good chance that one of them will.

As for when, it could be as soon as tomorrow or as late as several years into the future. From an investor's point of view, however, the "when" is not nearly as important as the "why." Since we now understand the why, the when becomes something we can avoid by being prepared. If we are a few years too early, so what? It sure beats being a day too late, especially since the foreign portfolios I suggest in this book will likely outperform domestic investments in the interim anyway. Since we will be collecting good dividends in strong currencies, being early not only has no opportunity cost, it provides priceless peace of mind.

I am a frequent participant in "bull and bear" debates, and when my bullish opponents begin taking on water, they will resort to calling my advice unpatriotic. If enough people followed my advice, they argue, the economy would suffer. The idea that I might single-handedly cause a massive flight to quality at the expense of the U.S. economy is certainly a flattering comment on my influence, but it is flawed economic logic in addition to being an unfair remark about my patriotism.

The economic reality is that only a small percentage of Americans will—or successfully could—actually do what I am suggesting. The ability to sell dollar assets requires a healthy pool of buyers and a limited number of competing sellers. Our artificially supported economy will collapse regardless of what readers of this book do with their investments.

The appropriate question to ask yourself is whether the country would be better off if you were in the depths of poverty along with everyone else. I personally think I can do a lot more for my country if I'm flush, not broke. Being patriotic does not mean going down with a sinking ship. It means helping in the rescue effort, and you can't do that if drowning yourself.

I realize that this book forecasts significant economic and financial hardships for millions of my fellow Americans, and I am personally saddened by what I see coming. But it is because I am patriotic that I want to use my expertise to help as many Americans as possible to safely protect their wealth through foreign investments. That is the only way Americans will retain ownership of financial assets that can then be repatriated in the aftermath of the collapse.

By that same token, you, the reader of this book, have a similar obligation, I strongly suggest, to share what you have learned with people you want to help. The impending economic collapse has been so long in the making, so complex as to be comprehended by only a small handful of economic analysts, and so skillfully concealed by parties who benefit from various elements of it that when it happens, it will happen suddenly and catch its victims unawares and unprepared. The consequences for the unprepared are potentially horrific, yet so easily avoided.

Do not assume that since you have protected your own wealth you are out of the woods. What about your relatives—your parents or adult children, siblings, or other extended family members? Do you really want to be in the position of being the only solvent person among your friends and family? Do you want to face the dilemma of either helping financially or turning down so many people, especially those you really care about? Even if you have a very charitable nature, if you try to help them all you might end up just as broke as they are.

To avoid this chilling scenario it is imperative that you help educate everyone who is important to you and encourage them to follow the same financial path to safety that you have taken. This may be the best piece of advice that I have given you. At a minimum, if the worst happens, you will have a clear conscience. Forewarned is forearmed.

For years the United States has been traveling a course the Nobel Prize-winning Austrian economist Friedrich von Hayek set forth in a book self-descriptively titled *The Road to Serfdom*. The coming economic collapse may finally bring Americans to that grim destination. But it is also possible that the same dire economic conditions will inspire a return to the country's constitutional traditions of sound money and limited government, the foundation upon which a viable economy can be rebuilt. There is a fork in the road to serfdom. One choice leads back to freedom, and it is my fervent hope that Americans will take it.

If we do, then out of the ashes of this collapse the country our founding fathers envisioned will reemerge, and America will once again be what Ronald Reagan eloquently called "that shining city on a hill."

2009 UPDATE

I knew several pins were out there and it was only a matter of time before our bubble economy found one. As I've said (ad nauseam, perhaps), I had been warning about it for years before I wrote *Crash Proof*, but the government's success in making problems look like progress had delayed the inevitable for so long that I was as surprised as anybody when it happened within a few months of the book's publication. I was even more surprised that the bursting, although devastating enough to create the crisis we're currently experiencing, didn't yield even greater fallout. Though I correctly anticipated that the powers that be, both here and abroad, would try hard to blow the bubble back up, I underestimated how effective their efforts would be. As a result, though some air has seeped out, a dangerous amount remains trapped inside. As long as these counterproductive and ill-fated efforts continue, so too will the slow leak. But sooner rather than later the rest of the air will come gushing out, and the real economic collapse will finally be upon us.

The bubble that found the pin turned out to be real estate, which had become particularly vulnerable because of its growing exposure in default-prone subprime mortgages. They were the weakest link in a defective chain, and once it broke, the chain reaction was unstoppable. The full magnitude of the crisis is still not generally appreciated, however. Fundamental structural flaws in the economy get lip service at best from our leaders who dismiss the current crisis as a credit crunch that can be remedied with the right combination of government expedients. The government's refusal to allow market forces to repair the damage will only weaken the structure further, making complete collapse inevitable.

The potential scenarios that I listed in bullet point in the original Epilogue have already partially played out. The housing bubble burst; consumers have cut back on spending; the recession began; debt defaults and bankruptcies are taking place (Lehman Brothers, General Motors, and Circuit City, to name a few); credit is contracting; Fannie and Freddie became insolvent; federal debt has exploded; and a derivatives-led chain of defaults, in the form of credit default swaps, overwhelmed AIG.

Much of the fallout has been postponed as companies deemed either too big or too interconnected to fail have been bailed out. But this borrowed time will cost us dearly. The rest of my scenario, where these events lead to a collapse in the dollar, surging long-term interest rates, and runaway inflation, has yet to unfold. However, given how many pieces have already fallen into place, I will be very surprised if the entire puzzle is not completed.

Considering what our leaders have already done, I can only imagine the bizarre things they will try as the situation worsens. In the meantime it is incumbent on us to protect our wealth and encourage others to do likewise. We must enlighten those Americans blinded by government propaganda. We must ensure that this economic crisis does not become a political crisis. If we allow our nation to abandon free market capitalism and surrender to the government's agenda of a centrally planned welfare state, prosperity will never return. More important, not only will our nation lose its wealth and standing in the global economy, but it will lose its soul as well. Let's do our best to ensure that this does not happen, and that our founding fathers' grand experiment does not end in failure.

Books for Further Reading

*These books are available on the Euro Pacific Capital web site at www
.europac.net/books.asp.*

OLDIES BUT GOODIES

Browne, Harry. *How I Found Freedom in an Unfree World: A Hand-
book for Personal Liberty.* Great Falls, MT: Liamworks, 1998.

Friedman, Milton. *Capitalism and Freedom.* Chicago: University
of Chicago Press, 2002.

Goldwater, Barry. *Conscience of a Conservative.* Washington, DC:
Regnery Publishing, 1994.

Hamilton, Alexander, James Madison, and John Jay. *The Federalist Papers.* New York: Penguin Classics, 1987.

Hayek, Friedrich A. von. *The Road to Serfdom,* Fiftieth Anniver-
sary Edition. Chicago: University of Chicago Press, 1994.

Hazlitt, Henry. *Economics in One Easy Lesson: The Shortest and
Surest Way to Understand Basic Economics.* New York: Three
Rivers Press, 1988.

Kindleberger, Charles P., Robert Aliber, and Robert Solow.
Manias, Panics and Crashes: A History of Financial Crises.
Hoboken, NJ: Wiley Investment Classics, 2005.

Mackay, Charles. *Extraordinary Popular Delusions and the Madness of Crowds.* United Kingdom: Harriman House, 2003.

Murray, Charles. *Losing Ground: American Social Policy, 1950–1980.* New York: Basic Books, 1994.

Rand, Ayn. *Capitalism, the Unknown Ideal.* New York: Signet, 1986.

Rothbard, Murray N. *America's Great Depression.* Auburn, AL: Ludwig von Mises Institute, 2000.

Rothbard, Murray N. The Case against the Fed. Auburn, AL: Ludwig von Mises Institute, 1994.

Say, Jean-Baptiste. *A Treatise on Political Economy; or The Production, Distribution, and Consumption of Wealth.* Ann Arbor, Michican: Scholarly Publishing Office, University of Michigan Library, 2005.

Schiff, Irwin A. *The Biggest Con: How the Government Is Fleecing You.* Hamden, CT: Freedom Books, 1977.

Schiff, Irwin A. *The Kingdom of Moltz.* Hamden, CT: Freedom Books, 1980.

Schiff, Irwin A., and Vic Lockman. *How an Economy Grows and Why It Doesn't.* Hamden, CT: Freedom Books, 1985.

Smith, Adam. *The Wealth of Nations.* New York: Modern Library Classics, 2000.

Sowell, Thomas. *Knowledge and Decisions.* New York: Basic Books, 1996.

Von Mises, Ludwig. *Human Action: A Treatise on Economics.* San Francisco: Fox & Wilkes, 1990.

Weaver, Henry Grady. *The Mainspring of Human Progress.* Irvington-on-Hudson, NY: Foundation for Economic Education, 1997.

Williams, Walter E. *State against Blacks.* New York: McGraw-Hill, 1984.

CURRENT BOOKS

Bonner, Bill, and Addison Wiggin. *Empire of Debt: The Rise of an Epic Financial Crisis.* Hoboken, NJ: John Wiley & Sons, 2006.

Bonner, William, and Lila Rajiva. *Mobs, Messiahs, and Markets: Surviving the Public Spectacle in Finance and Politics.* Hoboken, NJ: John Wiley & Sons, 2007.

Duncan, Richard. *The Dollar Crisis: Causes, Consequences, Cures.* Hoboken, NJ: John Wiley & Sons, 2005.

Fleckenstein, William, and Fred Sheehan. *Greenspan's Bubbles: The Age of Ignorance at the Federal Reserve.* New York: McGraw-Hill, 2008.

Folsom, Burton W. Jr. *New Deal or Raw Deal? How FDR's Economic Legacy Has Damaged America.* New York: Threshold Editions, 2008.

Mullen, Thomas. *A Return to Common Sense.* 2009. E-book available at www.lulu.com/content/5618680.

Panzner, Michael J. *Financial Armageddon: Protecting Your Future from Four Impending Catastrophes.* New York: Kaplan Publishing, 2007.

Paul, Ron. *The Revolution: A Manifesto.* New York: Grand Central Publishing, 2008.

Prechter, Robert R. *At the Crest of the Tidal Wave: A Forecast for the Great Bear Market.* Hoboken, NJ: John Wiley & Sons, 1995.

Prechter, Robert. R. *Conquer the Crash: You Can Survive and Prosper in a Deflationary Depression.* Hoboken, NJ: John Wiley & Sons, 2003

Rogers, Jim. *Adventure Capitalist: The Ultimate Road Trip.* New York: Random House, 2004.

Rogers, Jim. *Bull in China: Investing Profitably in the Opening of the World's Greatest Market.* New York: Random House, 2007.

Rogers, Jim. *Hot Commodities: How Anyone Can Invest Profitably in the World's Best Market.* New York: Random House, 2004.

Rogers, Jim. *Investment Biker: Around the World with Jim Rogers.* New York: Random House, 2003.

Schiff, Peter D. *The Little Book of Bull Moves in Bear Markets.* Hoboken, NJ: John Wiley & Sons, 2008.

Shlaes, Amity. The *Forgotten Man: A New History of the Great Depression.* New York: Harper Perennial, 2007.

Todd, Emmanuel. *After the Empire: The Breakdown of the American Order.* European Perspectives: A Series in Social Thought and Cultural Criticism. New York: Columbia University Press, 2003.

Turk, James. *The Coming Collapse of the Dollar and How to Profit from It: Make a Fortune by Investing in Gold and Other Hard Assets.* New York: Currency, 2004.

Wiedemer, David, Robert Wiedemer, Cindy Spitzer, and Eric Janszen. *America's Bubble Economy: Profit When It Pops.* Hoboken, NJ: John Wiley & Sons, 2006.

Wiggin, Addison. *The Demise of the Dollar . . . and Why It's Great for Your Investments.* Hoboken, NJ: John Wiley & Sons, 2005.

Woods, Thomas E. Jr. *Meltdown: A Free-Market Look at Why the Stock Market Collapsed, the Economy Tanked, and Government Bailouts Will Make Things Worse.* Washington, DC: Regnery Publishing, 2009.

Glossary

balance of trade Part of the *current account* of the balance of payments, which is the system governments use to keep track of monetary transactions with the rest of the world. The trade account is the difference between exports and imports of goods and services. The other part, called the income account, records earnings on public and private investments. Since the income account is a negligible part of the current account, the terms *trade* and *current* are often used interchangeably. Because the United States imports vastly more than it exports, it runs a huge *trade deficit*. It varies, but is typically around $65 billion a month or close to $800 billion annually. That figure represents the dollars being accumulated in foreign central banks after the companies from which we import convert dollar payments to their local currencies. A substantial portion of the U.S. dollars not on deposit in foreign central banks as reserves is used by the central banks to purchase U.S. Treasury securities, comprising some $2 trillion of our national debt.

budget deficit or surplus The federal budget deficit (or surplus) is the difference between what the government spends and takes in during a given fiscal year, essentially the difference between tax revenues and expenditures. Budget deficits are financed by either issuing government securities, in which case they add to the national debt, or by being monetized, meaning the Federal Reserve adds money to the economy, thereby creating inflation.

carry trade Borrowing at a given rate of interest and using the proceeds to invest at a higher rate of return. A favorable spread between the rate paid and the return earned is termed a *positive carry*, while the reverse is a *negative carry*.

central bank The government institution responsible for the monetary system of a country, such as the Federal Reserve System in the United States, or group of countries, such as the European Central Bank (ECB).

349

A central bank's functions include the issuance of currency, the administration of monetary policy, the holding of deposits representing the reserves of other banks, and the administration of functions designed to facilitate the conduct of business.

consumer price index (CPI)   Monthly index published by the Bureau of Labor Statistics of the U.S. Department of Labor that measures the prices of a fixed basket of goods bought by a typical consumer based on a 1982 value of $100. Also called the *cost of living index*, it is widely used as a gauge of price inflation and a benchmark for inflation adjustments in Social Security and other payments and tax brackets.

counterparty risk   The risk that either party to a contractual obligation will fail to live up to its terms.

current account deficit   *See* balance of trade.

deflation   Contraction of the supply of money and credit in an economy relative to the total amount of goods and services, resulting in a decrease in the general level of prices. Distinguished from disinflation, which is a reduction in the rate of inflation.

derivative   A contract whose value is based on the performance of another underlying financial asset, index, or investment. Derivatives afford leverage and are used in hedging strategies. They are available based on the performance of assets, interest rates, currency exchange rates, and various domestic and foreign indexes.

futures contract   An agreement to buy or sell a specific amount of a commodity, currency, or financial instrument at a particular price on a stipulated future date.

gross domestic product (GDP)   The sum total of the monetary value of all final goods and services bought and sold within the United States borders in a given year.

hedge fund   A largely unregulated pool of investment funds restricted to high net worth investors that aims to make money by identifying investments likely to rise and likely to fall and taking both long and short positions.

hyperinflation   Inflation that is rapid and out of control. Some sources define it as prices rising 100 percent or more annually, but there is no standard of measurement. The operative idea is that there is zero confidence in purchasing power.

inflation   Expansion of the supply of money or credit in an economy relative to the total amount of goods and services, resulting in an increase in the general level of prices.

monetary policy   Decisions by the Federal Reserve to expand or contract the supply of money or credit. Monetary policy is implemented through actions of the Federal Open Market Committee (FOMC) of the Federal Reserve. The FOMC's principal tool is the target federal funds rate, which is the rate banks charge each other for overnight loans to meet reserve requirements and which influences general interest rate levels. The Fed effectively sets the federal funds rate by expanding or contracting the money supply through its open market operations, that is, its purchase or sale of Treasury securities in the open market.

monetize   To finance with printed money (i.e., by expanding the supply of money or credit).

money supply   The total stock of money in the economy, primarily represented by currency in circulation and funds in checking and savings accounts, money market mutual funds, and other forms of near money. The Federal Reserve classifies money supply in three groups designated M1, M2, and M3, ranging from the narrowest definition of liquidity (such as currency and checking account balances) to the broadest, such as large certificates of deposit.

national debt   The sum total of government borrowings, which is to say the accumulated total of all past budget deficits net of the occasional budget surplus. The national debt is represented by (short-term) Treasury bills, (intermediate-term) Treasury notes, and (long-term) Treasury bonds held by individuals, businesses, governments, and other creditors and backed by the full faith and credit of the U.S. government. It excludes unfunded debt, such as obligations of government trust funds like Social Security and Medicare, or contingent liabilities, such as student loan guarantees. The national debt in late 2006 was around $8.5 trillion, which represents over 60 percent of the gross domestic product (GDP). Put in recent historical perspective, the national debt peaked at 120 percent of GDP in 1946 for World War II–related reasons, then steadily declined to a post–Great Depression low of 32.5 percent of GDP in 1981. In 1982 it began a sharp rise that reversed by 10 percent or so of GDP during the 1990s, but resumed in 2000 and is projected to end 2006 at a 47-year high.

negative carry   *See* carry trade.

positive carry   *See* carry trade.

printing money   Although the term literally refers to the actual printing and engraving of physical currency, it is more commonly used in an informal sense to mean actions by the government to expand the supply of money and credit in the economy.

reserve currency   Status given to the U.S. dollar by the Bretton Woods agreements of 1944 that made it the currency used by other governments and institutions to settle their foreign exchange accounts and to transact trade in certain vital commodities, such as oil and gold. Because other countries accumulate dollar reserves to facilitate transactions, the country enjoying reserve currency status is exempt from the free market forces that would otherwise force the adjustment of trade imbalances.

selling short   *See* short selling.

short covering   *See* short selling.

short position   *See* short selling.

short selling   Selling an asset, such as a stock or futures contract, that is borrowed and not owned at its current market price in anticipation that the market will fall and it can be purchased at a lower price, netting a profit after the borrowed stock is returned. The actual purchase of the asset by the short seller is called *short covering*. A situation where numerous short sellers engage in short covering at the same time, creating upward pressure on the asset price, is called a *short squeeze*. A short seller is said to have a *short position* in the asset involved as distinguished from having a long position or being long, which would indicate the asset is owned.

short squeeze   *See* short selling.

trade deficit   *See* balance of trade.

Treasury securities   Bills, notes, and bonds issued by the U.S. Treasury and directly backed by the full faith and credit of the U.S. government. Treasuries are distinguished from government agency securities, which are indirect obligations of the U.S. government.

Index

Acid-test ratio, 268
Action plan, 331–334
Adjustable-rate debt, 318, 323
Adjustable-rate mortgages (ARMs), 166, 171–172
Aggregate demand, 99
Agnico-Eagle Mines Limited, 305
Agricultural production, 12
Amaranth, 139
American Depositary Receipts (ADRs), 252–256
American International Group (AIG), 153
AMEX HUI Gold BUGS Index, 312
AngloGold Ashanti Ltd., 305
"An Update on the Status of the Economy and It's
    Implication for Monetary Policy" (Fisher), 95
Asian economies. *See also* China; foreign economies:
    beneficial structure of, 261
    gold redemption by, 73–74
    without U.S. indebtedness, 17–18
Asset bubble, 30
Asset liquidation, 86
Australia, 260, 306, 320, 326
Austrian school of economics, 111, 121
Automobile industry, 10, 26, 55
Automobile loans, 214–215

Bags (coins), 298
Bailouts, 26, 55, 59
Balance of trade. *See also* current account deficit;
    trade deficit:
    currency and, 75
    of United States, 36
    U.S. dollar value and, 75–78
Banking system, 67–68. *See also* central banks;
    Federal Reserve
Bank loans, 163
Bank notes, 68
Bank of America, 153
Bankrate.com, 175
Bankruptcy, 55, 152, 154
Barrick Gold Corporation, 305
Barter system, 65, 94
Bear markets, 129, 144–145, 149–150
Bear Stearns, 84, 153
Bema Gold, 305
Bernanke, Ben, 39–40, 53, 117, 314

The Biggest Con (Schiff), 67, 109
Bimetallic monetary system, 296
Black markets, 115
Board lots, 255
Bond bubble, 234
Bondholders legal status, 154
Bonds, 130, 234–265, 321
Bonner, Bill, 41
Boom-bust cycle, 112–113
    in Japan, 103
Bretton Woods agreement, 8–9, 70–71
Brokers, 132, 256–259
Budget deficits, 25, 73, 117, 321
Budget surplus, 31, 78
Buffett, Warren, 37, 150
Bullion, 299, 307, 323. *See also* gold
Bull markets and bear markets, 145
Bush, George W., 53, 120
Business cycles, 110, 143
BusinessWeek, 177
Buy-and-hold investing, 156–157, 282

Canada, 260, 263, 306, 320
Capital debt, 204
Capital gains, 131
Capital goods, 48
Carry trade, 290
Cash. *See* Liquidity
Cash dividends, 135
Cash-for-clunkers bill, 233
Cash in domestic currency, 319
Central bankers, 9, 287
Central banks. *See also* Federal Reserve; foreign
    central banks:
    gold reserves, 285–286
    interest rates, 313
Central Fund of Canada, 301
Central planning vs. free-market capitalism, 28
Chain-Type Price Index of Personal Consumption
    Expenditures (CTPIPCE), 101
China:
    accumulation of U.S. dollars by, 105–106
    currency peg, 77, 107
    currency risk in, 264
    dollar decline benefit, 18–19

China (continued)
  economy of, 18–20, 243
  future borrowing from, 234
  gold reserve increase, 311
  U.S. dollar redemption by, 107
  wage scales in, 240–241
Christmas clubs, 206
Chrysler bankruptcy, 154
Citigroup, 153
Civil War, 104
Coal, 265
Coinage, 68–69
Coins, 328–329
Collateralized debt obligations (CDOs), 26, 189
Collateralized loan obligations (CLOs), 150
Collateralized mortgage obligations (CMOs), 169
College education loans, 215–216
The Coming Internet Depression (Mandel), 49
Commercial real estate, 198
Commodities exchange, 303–304
Commodity futures, 303–304
Common stocks, 139
Computer technology and productivity, 47
Confiscation, 331
Conflicts of interest, 132, 137, 152–155, 167
Conglomerates, 151
Congressional elections, 34
Congressional Oversight Panel (COP), 54
Consumer confidence, 51–53
Consumer credit, 205, 206, 227
Consumer debt:
  charts of, 200
  damage caused by, 216
  demand for, 237
  Government spending and, 96
  as gross domestic product (GDP) component, 212
  lack of savings and, 204
  misuse of, 199–200
  vs. savings, 232
  securitization and, 29, 232
  societal effects of, 212–213
  trade deficit vs., 37
  and U.S. dollar, 79
Consumer goods vs. capital goods, 48
Consumer price index (CPI), 37, 40, 63, 91, 92
Consumer prices and deflationary pressures,
  124–125
Consumer spending, 2
Consumption. See also consumer debt; household
    debt; interest rates; savings rate; trade deficit:
  Asian economies and, 17
  chart of, 200
  China's economy and, 18
  excessive, 2
  of foreign oil, 42–43
  reserve currency status and. See also reserve
    currency status; service economy
  subsidization of, 31

U.S. economy driver, 7, 29, 31
U.S. government policy on, 7
Copper, 328
Core consumer price index (CPI), 182, 184
Core consumer price index (CPI) vs. consumer price
    index (CPI) and producer price index (PPI), 41
Core inflation, 99–100
Corrupt practices, 170
Cost-push inflation, 98
Costs of capital, 211
Counterparty risk, 304
Crash of 1929, 30, 145
Creative destruction concept, 12
Credit. See also consumer debt:
  appropriate use of, 214–216
  misuses of, 213–214
Credit card debt, 323–324
Credit contraction, 105
Credit crisis of 2008, 24, 84, 335
Credit securitization, 210
Critics/criticism, 278–279
Crowding out effect, 212
Currency. See also gold standard; reserve currency:
  balance of trade and, 75
  fiat currency, 64–65, 284, 288
  foreign, 251, 310, 320
  strength of, 75–76
  velocity of money, 115, 127
Currency gains as capital
    gains, 322
Currency pegs, 31, 77, 85, 107
Currency risk, 244–245
Current account balance chart, 3
Current account deficit, 76, 216
Current account surplus, 217
Current consumption costs, 218
Current ratio, 268

Dealer premiums, 315–316
Debt. See also consumer debt:
  good vs. bad, 204
  and liquidity, 323–324
Debt collateral, 39
Debt to equity (debt ratio), 270
Debt to total assets ratio, 269
Declining dollar, 63, 81. See also U.S. dollar
Decoupling, 274, 277, 280
Default risk vs. inflation risk, 88–89
Defaults, 25–26, 225
Deflation, 102–105, 122, 124–125
Demand for oil and energy, 101
Demand-pull inflation, 98
The Demise of the Dollar (Wiggin), 74
Democracy:
  China, 241–242
  vs. republic, 242
Department of Commerce, 101
Deposit Insurance Fund, 228

Deregulation, 13, 55
Derivatives, 291, 304, 320
Direct owner/lender negotiation, 195–196
Diversification, 252
Dividends, 140, 142–143, 252, 259, 265, 271
Dollar Index, 83
Domestic savings, 231
Domestic stock market, 130
Dot.com bubble, 39, 113
Dow/gold ratio, 294, 296, 314–315
Dow Jones Industrial Average, 145, 150
    vs. gold prices, 294–296
Down payments, 163
DRDGold Limited, 302
Dumping, 125

Echo-boomers, 176, 177
Economic collapse:
    consequences of, 329–331, 338
    consumer credit and, 228
    consumers shift to savers after, 20
    from currency crisis, 89
    forecast of, 24–25, 274
    inflation as cause of, 114
    living conditions after, 332–333
    national and personal debt leading
        to, 199
    timing of, 114–115
Economic growth, 200–201
Economic statistics, 33
Electric utilities, 262
Emergency cash holdings, 250–251. See also
    Liquidity
Empire of Debt (Bonner and Wiggin), 41
Employment, 52
Energy costs, 43. See also oil prices
Enron, 133
Entitlement programs. See Social Security:
Euro, 72, 244, 262
Euro Pacific Capital, 335
Europe:
    Bretton Woods Accords impact, 72
    decoupling, 31
    demand for euros, 262
    dollar collapse impact on, 262
    gold demands by, 74
    imports from as quality, 240
    markets in, 262
    purchasing power of, 49
    ROI in, 48
    trade surplus of, 244
European Central Bank (ECB) inflationary
    policies, 313
Europe on Five Dollars a Day (Frommer), 333
Euro zone, 244, 262
Excess profits tax, 307
Exchange controls, 336
Exchange rate, 258

Exchange-traded funds (ETFs), 301–302
Executive compensation, 133
Exploration companies, 305
External debt, 210

Fair Isaac and Company (FICO), 205
Falling prices, 103, 104
Fannie Mae (National Mortgage Association), 57,
    59, 167, 181, 192–193
Farm production, 12
Federal Deposit Insurance Corporation (FDIC), 228
Federal funds rate, 27, 58
Federal Reserve:
    data manipulation, 5
    establishment of, 69
    fiat currency, 284
    funds rate, 58
    gold standard and, 65
    inflation and busts, 113–114
    money supply expansion, 73, 91
    mortgage rates lowered, 38–39
    paper money for liquidity, 38–39
    on systemic risk regulation, 155
Federal Reserve notes, 70, 109
Fiat currency, 64–65, 284, 288
FICO score, 205
Final collapse and liquidity, 337–338
Financial Accounting Standards Board (FASB), 196
Financial businesses, 152
Financial Industry Regulatory Association
    (FINA), 155
Financial obligation ratio, 203
Fisher, Richard W., 95
Fixed-charge coverage, 270
Fixed-rate debt vs. adjustable-rate debt, 318
Floating currencies, 75
Ford administration, 108
Foreign bank account, 260
Foreign bonds, dividends and taxation
    paid on, 321
Foreign borrowing and gross domestic product
    (GDP), 51
Foreign central banks, 5, 31, 33, 170, 313
Foreign currency, 310, 319
Foreign demand for U.S. assets, 127
Foreign dividend yields, 249
Foreign equities, 272, 322
Foreign income producing assets, 147
Foreign investment future, 181
Foreign markets:
    broker selection and, 256–257, 272
    investing in, 254
    myths and fears about, 237
    real estate investing, 263
    variables affecting, 322–323
Foreign real estate trusts, 326
Foreign stocks, 276, 278–282
Foreign stocks and bonds, 237, 247–248, 255

Foreign stocks portfolio:
  cash account, 259–260
  commodities and natural resources, 263
  industrial sectors in, 262–265
  market selection, 260–262
  real estate, 263
  stock selection, 265–266
Forward price to earnings ratio (P/E), 149, 270
Franklin, Benjamin, 242
Freddie Mac (Federal Home Mortgage Association),
  57, 59, 167, 181, 192–193
Free-market capitalism, 28, 60
Frommer, Arthur, 333
Fuller, Ida M., 224
Fundamental analysis, 266–271
Futures contracts, 303–304

Gas utilities, 262
Geithner, Timothy, 29, 228
Gekko, Gordon, 59
General demand, 99
General Electric, 150–151
General Motors, 55, 151
Germany, 320
Ginnie Mae (Government National Mortgage
  Association), 167
The Global Investor (newsletter), 334
Global Investor, The (newsletter), 334
Gold. See also Dow/Gold Ratio; gold standard:
  character of, 67
  vs. fiat currency, 288
  and foreign currency, 310
  growth and speculation, 308
  price of, 284–286
  remonetization of, 296
  short covering, 290
  supply of, 291–292
  vs. U.S. dollar, 85, 123
"Gold and Economic Freedom" (Greenspan), 95
Gold Bullion Securities, 301
Gold certificates, 69
Gold coins as liquidity, 323
Goldcorp Inc., 305
Golden Star Resources, 305
Gold exchange-traded funds (GETFs), 301–302
Gold Fields Ltd, 305
Goldilocks economy, 283
Gold market, 286–293
Gold mining companies, 302
Gold money, 298, 302–303
GoldMoney.com, 302–303
Gold portfolio, 306–307
Gold prices, 79–80, 309
  vs. Dow Jones Industrial Average, 294–296
  in late 20th century, 285
  potential, 293–294
  and reserve currency status, 310–311
Gold redemption by Asian economies, 73–74
Gold Reserve Act of 1934, 69, 72

Gold reserves, 68, 285–286, 289
Gold selloff, 309–310
Gold/silver price ratio, 296
Gold standard, 9, 64–65, 287–288
Government bonds, 320–321
Government reporting:
  on consumer confidence, 51–53
  on deflation, 44–45
  on GDP numbers, 54
  on inflation, 35–44
  need for public confidence and, 51–53
  on productivity, 45–49
  on trade deficit, 25–27
Government spending:
  immense levels of, 28
  by Obama administration, 54
  prior to WWII, 31
  profligate, 6
  during World War II, 31
Great Depression of the 1930s, 29–30, 45,
  61, 229
Greenspan, Alan, 47, 48
  actions of, 108
  on credit crisis of 2008, 55
  on gold, 95
  as inflation creator, 39
Greenspan put, 61
Gross domestic product (GDP), 2, 49–51, 53, 54, 212
Gross national product (GNP), 49
Guns and butter policies, 72, 108

Haines, Mark, 12
Halberstam, David, 10
Harmony Gold Mining, 305
Hayek, Friedrich von, 111
Headline numbers, 100
Hedge book, 305
Hedge funds, 59, 154
  conflicts of interest, 137
  risk in, 137–138
Hedonics, 46–49
Home equity, 160, 207
Home equity lines of credit (HELOCs), 168
Home equity loans, 337
Homeowner options, 324–326
Home ownership, 188, 324–326
Home ownership and speculation, 182–183
Home values, 39, 54, 124
Hong Kong, 261, 321
Hoover, Herbert, 30
Household debt, 213
Housing. See real estate
Housing market speculation, 184
Housing prices, 174–177, 179
Hurricane Katrina, 50, 209–210
Hyperinflation, 45, 79, 161, 225, 235, 316

IAMGOLD Corporation, 302
Industrial sectors, 262–265

Inflation:
  Alan Greenspan as creator of, 39
  artificial demand created by, 93–95
  Ben Bernanke as creator of, 39
  and boom-bust cycle, 112–113
  core inflation, 99–100
  cost-push, 98
  debt reduced by, 225
  defined, 93
  expectations, 99
  Federal Reserve and, 113–114
  foreign equities as hedge against, 272
  hyperinflation, 161, 235, 316
  impacts of, 96–97
  indicated by consumer price index (CPI), 91
  indicated by money supply expansion, 91
  indicated by producer price index (PPI), 91
  interest rates and, 326
  measures of, 37, 40, 101
  Paul Volcker's war on, 285
  reasons for creating, 95–96
  risk, 244–245
  and slower growth, 117–118
  terms describing, 98
  Treasury inflation protection securities (TIPs), 238
  visibility of, 97
Inflation curve, 44
Inflation danger timing, 12?
Information technology, 11
Infrastructure spending, 27–2., 119, 216
Instrumental goods, 48
Interest only loans, 173
Interest rates:
  and ARM payments, 172
  bond prices and low, 23, 234
  China's concern with, 77
  consumer debt and, 54, 212
  housing bubble and, 82, 185
  inflation and, 96, 189, 326
  vs. national savings rate, 161
  reduction, 161
  stock market prices, 146
International Bank for Reconstruction and
  Development (World Bank), 71
International Monetary Fund (IMF), 71, 321
Investing vs. speculating, 131
Investment debt, 204
Investment horizon, 252
IShares COMEX Gold Trust, 301
IShares Silver Trust, 301

Japan, 61, 103, 261
Jingle mail, 186
Job creation, 28
Jobs. See also employment:
Johnson, Lyndon, 293
Johnson administration, 72, 108
JPMorgan Chase, 153
Junk silver (coins), 298, 335

Kennedy administration, 73
Keynes, John Maynard, 73
Kincross Gold, 305

Labor unions, 154
Layaway plans, 206
Lehman Brothers, 84, 153, 309
Lending standards, 163, 165–166, 185
Lereah, David, 175–176
Leverage, 137, 160, 303
Leverage ratios, 269–270
Limit orders, 259
Liquid assets, 319
Liquidity, 225
  bullion gold as, 323
  in cash, 276–277
  and debt, 323–324
  and final collapse, 337–338
  gold coins as, 323
  importance of, 185–186
  investments providing, 320–321
  longer-term investments providing, 321–323
  personal, 318
  required levels of, 319–320
  types of, 322
  update assessment, 335
  ways of maintaining, 335–336
The Little Book of Bull Moves in Bear Markets
  (Schiff), 281
Living standards, 7
Long-term debt to total capitalization ratio, 269

M-3 (money supply), 105
Made-in-America status, 239
Madison, James, 242
Madoff, Bernard, 155, 227
Malinvestments, 111, 112, 113, 118, 231
Mandatory conversions, 226
Mandel, Michael, 49
Manufacturing sector, 9–10, 20–21, 231, 239–241,
  252. See also consumption
Margins vs. prices, 104
Market makers, 255
Mark-to-market accounting rules, 189, 196–197
Martin, William McChesney, Jr., 108
Maturity extension, 226
Measures of inflation, 101
Medicare programs, 221
Meridian Gold, 305
Merk Hard Currency Fund, 320
Merrill Lynch, 153
Mining stocks, 304–305, 312–313
Mint Act of 1792, 69
Monetary policy, 41, 69, 92, 95, 111
Monetization (financing), 73, 88, 108
Money. See also currency:
  economic functions of, 66
  first uses of, 67
  origins of, 65–66

Money (continued)
    supply, 105–107, 123–124
    supply and business cycles, 110
Monthly Review, 48
Moral hazard, 170, 193–194, 229
Mortgage credit, 207
Mortgage meltdown, 84
Mortgage rates, 57, 162
Mortgages. See real estate
Mutual funds, 252
    absolute performance of, 136
    case against, 253–254
    foreign, 253–254, 320
    gold shares in, 290–291
    with mining shares, 308
    problems with, 135–136
    yield vs. past performance, 135–136

National debt, 2, 25, 219–221, 225
National default, 229
Nationalization, 306
National savings rate, 161, 336
Natural disasters, 209
Natural resources investment, 260, 338
Negative amortization ARMs, 173
Negative carry. See carry trade
Net asset value (NAV), 320
Net profit margin, 269
Newcrest Mining, 305
New Deal, 30
Newmont Mining, 291, 305
New York Times, 35, 159
New Zealand, 260, 326
The Next Century (Halberstam), 10
Nickel(s), 328
Nixon, Richard, 72, 74, 78, 108
No-documentation mortgage loans, 171
No-load mutual funds, 320
Nontraditional mortgages, 171–174
Northern Orion Resources, 305
Northern Trust Company report, 160
Northgate Minerals, 305
Norway, 260
Numismatics, 299

Obama administration:
    Congressional Oversight Panel (COP), 54
    on credit, 230
    economic plans by, 27
    General Motors, 55–56
    government spending by, 54, 56
    mortgage modification plan, 193
    stimulus plan by, 119, 120
    too big to fail designation, 155
    Troubled Asset Relief Program (TARP), 54
Oil prices, 42–43, 101, 263
Oil utilities, 262
Operating profit margin, 268–269

Option ARMs, 172
Order flow, 259
Ordinary foreign shares (ords), 255
Overseas investing. See foreign stocks and bonds:
Owen-Glass Reserve Act of 1913, 69

Passive foreign investment trust (PFIT), 321
Paulson, Henry M, Jr., 55, 153
PCE (Chain-Type Price Index of Personal
        Consumption Expenditures CTPIPCE), 101–102
Perma-bears, viii
Personal cash management, 319
Personal debt, 2, 76
Perth Mint, 300–301
Perth Mint Certificate Program (PMCP), 300
Pink Sheets LLC, 255
Political risk, 245, 260, 306
Ponzi schemes, 156, 222–223, 227
Portfolio:
    allocations of, in foreign investments,, 246, 250
    creation of foreign, 250–252, 259–266
    domestic, replicated in foreign currencies, 245
    of foreign securities, 237
    foreign stocks as means of diversification of,
        257, 271
    of non-dollar-denominated dividend-paying
        foreign stocks, 273
Positive carry. See carry trade:
Post-war economy, 71
Precious metals. See copper; gold; silver:
Prices, 98, 104, 157
Price stability, 104
Price to book value ratio, 270–271
Price to earnings ratio (P/E), 141, 270
Price to sales ratio, 271
Producer price index (PPI), 37, 40, 91
Productivity, 46–47
Profitability, 45
Profitability ratios, 268–269
Pro forma earnings, 42
Property trusts, 263
Public utilities stock, 142
Purchasing power, 244–245, 332

Qualifying dividends, 321
Quick ratio, 268

Rating agencies, 132
Ratios:
    forward price to earnings ratio (P/E), 149, 270
    leverage ratios, 269–270
    of paper to reserves, 68
    price to earnings ratio (P/E), 141, 270
    profitability ratios, 268–269
    stock valuation ratios, 270–271
    trailing price to earnings ratio (P/E), 149, 270
    valuation ratios, 141–142
Reagan administration, 108

Real estate:
  chart of housing starts, 176
  collapse of and aftermath, 25–27, 54
  foreign stocks portfolio in, 263
  home builders and, 174–175
  home equity and consumer debt, 26, 124, 159, 168
  lending standards and, 162–163
  nontraditional mortgages and, 171–174
  securitization and, 162–163, 167
  temporary appreciation vs. wealth, 124
  traditional loan process and requirements, 162–163
Real estate bubble, 24, 54, 56, 109–110, 160–161, 174–175, 177–182, 189–191
  U. S. government response to, 191–192
Real estate mortgage investment conduits (REMICs), 169
Real estate prices, 184, 185, 194–196
"Real Estate Review 2006" (Bankrate.com), 175
Recessions, 111, 334
Regulation:
  in Asian economies, 261
  bypass of, 132
  in China, 241
  economic burdens of, 158, 254
  historical impact of, 10, 12
  impact of, 155, 202, 334
  imposition of, 59
  relief of, 20, 240
  of Securities and Exchange Commission (SEC), 258
Remonetization of gold, 296
Rental housing prices, 183
Reserve currency, 311. See also world reserve currency
Reserve currency status, 8, 72, 77
  and gold prices, 310–311
  and national debt, 225
  timing of loss of, 317
Return on equity, 269
"The Revolution in Information Technology" (Greenspan), 47
Rising interest rates impact, 146
Rising oil prices, 108
Risk, 137–138, 246, 252
Risk hedges, 232
Roosevelt, Franklin Delano, 30
Royalty trusts, 263
Rubin, Robert, 153, 246
Russian default, 6

Saving(s), 207, 326–327
  chart of rate of U.S., 8
  rate, 2, 76, 202, 209, 211
  vs. consumer debt, 232
  two paycheck situation, 163–164
Say's Law of Markets, 94
Schiff, Irwin, 67
Schumpeter, Joseph, 12

Secondhand consumer goods, 327
Secular markets, 144
Securities and Exchange Commission (SEC), 155, 258
Securitization:
  conflicts of interest through, 167
  higher housing demand and prices from, 167
  impact of, 231
  process of, 162
  real estate debt and, 163
  risk distribution through, 232
  root cause of the real estate bubble, 167
  as source of funds, 29
  tapping foreign savings through, 232
Sedative, 58
Selling short, 275
Service economy, 9–10, 11, 231
Short covering, 290
Short selling, 275
Short-term U.S. debt vs. long-term U.S. debt, 37
Silver, 296–306, 335
Silver certificates, 69
Singapore, 261, 321, 326
Snow, John, 35–36
Social Security, 202, 221, 223
South Africa, 260
South Korea, 261
Speculation, 330
  ARMs and, 173–174
  and home ownership, 182–183
  in housing market, 184
  vs. investment, 131
Spiders. See Standard and Poor's Deposit Receipts (SPDRs):
Spread, 255
Stagflation, 7, 78, 181
Standard and Poor's Deposit Receipts (SPDRs), 301
Standard of living, 202
"stated income" mortgages, 171
Stevens, Thomas M., 176–177
Stimulus plans, 58, 119, 120, 233
Stock exchanges, 139
Stocking up, 328–329
Stock market:
  bubbles, 108–109
  conflicts of interest in, 152–155
  domestic, 130
  exchange-traded funds (ETFs), 301–302
  gold exchange-traded funds (GETFs), 301–302
  shorting, 146–147
  values of, 54, 208
Stock ownership risk, 140
Stock price appreciation, 133–134
Stock repurchase program, 133
Stock valuation ratios, 270–271
Streettracks Gold Shares, 301
Subprime mortgages, 25, 57, 169, 170, 188
Suitability rules, 132
Systemic risk regulation, 155

Taseko Mines, 305
Tax code, 203, 251
Tax cuts, 161
Too big to fail designation, 6, 26, 155, 232
Toxic assets, 191, 228
Trade deficit. *See also* balance of trade:
    current level of, 218
    growth of, 35–37
    level of, 2
    parable about, 21–23
    reserve currency status and, 9
    service economy and, 11
"Trade Deficit at New High, Reinforcing Risk to
    Dollar" (*New York Times*) , 35
Trading multiple, 141
Trailing price to earnings ratio (P/E), 149, 270
Tranches, 169
Transaction requirements, 259
Treasury inflation protection securities (TIPs), 238
Troubled Asset Relief Program (TARP), 27, 54
Tuition, 215–216
Túrk, James, 302
Two paycheck situation, 163–164

Underwriting and investment-banking fees, 139
Unemployment, 48
Unfunded liabilities, 292
United Kingdom:
    European markets, 262
    interest rates in, 313
    spread in stocks, 255
    utility dividend yield in, 142
United States:
    comparative advantage of, 242
    vs. Japan, 10
    manufacturing sector in, 239–241
    manufacturing sector vs. service sector, 76
    national debt, 16
    post-wartime economy of, 18
    regulatory burden in, 241
    savings rate in, 76
    tax code, 251
    trade and financial imbalances of, 1
    wage scales in, 240–241
    wartime economy of, 18
U.S. assets, 126
U.S. Constitution, 110
U.S. dollar. *See also* currency:
    collapse of, 147–148, 227
    devalued, 20
    establishment of, 88
    flight to safety, 309–310
    foreign countries' response to decline of, 180–181

vs. gold, 85, 123
    impact of collapse of, 17
    impact of strength in, 126–127
    money flow into, 87
    origins of, 68–69
    redemption of, 70–71
    as reserve currency, 71, 77
    reserve currency status, 7, 31, 83
    strength of, 76, 276
    value of, 63
U.S. dollar index chart, 78
U.S. exports, 11
U.S. government:
    AAA-rating, 230
    and dollar strength, 80–81
    economic statistics, 33
    expansion of, 201–203
    increases in debt, 233
    inflation as policy, 107–109
    inflation hiding, 96–97
    moral hazard created by, 193–194
    post-collapse options, 330
    response to real estate bubble, 191–192
    trust funds, 221–222
    unfunded liabilities, 292
U.S. Treasury bonds, 234–235
U.S. Treasury securities, 31, 186–87
Utilities, 142, 262

Valuation factors and the market outlook,
        147–148
Valuation ratios, 141–142
Velocity of money, 115, 127
Volcker, Paul, 108, 285
Von Mises, Ludwig, 111, 212

Wage-price spiral, 98
Wages and price controls, 79
Wage scales, 239
Wall Street, 156–158
"Wall Street Unspun" (radio program), 333
War on inflation, 285
Wealth effect, 123, 232
Wealth vs. consumption, 2
Wiggin, Addison, 41, 74
World financial capital, 157–158
World reserve currency, 243, 311. *See also* U.S. dollar
World War II, 31, 71

Yen carry trade, 86
Yield, 142
Yield curve, 44
Yuan as world's reserve currency, 243